GOING DEEPER

GOING DEEPER

How to Make Sense of Your Life When Your Life Makes No Sense

JEAN-CLAUDE GERARD KOVEN

PRISM HOUSE PRESS

Rancho Mirage, California

Going Deeper: How to make sense of your life when your life makes no sense by Jean-Claude Gerard Koven. Copyright © 2004 hardcover edition, 2006 paperback edition by Jean-Claude Gerard Koven

First Edition   Publication Date: October, 2004
Paperback Edition Publication Date: October, 2006

Prism House Press
36101 Bob Hope Drive, Suite E5/PMB305
Rancho Mirage, CA 92270
Tel. +1.760.324.3072
www.prismhouse.com
E-mail: info@prismhouse.com

Library of Congress Cataloging-in-Publication Data
Koven, Jean-Claude.
   Going deeper : how to make sense of your life when your life makes
no sense / Jean-Claude Gerard Koven. — 1st ed.
   p. cm.
   LCCN 2004091586
   ISBN 13: 978-0 9723954 0-3 (pbk)
   ISBN 10: 0 9723954 0-7 (pbk)
   ISBN 13: 978-0 9723954 5-8 (hdbk)
   ISBN 10: 0 9723954 5-8 (hdbk)

   1. Consciousness—Fiction. 2. Joshua Tree National Park (Calif.)—
   Fiction. 3. Metaphysics—Fiction. I. Title.

   PS3611.O747G65 2004   813'.6
                              QBI04-700092

Printed and manufactured in the United States of America

9 8 7 6 5 4 3

Book Design by Dotti Albertine

Cover photograph by Ellie Tyler © 2001. Relationships — *Juniper and Monolith*, Joshua Tree National Park.

◎ CONTENTS

⚜ CONTENTS ⚜

This book is dedicated

to my beautiful wife, Arianne,

without whose loving support and

companionship my journey

would have seemed extremely lonely

◉ INTRODUCTION

If you . . .

> *are deeply saddened by the way humans treat each other,*
> *suffer from allergies and other sensitivities,*
> *feel somewhat alienated, even from friends and loving family,*
> *love to gaze out at the stars,*
> *find yourself thinking that UFOs and channeling might be true,*
> *are more comfortable with plants or animals than with people,*
> *have a sense that you came here to do something important . . .*

you may be one of the seventy million Wanderers who
are here to assist with the impending shift. These cosmic servers
have come to Earth from other dimensions through the Veil of
Forgetting. The information in this book is structured to restore
their memory.

If you are one of them, this book is meant for you.

It has long been predicted that the world as we know it will soon come to an end. The Bible speaks of a great battle, Armageddon, as the omega and alpha—the cessation of chaos and the dawn of a millennium of peace. The Hopi, Mayans, and numerous other indigenous cultures are replete with calendars, legends, and assorted predictions targeting the same moment in time—somewhere between now and the end of 2012—as the termination of civilization.

These early writings—for the most part by unsophisticated and relatively primitive people—are turning out to be astonishingly accurate. According to an increasing flow of esoteric information channeled by psychics all over the world, our entire solar system is indeed passing through the last segment of a great arc representing the final moments of its current state of awareness. We are being told that within a few years, a great shift in consciousness—affecting all forms of Creation—will engulf us like a tsunami advancing inexorably toward our shores.

Apparently, many advanced beings who live well outside the illusions of earthly existence have also known about these precipitous events for some time. Our planet, orbiting one of the larger suns on the remote fringes of one of the 125,000,000,000 galaxies in this physical universe, has long fascinated intergalactic observers. The experiment conducted here has been rich beyond expectation, yet in many ways deeply disturbing.

When the illusion that humans choose to call "reality" was first envisioned, it was meant to be a game board upon which highly evolved beings would "pretend" to forget who they are. There they could play at creating new experiences possible only in the crucible of duality and polarity where belief and emotion are the prime forces of motivation. It soon became apparent that the illusion was too well crafted. The experiment, while interesting, was not going as planned; with each successive incarnation, souls were experiencing greater levels of pain and suffering. Several times in the history of our planet, advanced beings incarnated on Earth to help shift consciousness and offer expanded choices. In each instance, their higher teachings were appropriated by the priesthood and ultimately created more harm than good.

Now that we are well into the anticipated shift, more than seventy million of these advanced beings have already incarnated on Earth. Unlike their predecessors, who kept their full awareness during their time on this planet, these Wanderers—as entities from higher densities are called—agreed to pass through the Veil of Forgetting as they entered the illusion. This means that they took on limited human awareness as well as human form.

They thought that their advanced state would permit them to quickly resolve the distortions of the Veil.

They were wrong.

At present, fewer than nine percent of these Wanderers have succeeded in cleansing the sleep from their eyes. Like the six billion souls they came to serve, the rest are trapped in the illusion, unable to break free. However, the effect that this small percentage of awakened beings has already made is considerable. Many of the predicted calamities appear to have been averted or at least ameliorated. The massive Earth shifts envisioned by several seers have not occurred, nor have the cataclysmic volcanic eruptions. Yet all around us—even on the physical plane—the evidence of the shift is unmistakable.

Unfortunately, our scientists are less than forthright. Under extreme pressure by their employers, they are refusing to share openly the grave fears that consume them behind closed doors. A short list of irrefutable scientific facts speaks volumes: the recent sunspot activity exceeds any previous measurement; a report leaked from the Russian National Academy of Science reveals that our solar system has moved into a "different area of space" with higher and more aberrant energy levels than previously noted; the sun's heliosphere (the magnetic "egg" radiating from the sun) is now ten times its normal size, creating a glowing, excited plasmic energy field at its leading edge; the atmospheres of five planets (including Earth) are undergoing significant change; several planets have recently undergone shifts in their magnetic pole positions—one of the turbulent changes also predicted for Earth; magnetic shifts on our planet are already so significant that the aeronautical maps used by pilots have had to be revised.

This list could be expanded many times over with more corroborative information. The point is clear: the predicted changes are not in our future, they are here now. The governmental and scientific communities, although well-informed, are at a loss as to what to do. In their desire to keep us calm and secure, they are choosing to conceal rather than admit impotence. Yet despite the confusion within the establishment, what is happening now is no mystery. It is exactly as it was meant to be, and, with full acknowledgment to the Mayan, Hopi, and other seers of the past, it is right on schedule.

To those still struggling beneath the weight of the Veil, breaking free seems daunting. In fact, it is surprisingly simple. All one needs to do is shift the point from which one views and the solution is immediately obvious. The trick, of course, is being willing to let go.

Although bits and pieces of the information contained in *Going Deeper* have long been available in various teachings, they were not easily integrated. In a sense, it's like saying all of Shakespeare's sonnets are contained in a can of Campbell's alphabet soup—one simply has to know how to rearrange the letters. I realize now that every step in my life was orchestrated to prepare me to become the scribe, so the information presented in this book could arrange itself like the tumblers in an elaborate lock.

This book is offered primarily to those Wanderers and those precious souls within the illusion who have wielded their spiritual machetes sufficiently to hack through the tangles of the Veil and glimpse the first rays of light. Our collective mission on this planet at this time is clear: to help the beings currently trapped within the illusion to move forward—should they wish it. If you are such a person—a Sleeping Beauty who has descended into the dream state behind the Veil of Forgetting—then prepare for the kiss of your prince.

You are about to awaken.

CHAPTER 1

In the Beginning Was the Ad

Larry was always amused by the way dogs and their owners appeared as a perfect match. They could look astonishingly alike, as if identical twins were manifesting in different forms—like a Mozart symphony and a perfect sunset. He wondered if they started out so—people unconsciously drawn to themselves in their pets—or if animal and human found common ground over time as their relationship deepened.

He also wondered if others could see how much he and Zeus had in common. Zeus was a genetic marvel—part everything. He was a shade too big for a border collie, but nowhere near the size of a German shepherd. He had the hunting instincts of a springer spaniel and the intelligence of a French poodle. He was part all of them—and probably more. The vet declared him as decidedly "something else" and said the dog definitely would not win best of breed in any AKC event, although he could probably be entered in at least four categories, maybe six.

Larry had had absolutely no intention of getting a dog; the idea had never crossed his mind. Even in retrospect, he couldn't fully rationalize the improbable series of events that brought them together. The odds must have been a billion to one. But in fact the outcome had already been determined; Zeus and Larry were destined to be together. In a very real sense, the fate of the world depended on it.

On the third of May, 1999, a freak tornado tore through the Wistful Willows trailer park some thirty miles southwest of Norman, Oklahoma, leaving several people dead, over eighteen mobile homes destroyed, and a litter of three six-week-old puppies stranded with no mother. The pups were rescued by Lucille Douglas, a volunteer emergency medical technician assigned to the team serving Norman Regional Hospital. She was at home glued to the TV set, like almost everyone else within a hundred-mile radius, when she took the call from the EMT team. It was well into the early hours of Tuesday morning. The call came as no surprise, as both KFOR and KWTV had been broadcasting tornado watch warnings and preliminary damage reports for the past twelve hours. Luckily, most people in the storm's path had plenty of advance notice and were able to get out of harm's way. But not everyone escaped what was later classified as the most damaging twister in U.S. history.

It rated an F5 on the Fujita scale, with truck-mounted Doppler radar clocking wind speeds of 318 miles per hour—the highest ever documented anywhere on earth! Several days later, after James Lee Witt, head of the Federal Emergency Management Agency, declared eleven surrounding counties eligible for federal aid, the local officials began finalizing the tallies: over thirty dead, more than three thousand homes severely damaged or destroyed, and losses exceeding 1.5 billion dollars.

Lucy threw on her EMT overalls and drove the short distance down Porter Street to Norman Regional to join one of the ambulance crews assigned to the disaster scene. Bridge Creek was less than sixteen miles from the hospital. The drive down I-35 to OK-9 should have taken no more than forty-five minutes. This trip, even with the flashing lights and sirens clearing the way, took the team over an hour and a half. The state police and sheriff's department had their hands full providing access to the disaster scene for the highway maintenance, phone, power, and emergency vehicles while keeping the press, curious onlookers, and distraught relatives at bay.

Lucy thought herself lucky to be on a team with Roger Thornton, widely acknowledged as the state's most experienced disaster specialist. Roger was also well-versed on tornadoes and gave the group an insider's view of these quirky weather patterns as they picked their way along rubble-strewn roads. He was obviously concerned about the storm-chasing "tourists" whose only training, he surmised, was viewing the movie *Twister*. "These idiots will get themselves killed for the chance of having one of their homemade videos make the six o'clock news. They not only risk their own lives, they put the real pros in jeopardy by clogging up the roads." On the other hand, he couldn't heap enough praise on the way the people at the Storm Prediction Center and the press were handling information dissemination. Thanks to their cool professionalism, he estimated, hundreds—if not thousands—of lives were saved.

The last stretch of road leading to Bridge Creek off OK-9 was ironically called Lovers' Lane. The current scene of tangled debris and fallen branches made a mockery of the twisted road sign—a biting reminder of gentler times. Roger's calm voice provided welcome assurance. His last piece of advice concerning the "four P's" of emergency evacuation turned out to be prophetic.

"This is probably the hardest hit area of the most devastating storm ever recorded in Oklahoma, if not the entire United States. I understand the trailer park's been hit pretty hard. From what the sheriff's people reported, it won't be a pretty sight. The good news is we're not the first on the scene, but we're going to have our hands full. Hope for the best and be ready for the worst, and don't forget to take care of the four P's, the possessions that people value most: pets, pictures, pills, and PCs."

Lucy subsequently told Larry that she heard the puppies long before she saw them and that the gut-wrenching pain caused by their cries will stay etched in her body memory forever. She followed the shrill sounds to three little bodies huddled against each other, pressed into the lifeless form of their mother who had birthed and nurtured them in a shallow furrow beneath a tangle of brush under a black willow tree, some thirty yards from the nearest structure. Mama would probably have been fine except for the unlikely shard of glass embedded deep in her neck. In Lucy's mind, she died saving her litter, and that made her a super mom and each of her puppies one of destiny's chosen children.

That thought—and Lucy's flair for the dramatic—explained the rather strange ad Larry saw in Sunday's paper, less than one week after the tragedy:

PHOENIX RISING! Three miracle puppy survivors of the WW disaster, ascending out of the ashes to help us embrace the winds of change. Each will be placed in the partnership/care of an equally special human. You will know. Reply by e-mail only: PhoenixPups@aol.com.

Everything about the ad was strange. It appeared under "Employment Opportunities," sandwiched between job offers for a paralegal and a plumber's assistant. It made no mention of breed. It contained none of the usual clichés like cute, adorable, needs a good home, loves children, and the like. It almost challenged response by providing no contact information beyond the e-mail address.

Larry was hooked the instant he read it, even though every part of his rational mind yelled at him to turn the page. Even from the vantage point of $^{20}/_{20}$ hindsight, he never understood what made him notice Lucy's ad in the first place. Larry had started that particular morning as he had begun each day during the eighteen months since his divorce became final. He retrieved the paper from wherever it was tossed, poured a glass of ruby-red grapefruit juice, and scanned the sports pages.

This mini ritual was simply a prelude to the real business at hand—matching wits with the grand master expert play in the bridge column and doing the daily crossword puzzle. Every so often, for reasons Larry could never understand, he was drawn to the horoscope on the facing page—almost as if there was a secret message waiting. Today was one of those occasions. "Now that spring is on the descendant, it is time for you to clean house like never before. Summon the resolve and courage to surrender the old and emerge like the Phoenix, from the ashes of your past. Prepare for great adventures. Your time has come."

The horoscope reminded Larry briefly of Marianne, and without bitterness he wished her well. Their seven years together had opened like a heart-stopping Disney A-ride and gradually faded into two people conversing in different languages across a widening chasm. They both deserved better. Unlike Larry, Marianne knew exactly what she wanted out of life, and her meteoric career as a clinical psychologist eloquently confirmed her ability to get it. Her many articles in women's magazines and regular talk-show guest slots had made her a minor celebrity, caught in the whirlwind of her own success.

All Larry knew with any degree of certainty at the time of their divorce was that he was somewhere between his thirty-seventh and thirty-eighth birthdays and his life wasn't working. His partnership with Cresswell, Timmons, and Baker paid well but offered little else. There was the little cabin in Idyllwild, two cars, a substantial investment portfolio, no children, and a community property state. Although he and Marianne still loved each other, both knew it was time to move on. This made the mechanics of the divorce relatively easy. It was completed almost before it began; Marianne never missed a beat, and Larry lost his codependent crutch. The last eighteen months had been, as he liked to call it, a prolonged time of healing.

The horoscope hit home. He briefly toyed with the idea that it was a plant, paid for by Mark Marston or one of the other goofballs from the Poker, Drinking, and Quipping Society—a group of intelligent, successful, and otherwise dignified men who met monthly on the first Thursday after the full moon to relive college memories of their misspent youth.

Any one of the PDQ Society's six members could have paid the newspaper to load Gemini with secret messages for a year. But they hadn't. Nor had they paid off Ming's Chinese Palace to give Larry a rigged fortune cookie the night before that read: "Good fortune, like Phoenix, arise in proper time." Larry briefly cultivated the notion that the world was covertly run by the Peking Noodle Company, whose clandestine messages were delivered by undercover agents, disguised as Chinese waiters, informing us on a need-to-know basis. Last night he had added the fortune to a small collection of $\frac{5}{8}$"x $2\frac{5}{8}$" coated white papers inscribed with Chinese wisdom that he kept in a beige suede pouch along with Indian sacred objects from Taos in his desk's top right-hand drawer. After reading the horoscope and the classified ad, he got up to check. Sure enough. Last night's Phoenix message was still there.

Larry was keenly aware that for the third time in twenty-four hours the word "Phoenix" had played a prominent role in his consciousness. If it was a conspiracy, it had to involve a lot of people, including whoever had caused America's most devastating tornado to trigger the events culminating in the appearance of the four-line ad in the *Los Angeles Times*. The instant he read it, Larry knew the ad was meant only for him.

He went to his laptop and composed the first of many e-mails to Lucy:

Dear Phoenix Pups,

   I too am an arising Phoenix preparing for the next phase of my adventure. I have been waiting for this transformation and your arrival for thirty-seven years. Please let me know when we can meet. Reply by e-mail at earliest convenience.

A slew of e-mails followed, in which the two shared thoughts on life, philosophies, favorite foods, movies, and the wackiest political moments throughout history. Over the next few days, Larry confided more to Lucy about his personal life than he had to close acquaintances. Somehow, the anonymity of electronic mail and the sincerity of Lucy's perceptions made it easier. Lucy also learned much more than the facts Larry chose to share. She delighted in his offbeat sense of humor, his display of tenacity and flexibility in playing her "take-away" e-mail game, and, above all, his genuine desire to make a difference on this planet.

What Lucy didn't share with Larry was that she was reading his e-mails alongside those from other respondents. She explained later that she had been "informed" by some inner voice to keep one of the puppies for herself and give away the other two to "special people" who were waiting for them on either coast. Lucy claimed this inner voice had directed her to place the same Phoenix Rising notice in the "Employment" section—once only, and definitely not under "Pets"—in the May 9 Sunday edition of the *Boston Globe*, the *Los Angeles Times*, the *Seattle Times*, and the *Savannah Morning News*.

She must allow the puppies to choose their own partners. This, she was told, especially applied to the puppy she was eventually to keep for herself. Her next task was to name them. Because of the unprecedented magnitude of the tornado that had torn through their collective lives, Lucy was inspired to give each the name of a god. The sole female in the litter—the one that ultimately became hers—Lucy named Sekhmet after the Egyptian goddess of fire, who has the body of a woman and the head of a lioness and is typically portrayed seated on a throne. The two males she named Rama, to honor the attributes of the Indian warrior god who conquered the demonic Ravana; and Zeus, who ruled Olympus as the Greeks' supreme god of the sky and was thus directly responsible for the terrible twisters that had begun this improbable chain of events.

As e-mail responses arrived from the four cities, Lucy felt like the International Olympic Committee accepting bids for future venues. Any doubts or concerns were swiftly allayed by some higher awareness deftly instructing every aspect of the process. Lucy was comfortable surrendering herself to this higher knowing. She was too intuitive to allow her ego to override the extraordinary flow of events sweeping her along.

At Lucy's suggestion, her final communication with Larry, nine days after the ad appeared, was by telephone. By the time Larry learned that Lucy and the pups were half way across the continent, he was too far gone to care. He would gladly have traveled to Panama if that was part of the deal. Lucy also laid out for him three final "challenges"—a mini version of the trials of Hercules, as she laughingly likened them—that would prove, mostly to himself, his degree of commitment.

One: He could not fly. He had to make the 1,350 mile journey by car, driving alone. Certain processes—Lucy used a few new-age buzz words like "reprogramming," "frequency tuning," and "downloading"—needed to take place during the journey to attune Larry and his partner to their new relationship.

Two: He and his pet must first see each other within twelve hours of the full moon, which would occur in Norman, Oklahoma at precisely 6:40 a.m. on Sunday, the thirtieth of May. By Larry's calculations, then, he had to arrive at Lucy's house some time between 6:40 p.m. on Saturday and 6:40 p.m. Sunday.

Three: The final selection process was up to neither Lucy nor Larry. If one of the puppies did not clearly select him, the deal was off and he would have to return home alone.

Larry arranged his work schedule so he could take extra vacation time, padding the long Memorial Day weekend into a six-day trip. He decided to allow two days for the journey east, one day to visit Lucy and pick up his new companion, and three days to return home. If some arcane force was tampering with his inner circuitry while he navigated the endless ribbon of concrete interstates constantly receding before him, he wasn't aware of it. All he knew was that the smooth jazz of 94.7 FM was soon replaced by country music and stayed that way until he reached his destination. He made a mental note to stock CDs on his next trip.

Lucy appeared pretty much as she had described herself: in her late forties, pleasant-looking, with a trim, athletic build and strawberry blonde hair that she kept in a pony tail. However, certain qualities transcended her physical appearance and spoke volumes about who she really was. Her eyes were grayish-green, and when she looked at Larry, he felt he could trust her implicitly. She managed to convey a highly improbable mix of guilelessness and impeccable discernment. Her smile could turn an iceberg into a gentle puddle.

The two liked each other instantly. It appeared both had been completely honest in their communications, and they were comfortable dealing at a level of trust uncommon in the first twenty years of a "normal" relationship. Perhaps the fact that they connected only at the level of the Phoenix Pups, with no innuendo of personal relationship, helped.

Their get-to-know-each-other cup of coffee was interrupted by the sound of scratching at the back door. "Ah, the time has come," Lucy said, "to meet the brood. Apparently your arrival has not gone unnoticed, and one of the puppies appears to be anxious to meet you firsthand." With that she opened the door to her back yard and a little ball of fur scampered in, jumped up on the couch, and began licking Larry's face.

"Well, I guess that takes care of the third condition. Larry, meet Zeus. Zeus, it seems you already know Larry. I had a feeling the two of you were destined to be together. I'm glad I was right."

Larry was introduced to the other two members of the litter, who, however, seemed more interested in playing with a blue ball that jangled as it rolled. Zeus, on the other hand, never left his side. The three spent the rest of the day driving out to Bridge Creek, tracing the route Lucy had covered with her EMT team nearly four weeks earlier. The roads had been cleared of broken branches and downed power lines, but visible reminders of the devastation were everywhere. The badly bent pole with the hanging road sign identifying Lovers' Lane was exactly as Lucy recalled it. So was the Wistful Willows trailer park. Unfortunately, not one of the graceful thirty-year-old trees for which the lower-income community was named remained undamaged. Jagged, broken trunks provided poignant proof of the F5 twister.

They walked through the remnants of destroyed lives in reverent silence. Zeus quietly left Larry's side and disappeared behind a pile of twisted rubble. When they found him, he was sitting next to what was left of the black willow tree where Lucy had discovered the litter. He didn't move a muscle. He sat mutely, doing whatever dogs do when they know the exquisite sadness of losing the one presence they loved most.

They left the little puppy there alone, allowing him whatever he needed to create closure. Somehow, Zeus seemed to know his life was about to move in a decidedly different direction and he would never return here again. The three exited the trailer park without saying a word.

It struck Larry when he first met this funny-looking little puppy that he was no ordinary dog. It would take almost two and a half years to discover how much of an understatement this was.

Many of us spend our whole lives
Running from feeling
With the mistaken belief
That you cannot bear the pain.
But you have already borne the pain.
What you have not done
Is feel all you are beyond that pain.

— KAHLIL GIBRAN

CHAPTER 2

9/11—The Day the World Changed Forever

A long with the other 6.17 billion passengers on planet Earth, Larry's world irrevocably changed on Tuesday, the eleventh of September, 2001.

When he first saw the live television broadcasts showing what seemed to be model planes crashing into replicas of the twin towers, he thought of Orson Welles's historic 1938 Mercury Theater on the Air broadcast of the Martian invasion. He especially remembered the crackling voice of the CBS announcer reporting from atop the broadcast building, telling a horrified audience of the fateful discharge of poisonous smoke that was about to annihilate the population of New York. Everyone in the city died that night, only to be reborn the next morning. "Rising," Larry later mused, "from the ashes of their own imaginations."

This time was very different. Thousands of people died and there was no resurrection. Instead, there was shock, disbelief, grief, anger, and an incredible feeling of impotence. For the next several days Larry was stunned, reflexively going through the motions that carried him from bed to shower to office to home. By Friday, the Novocain-like numbness had begun to wear off, exposing the underlying pain and the realization that the world was in deep trouble. The tragic event was a major turning point in Larry's life, but its significance paled in comparison to what would happen that weekend.

Larry left the Santa Monica offices of Cresswell, Timmons, and Baker just before noon on Friday. He wanted some time away and had decided he and Zeus would "go bush"—one of those wonderfully rich Aussie phrases that simply means to wander off into the outback, to hang out away from civilization and commune with nature. Man and dog needed to do some serious thinking. Larry's only plan was to leave early and head east on Interstate 10, well ahead of the rush-hour traffic that lately seemed to pour onto the freeways around four in the morning and thicken through the day into the hard-set parking-lot syndrome of late afternoon. Larry reckoned he was early enough so he could flow through the 210 interchange with the consistency of a creamy Hollandaise.

He loaded the car with sleeping bag, tent, and assorted yuppie victuals carefully selected at Trader Joe's. Larry had no plan in mind except to head towards Phoenix. He didn't intend going there; he just relished the symbolism in light of the Phoenix trinity that had brought Zeus into his life. Besides, if he tried to go west, there was nothing but a lot of Pacific Ocean.

There's a long, gentle descent marking the eastern slope of Banning Pass, starting at White Water all the way down into the Coachella Valley and the rich excesses of Palm Springs, the "Land of 100 Golf Courses." Beyond, the road stretches past the Salton Sea and begins its climb towards the Arizona border. Along the way, miles of nothing. Larry was busy conjuring scenes of turning his RX300 off the main drag, finding an unmarked dirt road, and exploring some of the volcanic mounds he remembered from his frequent cross-country flights.

"Stop thinking so much, already. You're giving me a headache!" The voice in Larry's head was sudden and frighteningly clear.

"What?"

"Thank you. That's much better," the voice said. "By the way, take the next exit. It's coming up in less than a quarter of a mile, so get over to the right as soon as you can." Despite his shock, Larry maneuvered to the off-ramp, left the freeway, and pulled over.

"Zeus, did you hear anything, or am I going crazy?" Zeus, hearing his name called, arose from his bedding in the back of the SUV, wagged his tail, and jumped onto the front seat to lick Larry's face.

Thank God for Zeus. In the little over two years since Larry had driven out to Oklahoma to formally adopt him, the two had been virtually inseparable. Funny, all the members of the PDQ Society had remarked how much Larry had changed after that. It was more than getting over Marianne; it was hard to define. He seemed "the same, but different," as they lamely put it.

Larry not only read more, he read books about bizarre material that had never interested him before. He had sudden urges to go to lectures and workshops, or surf the Internet looking up the oddest topics. He found himself browsing the shelves of the Bodhi Tree bookstore in West Hollywood. He listened to tapes by Deepak Chopra and Marianne Williamson. Little by little it was dawning on him that reality doesn't lend itself to containment in tidy packages. Certainty was receding, replaced by a newborn voice in his psyche that demanded answers to a host of unspoken questions. Despite all his education and apparent success, the life he'd constructed for himself didn't quite make sense to him any more. Something about it was a complete sham. Whatever he was doing now, whatever he had done in the past, no longer had much relevance. And he had no answers. The events of September eleventh seemed to bring it all to a head. Larry had come to the disquieting realization that he, too, was in trouble.

After making sure his master was okay, Zeus returned to the comfort of his blankie, the tattered remnant of a maroon blanket with the faded letters PROPERTY OF SAN QUENTIN still visible to the discerning eye. For some inexplicable reason, Zeus preferred this Ghirardelli Square tourist artifact to any PetsMart bed Larry had ever brought home.

"You feeling okay?" There was the voice again!

"Are you real?" Larry asked. "Who are you?"

"Of course I'm real. You're talking to me, aren't you? As to who I am, we'd better handle that question a little later. This isn't the best time or place. For now, go to the end of the ramp and head north on 62. By the way, are you okay?" There was a tone of genuine concern.

"I guess so." Larry pulled off the shoulder and turned left, starting the long ascent toward Morongo Valley and the high desert nestled in the foothills of the San Bernardino Mountains.

"This is crazy," Larry said more to himself than to the voice.

"No more crazy than that," said the voice.

"What?"

"If this is one level of reality and that is the part of reality that isn't this, then that is no less crazy than this," the voice said.

"What?"

"Forget it. Besides, you're beginning to sound like a What-What bird."

"A what?"

"See, there you go again. A What-What bird. You'll probably get to meet one later. For now, you're doing just fine. Keep driving north on 62. I'll let you know where to turn off."

"Do you mind telling me who you are and where we're going and why you're giving me all these instructions?"

"No."

"This is getting silly. No, what?"

"Sorry. No, Larry," the voice said. "I didn't think I had to use your name every time I spoke to you. Am I wrong about that?"

"No, you don't have to use my name at all, unless you want to. Now please answer my questions."

"I did," the voice said. "I am totally literal, you see. So you have to be very, very precise when you ask me things. Unlike you, it's not in my nature to assume anything. You asked me if I minded providing you with certain information, and I told you I didn't mind at all."

"Well?" asked Larry.

"Now that's a deep thought," the voice said. "What do you suppose is at the bottom of it?"

"The bottom of what?"

"The well, of course!"

"This is like *Alice in Wonderland*," Larry said. "Only I haven't fallen into a hole or gone through a mirror or eaten magic mushrooms—or followed a tardy rabbit, for that matter!"

"In a curious way, Larry, over the past two years you've done all of those things. And now your world has expanded to include me in a new way. And that makes me very happy."

Time seemed to dissolve as Larry patiently endured the 40-mph speed limit and the stop-and-go traffic of Yucca Valley on the way toward the little town of Joshua Tree. Deep in thought, he simultaneously realized nothing and everything. He exploded into a wordless, timeless void, watching his mind race like a spinning roulette wheel, never allowing the ball to settle into a numbered slot.

"You're doing fine," the voice said. "Hang a right at the next light, onto Park Boulevard."

Larry complied and found himself on a rising, turning road headed toward the west entrance station to Joshua Tree National Park.

"What do I do here?" he asked.

"Pay the ranger and drive in. Relax. You've already handled the tough part. It'll all start making sense once we can really talk inside the park."

Following the voice's instructions, Larry made a sharp right off the main park road and pulled into the Hidden Valley parking area. Zeus had already made his way onto the front seat, leash in mouth, tail wagging like a metronome on speed.

"Cattle thieves," the voice said.

"What?" At the sound of Larry's voice, Zeus turned and looked straight at him.

"There you go again. What's with the whats?"

"What about cattle thieves?" Larry asked, all but ignoring Zeus.

"Oh! Whoopee-ti-yi-yo, get along little dogies," the voice began singing the old cowboy refrain. "That's my theme song down here. Did you know that?"

"Give me a break. Can't you say anything that makes any sense?"

The voice smiled. But Larry had no way of knowing that. Man and dog walked in silence, Zeus leading the way, Larry blindly following. Larry removed Zeus's leash, and the dog spent a few minutes sniffing the air and exploring nearby rock outcroppings before returning to Larry. He circled Larry completely three times counterclockwise, then three times clockwise, and, using his front right paw, drew an arrow in the sand. Larry's jaw dropped. It wasn't just a line; it was a real arrow pointing in a real direction, marking the way Zeus began walking. The voice in Larry's head simply said, "Follow."

Larry tagged behind Zeus in total disbelief. Things, as Alice quite properly observed, were getting curiouser and curiouser. The two clambered over boulders and up steep inclines. They left any semblance of a trail as scrambling gave way to picking then to climbing up one of Joshua Tree's steeper rock formations. Larry's body would have preferred a more leisurely stroll, but he comforted the nagging aches with the thought that the view from the top would justify the journey's sacrifices.

As if reading his mind, the voice said, "Wrong. And wrong."

"What do you mean by 'wrong and wrong'?"

"Why, wrong on both counts, of course," it replied.

"What counts?" Larry asked.

"Everything counts, Larry. Absolutely everything, as you will soon understand."

"Never mind the counts. Tell me about the wrong part," Larry demanded. He was becoming impatient, the stress of the climb loosening his grip on his usual sense of humor.

"Couldn't resist. Sorry about that. I suppose we'll have to get used to how each of us plays head stuff. When I said 'wrong and wrong,' what I really meant was 'wrong and wrong.' I may have been too literal. You thought—which is the same as speaking to me—and I responded.

"When you said you were willing to trade the pain of the journey for the reward at the top, you made two errors of assumption. First of all, we're not going to the top, so there will be no view. At least not the sort you're thinking about. And second, you were so focused on reaching some imagined destination that you were completely missing the gifts of the journey.

"You didn't see the little lizards turning in the sun, displaying their iridescent skins, or hear the welcome of the rocks or smell the perfume of the sage. You locked yourself into a tiny closet deep in the bowels of your lower 'I' and traded the magic of the present for the fanciful mirages of the future. You willfully shielded yourself from the infinite expression of All That

Is. If you do that repeatedly, it gets harder and harder to leave the closet."

"Well, it was starting to hurt," Larry said.

"So kiss it better," came the chuckling reply.

"Huh?"

"Not bad. At least you didn't say 'what.' That's a sign of improvement, don't you think?"

"Think about what?"

"Whoops, I may have spoken too soon. Never mind. Why does the muscle ache? It aches to speak to you. It aches to say, 'I'm not used to this much activity. It's straining my ability to bring in oxygen and release wastes.' It aches to tell you to eat your banana. It aches to tell you it is a part of you and needs your attention and acknowledgment.

"Consider this: When a mother kisses a booboo better, she becomes a radiant conduit of divine love. In that moment, child and mother and God merge, and time is commanded to stand still. Only when she removes her mouth may the sands resume their journey through the glass. By then, the healing is complete and the tears are replaced by a smile and soul touches soul and she hears the sweetest words of all: 'I love you, Mommy.'

"Does your body, the exquisite chariot that transports you through this kaleidoscopic realm of events, merit less? Of course not! Your body needs you to kiss it better."

Larry looked confused. "Part of me gets it and part of me is totally confused. I think I need your help. What do you really want me to do?"

"Bravo! I really mean it. Bravo! That was the most profound statement you've made so far, and I applaud you for it. Asking for help is one of the most accessible bridges available. Nothing is more powerful. When you ask, truly ask, from the innocence of your heart, the Universe must respond. This, Larry, is an immutable law. This is not asking from the mind, like asking someone to help you move a heavy box. This is an asking that shifts the lower I and makes room for a higher state of connectivity. I will do all I can to help. In fact, when you ask from that place, it becomes my honor, my duty, and my absolute pleasure to serve. Thank you for asking."

"One thing before you begin," Larry interjected. "What is the lower I you keep talking about?"

"Interesting question," the voice said. "I'll beg off answering that until you've had a chance to listen to my good friend Rocky. The lower I is a function of your 'tudes. And there's no one in all of God's vast kingdom—at least the parts I know about—who knows more about 'tudes than Rocky. Why hear it from me when such a master is near at hand?

"Let's rather speak of kissing your body better. You can start by peeling one of the bananas in your backpack. Plain ol' common sense tells you a quick shot of potassium can't hurt none," the voice shifted suddenly into a Western drawl. "You might wanna find yourself a comfortable place t' perch. Looks like we're fixin' t' stay here a spell."

Larry found a relatively flat rock shielded from the glare of the high desert sun, removed a banana from his pack, and sat. His wrist felt sweaty, prompting him to take off his watch and towel down his arms and face. It was already 4:17, and Larry briefly wondered what would happen if he and Zeus got lost and had to spend the night here among the rocks. Magnificent monzogranite boulders loomed on all sides. He was completely cocooned, unable to see more than ten yards in any direction, and for sure no one could see him. He was about to call Zeus when he saw the dog rounding a nearby rock, returning on cue, as if he had been privy to Larry's thoughts. "Damn, that mutt sometimes actually seems human," Larry thought.

Zeus turned toward Larry and smiled. His mouth never moved but he smiled. Maybe it was in his eyes or the tilt of his head. Then he lay down in a patch of sand cooled by the shade of a juniper tree and the lengthening shadows of the hour. His eyes stayed open, focused on everything and nothing in particular, the way wise dogs sometimes look.

The voice continued: "Go into your body now. Tell me what you feel."

Larry closed his eyes, as if in meditation, and responded, "I can feel a dull ache in my lower back and my legs are throbbing."

"Okay, let's start with the back. Begin breathing into it."

"That's silly," Larry said. "How can I breathe into my back when I breathe through my front and my back is behind me?"

"Horrors! Heah I was takin' you to yo' first day at kindergarten when you are only in yo' secon' month of nursery school." The voice continued with its distinct and very hammy Southern accent. "I do declare! What possibly could have come over me? I swear, I must be having a touch of the vapors. Larry, *do* forgive me, won't you? Now there's a sweet boy. Promise me you won't tell a livin' soul and let it be our little secret."

Larry burst out laughing.

"Welcome to the present," said the voice. "There's nothing like a little humor to band you back to the present."

"Band you what?"

"Band you back—much like your back, only completely different. That's what's so confusing about having to use words. They sound like each other but mean different things—especially to different people at different times. Words can make people think they know what is meant when in reality they don't because the people speaking them can't get them right enough to convey what they actually want to communicate and they end up compromising what they really mean to suit the words they think they know."

"What?" Larry said.

"There you go again with the whats. All I'm trying to say is that when you really want to communicate, words don't always do the job.

"That said, let's focus on the phenomenon of banding back, which, as it turns out, is the real gift of humor. You see, Larry, linear time is analogous to a rubber band. From where you always are—in present time or the Infinite Instant or the now, as it is often called—you can use your mind to project into the past or future. This stretches the band. If your mind is kept there too long, the band weakens and loses elasticity. In extreme cases it may break. Disease, stress, encysted emotion, negativity of any kind—either mental or physical—are always functions of persistently stretching the rubber band out of the infinite instant.

"There are many ways to return to the I-squared moment. We call it that because the infinite instant has no physical measurement. It folds itself simultaneously in and out of the illusion of space/time. The instant and infinity are two sides of the same nonexistent coin, making their product the square of either one. In your language, this circumstance is represented by the extraordinary word 'is,' which at one level refers to a state of being but at a higher, esoteric level actually refers to a *State of Being*: the infinite instant of the I-squared now.

"As I said, there are many ways to band back to the present. Sudden danger. Intense pleasure. Meditation. Personally speaking, intense pleasure comes in second. The best, in my book, will always be humor. Did you know there are documented cases of people curing themselves of cancer by watching Marx Brothers movies?

"Humor is the sudden, unexpected intersection of two planes of thought at a single point in the now. You slide down both planes simultaneously, coming from two directions in a joyous ride, and crash into yourself. The steeper the planes, the funnier the joke. Unless they become so steep that you aren't able to join them at their point of impact and you don't 'get it.'

"It's never quite as funny when it has to be explained because that reduces the steepness of the planes, so when they meet it's more like a gentle bump than an atomic explosion. By the way, when was the last time you saw a Marx Brothers movie?"

"Wow." That was all Larry could muster. "Who the hell are you?"

"Ah, the planes become steeper and steeper. I only request that you be there when they finally meet so you can find all this as supremely humorous as I do."

The voice lapsed into a clipped British accent. "But we wander far afield, and your sincere request for assistance begs resolution. Let's move on to the concept of breathing into your back, shall we? The breath, as you will discover, is one of the two great gifts to humankind—the other, by the way, being water. Breathing is so obvious, all but the most wise and most foolish among you overlook it. Humans take about 17,280 breaths a day, and they are probably not conscious of a single one unless they have asthma or find themselves in a noxious environment. On the other hand, dogs—of which Zeus is one of the more exquisite examples—can cycle over 30,000 breaths per day and are conscious of every one of them. Their sense of smell is a million times more acute than yours, which makes their infinite instant far richer than anything you can imagine. You have much to learn from Zeus, and from all the others.

"But I digress again. Let's return once more to your breath. Breathe in deeply and follow the breath. Now tell me where it goes."

"Into the lungs, of course."

"No. You are speaking of the air. I am speaking of the breath. Only at the surface are they the same. Go deeper and tell me what you feel as you breathe in."

"My chest and belly rise and fall."

"Okay, that's a start. Go deeper still. Tell me about the texture, the flavor, the color of the breath."

Larry sat in silence, eyes closed, as he watched his breath enter and leave his body. "Curious. It feels cool as it passes my nostrils on the way in and velvety warm as it passes the same spot on the way out."

"Excellent. Continue. What else do you perceive?"

"This is strange! I don't know if I am imagining it or it's real. I can almost feel energy on the breath, as if I were breathing in life. How weird."

"Not at all. What's really strange is that this is so new to you. Where have you been, man? Seventeen thousand breaths a day, every single day of your life, and you finally show up. Now *that's* weird! But you're definitely moving in the right direction. Don't let the mind confuse you into believing that reality and imagination are so different. I promise, their margins leak far more than you imagine. In fact, the two depend greatly on each other for their existence. Forget the thoughts. Simply stay with the breath. Move past viewing it as molecules of air and tell me what you sense. Go deeper. Just say whatever pops into your mind without filtering it through your preconceptions. Go deeper and tell me what you see."

"Okay." Larry's eyes remained gently closed. His face gradually relaxed, melting as if it was no longer defined by muscle and bone. His breathing became connected, with no discernible pause between in-breath and out-breath. He began speaking, barely louder than a whisper. But the voice heard every word.

"It's as if I'm breathing in light. There are flecks of iridescence reflecting a hidden light source. Golds and whites and very light purple. I am not certain whether I see them as waves or flecks . . . sometimes both. I can hear the light as well. Wow! There's beautiful music. No melody; just music resonating with the most incredible tones . . . unlike any instrument I know. I don't actually hear this music. I seem to feel it. My body resonates to it. Almost as if the music is language and it's the way the Universe and I really communicate."

"Excellent. Now continue. Where does the breath go?"

"Let me see. It appears to go everywhere. It goes throughout my entire body. I think of a part of me and the breath seems to concentrate right there. Wow."

"Wonderful. You're beginning to explore the outer reaches of the Great Mystery. The breath is Consciousness, just as you are Consciousness. These two planes of Consciousness intersect more than seventeen thousand times a day. Your only job is to show up and experience the joy at the instant of their meeting. It's like a joke. Show up and laugh, or you miss the moment and don't get it.

"Now direct the breath to your back. Tell me what you see."

"There's darkness, like a knot. And the breath is stroking it with light, like gentle waves lapping on a shore. Wow. The knot is actually dissolving. Now it's getting smaller . . . and smaller. It's gone, completely gone!"

"And how does your back feel?"

"It feels terrific. No pain whatsoever. In fact, it seems to be glowing with strength and giggles. My back is actually telling me it's happy!"

"And it is happy. Now do you think you can make you poor legs happy too?"

Larry focused his breath on his legs—and his chest and his arms and his head and his mind and his emotions and everything else he could think of. The voice watched and waited and smiled.

"Judging by the grin on your face, I gather you're done?"

"Oh, yes. Oh, yes. . . . Holy cow!"

"You can do this any time you wish. You don't need me or this place or anyone's permission to move past the local self—or lower 'I,' as I prefer to call it. Being physically in this place with my energies to guide you made the process easier. But they are no longer necessary.

"Now that we've taken care of your body's immediate needs, let's move on to the real reason you're here. Turn your attention from your breath and focus on Zeus. What do you see?"

"Should I open my eyes?" Larry asked.

"It actually doesn't matter. It will be the same either way. Perhaps you would be less tempted to doubt this is happening with your eyes open. But the choice is yours."

Larry opened his eyes. Zeus was sitting some ten feet away, facing him. His gaze was focused squarely on Larry's left eye. Behind Zeus, hovering some four feet above the ground, was the figure of an American Indian warrior, complete with chiseled features, prominent hooked nose, deep copper skin, full headdress, war paint, and fierce, piercing eyes. He was carrying a drum in one hand and a spear in the other.

Larry gasped. Even as he looked, the shape before him changed, flowing from one tribal representation to another, embracing Iroquois, Apache, Crete, Hopi, Navajo, Mohawk, Sioux, Seminole, Pawnee, and others defying description. Larry felt he was watching a movie projected onto billowing smoke.

The figure transmuted again and again, embracing all the indigenous peoples from the beginning of time: Australian, Asian, European, African, Pacific Islander, as well as Native American. A sudden, chilling breeze swept through the boulders, sending shivers down Larry's spine. He looked up into the sky to see a solitary bird—a majestic *chrysos aetos,* a golden eagle, with a seven-foot wing span—hovering on invisible currents no more than thirty feet above their heads.

The Indian spoke: "It is good. Wind Spirit has blessed our circle." His form was gentler now and smaller in stature. The piercing gaze shifted to a look of deep kindness as the illusion of smoke dissipated and the Indian descended onto solid ground. His voice was gentle and welcoming. "I am Gathering Cloud Salgado. I speak for my people, the Morongo, who once walked these lands freely. I speak also for my brothers and sisters who have been keepers of the sacred wisdom from the beginning of time and knew great riches. I speak now because it is time and because if I do not, it will soon be too late."

Gathering Cloud stepped in front of Zeus and drew a wide circle in the sand between man and dog, placing a large stone at each of the four cardinal directions. Then, entering the circle from the east, he began to softly chant an old Indian prayer:

We now put our minds together as one. We turn our thoughts to On-Gwa-Ya-Dis-Un, the one who made me. We choose our finest words to greet and give thanks to the Creator, for the Creator has prepared all things on the Earth for our peace of mind. The Creator has said, "No one will know my face, but I will be watching over all the people who move about the Earth."

Gathering Cloud walked counterclockwise along the inside

of the circle, representing the direction the Earth turns. The muffled beat of a drum, slow and steady, accompanied his journey. At each compass point he bent down to touch the Earth, then straightened and looked upward to the Creator.

At the north, he said:

Our thoughts now turn to the sky, where we see the sun, the source of life. We are instructed to call him our Eldest Brother. With the sun we can see the perfect gifts, for which we are grateful. Our Brother nourishes Mother Earth and is the source of light and warmth. Our Brother is the source of all fires of life. With every new sunrise is a new miracle. Now our minds are as one, O-nahn oh-kwat-neh-goon-wah.

To the west, he offered:

During the night we see the moon, who we have been instructed to address as Grandmother. In her cycle she makes her face in harmony with other female life. Our Grandmother still follows the instructions of the Creator. Within these are the natural cycles of women. She determines the arrival of children, causes the tides of the oceans, and she also helps us measure time. We are grateful and express our thanks. Now our minds are as one.

To the south, he said:

The stars are the helpers of Grandmother Moon. They have spread themselves across the sky. Our people know their names and their messages of future happenings, even to helping mold the individual character of mankind. The stars provide us with guidance and they bring dew to the plant life. As we view the beauty of the stars, we know that they are following the instructions of the Creator. Now our minds are as one.

To the east he prayed:

The four powerful messengers who have been assigned by the Creator to guide us are called the Sky Dwellers. Our Creator directed these helpers to assist him in dealing with us during our journey on Mother Earth. They know our every act and they guide us with the teachings that the Creator established. We give our greetings and thanks to the Sky Dwellers for their power of direction. Now our minds are as one.

Gathering Cloud turned toward the setting sun and said:

We who have gathered together are responsible that our cycle continues. We have been given the duty to live in harmony with one another and with other living things. We give greetings that our people still share the knowledge of our culture and ceremonies and are able to pass it on. We have our elders here and also the new faces yet to be born, which is the cycle of our families. Now our minds are as one.

Gathering Cloud stepped out of the circle and resumed his position behind Zeus. He spoke directly to Larry: "There has never been a time such as this. There is a gathering in all the realms unlike any told or sung about before. Know that you are loved and blessed. All my ancestors sit in council to support and advise. We salute you for the task you are about to perform. We are here to help you with each step on your journey. However the law that governs us all honors, above all else, your Free Will. The asking must come from you. We wait and pray.

"We now see that all things are faithful to their duties as the Creator instructed them. We therefore gather our minds into one and give thanks to the Creator for all that has been given to us. Ho!"

Larry saw five piles of sacramental offerings appear within the circle: pine nuts to the north, tobacco to the east, sage to the south, corn meal to the west, and in the center of the circle, several sprigs of juniper. Gathering Cloud was gone. He was replaced by another, almost familiar voice that continued his prayer. "Thank you, Mother Earth, Father Sky, for nurturing us. At this time we ask Great Spirit,

Give us hearts to understand:
    Never to take from our Creation's beauty more
        than we give;
    Never to destroy wantonly for furtherance of greed;
    Never to deny to give our hands for the
        building of Earth's beauty;
    Never to take from her what we cannot use.

Give us hearts to understand:
    That to destroy Earth's music is to create confusion;
    That to wreck her appearance is to blind us to
        beauty;
    That to callously pollute her fragrance is to make a
        house of stench;
    That as we care for her, she will care for us.

Give us hearts to understand:
>   We have forgotten who we are.
>   We have sought only our own security.
>   We have exploited simply for our own ends.
>   We have distorted our knowledge.
>   We have abused our power.
>   Grant that our minds be as one. Ho!

The last line of the Indian prayer had barely drifted out of the circle when the new voice spoke to Larry. This time it sounded exactly like the one he had heard in the car. "Now it is time. We need to talk." The words came directly from Zeus.

Larry was awestruck. No words would form in his mind. His mouth offered only incoherent noises.

Zeus didn't move a muscle, but his gaze bore deeply into Larry as he spoke. "Get a grip, man. Pull yourself together. We've been talking for years. Now we're just using words. No biggie."

Larry tried to piece together a few sounds. "Dog? Talk? Real? Huh?"

"Stay in your mind," Zeus said. "You don't need words, just thoughts. Keep them simple for now. You can add the fancy stuff once you get the hang of it."

Larry nodded.

Zeus continued, "This is real. In fact, it's more real than you know. I am a dog. Actually, I like being a dog, especially your dog. At least that's my part in the projection for now.

"Look, you seem a bit out of it, and for what's soon to come you'll need to be one hundred percent present. What do you say we call it a day? Let's head back to the car before it gets dark."

Larry looked at the watch lying by his side. It was 4:19 P.M. Only two minutes had passed since he had taken it off several hours ago . . . or several lifetimes ago . . . or was it several reality bands ago?

"Ah, the illusion of time. Deep stuff, that. We'll dig into it a bit tomorrow and play with the relativity of it all. For now, wagons ho!" Zeus turned to exit stage right. Larry staggered behind as best he could.

We must never cease from explorations.
and at the end of all our explorings,
Will be to arrive where we began
And to know the place for the first time.

— T. S. ELIOT

CHAPTER 3

Calling It a Day

The walk back to the car was timeless. If asked, Larry wouldn't have been able to remember a single thing except that he somehow ended up next to his SUV with his dog standing by his side, tail wagging.

"Howya doin', pardner?" Zeus asked, looking up at his master, giving it his best John Wayne drawl.

"Is that really you?"

"This is truly a Kodak moment lost. Your very first sentence and no camera! What's a poor dog to do?"

"My God, this is nuts. I'm going bonkers!" Larry said to no one in particular.

Zeus gave no reply and simply jumped into the car the instant Larry opened the door. He promptly scampered into the back and curled into his blankie, just the way he always did. Larry slid into the front seat and stared. "So help me, I'm going crazy!"

After a few minutes, regaining a semblance of composure, he turned to the back of the car. "Okay, let's say this is really happening. What's with the cowboy twang?"

"It makes me feel a part of history. Both this place's and mine. You noticed how easy it was to disappear from sight among all the rock outcroppings? I know you did because I caught some of your thoughts about it as we were walking. The place where we were is called Hidden Valley because it can't easily be seen from anywhere. That's why cattle rustlers used it back in the 1880s. Since I was orphaned myself, and I am a dog, I adopted the song 'Get Along Little Dogies' as my personal theme." Zeus began to sing the cowboy ditty, amused at the thought of being a doggie-dogie.

"You can read my thoughts?" Larry blurted.

"Of course I can read your thoughts. I told you that earlier. You don't have to shout at me. I can hear your mind just fine. In fact, I can generally make out what you are thinking even before you know it yourself. When you hear me talking, you're doing the same thing. The only difference is I project to you. You couldn't handle free access to my mind. My sense of smell alone would put you out for a week!"

"You mean you know everything I've been thinking?"

"Yep. Everything from the time you sent the first e-mail to Lucy. She read me your reply, I tuned in and telepathically let her know you were the one. She's a very gifted intuitive, so I didn't have to use words. In her mind, she just knew."

"Everything?"

"Oh, give it a rest, already. Start the car. We both need a break," said Zeus.

"Where's the park map? I need to find a campsite before it gets any darker."

"Forget the camping business. You're as much a boy scout as I am about to win Westminster Best of Show, if you care to remember the immortal words of Dr. Do-little when you got me my shots. What you need is a hot bath, a soft bed, and dropping off the planet for a while into the Bermuda Triangle. This world has just gotten much too complicated for you to handle without a good rest. Backtrack on the same road you entered and make a left turn onto 62 toward Yucca Valley."

"You've got to be kidding. Where are we going to find a

place to stay at this hour? Especially one that will take a wise-cracking dog!"

"I'll take that as a compliment, thank you. As to the rest, have no fear. It will be as it will be."

They drove in silence, Larry's mind capable of only disjointed fragments and Zeus apparently sound asleep in the back of the car, dreaming doggie dreams. "Slow down. It's coming up on the left."

"What's coming up on the left?" Larry asked.

"You'll see. Turn here."

Larry maneuvered the car into the steep driveway of the Oasis of Eden Inn and Suites. The sign clearly said NO VACANCY. Larry, at Zeus's insistence, opened the car door, got out, and approached the office. Maybe someone could offer a suggestion.

The office was empty, and the phone began ringing just as Larry walked in. A rather attractive woman entered the reception area and picked up the receiver, simultaneously smiling and nodding at Larry, indicating she'd be with him in a minute.

"Good evening. Oasis of Eden. May I help you? . . . Oh, yes, Mr. Halverson. . . . Okay, Michael, I do understand. I'm so sorry to hear about the break-in. . . . Of course I understand. However, our cancellation policy requires forty-eight-hour notice. You know we're booked out weeks in advance for all our theme rooms, especially over the weekends. . . . Okay, I'll hold." She turned to Larry, cupping the receiver.

"Can I help you?"

"I'm looking for a room. Your sign said you're full. Could you suggest any place we could go?"

"Don't move," the lady said. "You may be the luckiest man in Yucca Valley." She returned to the phone while Larry marveled at the photos lining the reception area walls. Each was of a different room, decorated as if on a movie set. The brochure on the desk described the fourteen "Theme Rooms with In-Room

Spas" available—an à la carte menu of tempting fantasies: the Jungle Room; the Cave, complete with stalactites, designed by a Hollywood prop man; the Art-Deco Suite; the Esther Williams Suite; the New York, New York Suite; plus Persian, Oriental, Grecian, Roman, plantation, safari, Tahitian, desert oasis, and . . . the Bermuda Triangle Room!

"Okay, hold a sec," the lady said, once more cupping the phone and speaking to Larry. "You won't believe this, I have just had a most unlikely cancellation. . . ."

"Let me guess," Larry said. "The Bermuda Triangle."

"Why, yes. How could you have possibly known that?"

"Please, don't ask. I'm dreaming. You're part of my dream. The script is playing itself out, and I'm hitting all my marks and saying all my lines on cue. I'll take the room so I can sleep and wake up to find myself in a new dream."

The lady gave Larry a very strange look.

"Only kidding. This has been a weird day and I've been walking around Joshua Tree. A bit too much sun, maybe. Just tired me out. Where do you suggest I go for a quick bite to eat?"

Larry went through the check-in formalities, got the key to room 209, and found a parking place at the rear of the motel. When he opened the door, he all but burst out laughing. He felt like he was in the twilight zone, stepping from the high-desert evening into a lush tropical paradise. It was absolutely surreal, a perfect ending to the events of the day. Billows of white clouds covered the ceiling, palm trees and waves covered the walls, instantly transporting Larry into a fantasy heaven, without the sand flies. In the corner of the room, off to the side of the king-sized bed, was the largest indoor hot tub he had ever seen. It was at least six feet across and more than four feet deep. And he was sharing this dream place with . . . a dog?

"Don't even think of it," Zeus said.

CHAPTER 4

The Lessons Begin in Earnest

The next morning when he finally realized that he was neither dreaming nor hallucinating, Larry barraged Zeus with a steady volley of questions. Zeus deflected each in turn.

"Ease up there, good buddy. I promise it will all come together very soon. Once you've reached a better level of acceptance, your questions will have more meat on them."

"Acceptance! *You* can speak . . . Indians and eagles appear out of thin air . . . my world gets turned inside out, and you talk about acceptance?"

Zeus didn't even try to muffle his laughter. "Larry, you ain't seen nothin' yet. All you got was a glimpse of the gift wrapping. Think you're ready to peek inside the box?"

"Wha . . . ? I . . . I . . . ." was Larry's best reply.

"I'll take that as a yes. Well, then, let's get the show on the road. It's time we headed back to Hidden Valley."

In the car Zeus asked Larry to remain silent. "This is not the time for understanding. It's the time for centering as best you can. As you drive try to keep your mind still by concentrating on your breath. Just watch the inhalations and exhalations and let any thoughts drift past without clinging to them."

Larry simply nodded. By the time they got out of the car in the Hidden Valley parking lot that Saturday morning, it was already 9:30. They walked in silence, Zeus trailing slightly

behind Larry, allowing his master's instincts to find the way back
to where they had met Gathering Cloud. "Well done," Zeus said.
"How did you know where to go?"

"I didn't. Come to think of it, I never gave it a thought.
Wasn't I following you?"

"No. You were following *you*. You completely bypassed
your mind and allowed a more powerful knowing to take over.
It seems they weren't wrong," Zeus said.

"Who wasn't wrong, about what?"

"The Council. About you. Let's keep it at that for now. We
have work to do—ground rules, fine print—you know, the CYA
stuff you lawyers use for disclaimers. But first, don't walk any
farther. Look around and tell me what you see."

"Someone's been here. I'd say they've been pretty busy."
Gathering Cloud's simple circle in the sand had been made much
larger. Small rocks lined the entire perimeter; a cairn of neatly
arranged stones, several feet high, now stood at center; eight
spokes, marked with smaller rocks, radiated out from the mid-
point, three of them aligning with three smaller cairns placed
irregularly along the circumference.

The offerings of pine nuts, tobacco, sage, corn meal, and
juniper had disappeared. There were two new mounds on either
side of the central cairn: sweetgrass and cedar.

"This wheel is excellent, exquisite. Even better than I had
expected," Zeus said. "It's the embodiment of Bighorn, Moose
Mountain, Cahokia. It is Stonehenge, Cheops. . . ."

"What does all this mean?" Larry interrupted.

"Ah," Zeus replied, adopting a tone reminiscent of an
overzealous tour guide, "this is a medicine wheel, or sacred
hoop, used in one form or another since ancient times. It represents the constant search for the Beloved . . . for Wakan Tanka
. . . for the One Supreme Infinite Creator . . . for the Great

Unknowable Mystery. It symbolizes the wheel within the wheel and provides visions into the Great Bottomless Pool.

"For those content with a simple explanation, the four larger rocks Gathering Cloud placed yesterday mark the four directions of the wind. The east is the direction of new beginnings and new knowledge. The south is the direction of growth, where everything is replenished and comes to full bloom. The west holds the gifts of reflection and insight into yourself and the Creator; dreams and visions come from the west. The north offers purity, stillness, and the wisdom of the elders; healing cures are found there. The four directions also map the four elements—air, water, fire, and earth—and the four stages of life: infancy, childhood, adulthood, and old age. At a deeper level they represent the spiritual, mental, emotional, and physical aspects of humankind. Notice the smaller cairns positioned at the edge of the circle. Each aligns with the center to point directly at an astronomical event important to the keepers of the wisdom; these might be the summer solstice or the dawn rising stars—Aldebaran, Rigel, and Sirius.

"The medicine wheel is a metaphor for Consciousness embracing all Creation. It connects the essences of the kingdoms: mineral, plant, animal, as well as human and spirit. The center represents the white hole from which all manifestation springs and the black hole where All That Is eventually returns. It signifies the stillness preceding Creation—the moment containing the unexpressed seeds of infinite possibility before time sprang into existence.

"This sacred hoop, cached here within the energy grid of Joshua Tree, is unusually powerful. Can you sense something different, Larry?" Zeus asked. "Tell me what you notice."

"Wow. This is weird. It feels like the hair on my neck is standing on end . . . like there's some sort of electric current moving through me. It feels strange but nice. Am I imagining it?"

"No, it's not imaginary. The energy you feel is quite real. Joshua Tree is no ordinary place. Because of their proximity to the San Andreas and Lavic Lake fault systems, these hills are on powerful ley lines. This is a grade-A, super-prime power spot!"

"Whoa, slow down there, pardner. What are you talking about?"

"Do you understand the concept of acupuncture meridians?" Larry's blank face told Zeus he should assume nothing. "They're like map lines tracing circuits of increased electrical conductance in the body. In a sense, they're like an anatomy chart detailing the nervous system, or perhaps the circulatory or lymphatic system. But instead of delineating actual tissue, the meridians trace energy flow lines. Healers activate specific points along them to remove blockages and restore the balance of the five elements. This allows the body to reestablish its innate harmony.

"Ley lines are similar to meridians, except they trace the energy grid of the planet. Power spots on the earth are analogous to the meridian activation points. Some well-known power spots, like Sedona in Arizona or Mt. Shasta in northern California or the Great Pyramid at Giza, have been used for millennia as sites for sacred ritual and prayer.

"Sensitives—people with inner sight—can 'feel' these spots just as you are feeling this energy now. Many houses of worship and other sacred structures have been built at the intersections of ley lines to take advantage of the energy acceleration potential there. Certain megalithic stones, menhir, and cairns in the British Isles, such as Stonehenge, Avebury, and Iona, are rather well known. But megalithic structures are found all over the world—from Novorossiysk and Lazarevskoe on the Black Sea to the magnificent statues on Easter Island. They remain mysteries only because researchers insist on looking for explanations that fit neatly into their structured view of reality.

Funny how often the need for form obscures the obvious."

Zeus looked deeply into Larry, as if focusing on something six to eight inches behind his eyes. "You getting any of this?"

"I think so," Larry responded. "Ancient people who had the gift of sensing energies—probably the priests and the soothsayers—built places for ceremony on power spots located on the Earth's energy grid so they could amplify the juice for ceremonies or rituals they wanted to perform."

"Well done, Larry. *Mes compliments!* You have the first half of the story. Now let me ask you a question: Where is the dumbest place to stand during a lightning storm?"

"Under a tree."

"And why is that?"

"Because lightning will strike the highest attractive object it can find."

"Excellent," Zeus said. "Now let's go deeper. Your scientists might explain the process as follows: All thunderclouds are made up of billions of water droplets and ice crystals. Great shear drafts create sudden, massive movement within these clouds, causing static electricity to build. As the water droplets and crystals crash madly into each other, they exchange some of their electric charge. The larger droplets take on a negative charge and migrate to the bottom of the cloud. This charge repels the negative charges on the trees below.

"As a result, positive charges begin to build in the trees. An electric potential now starts building between cloud and tree. This would drive the cloud's charges towards the earth, except that the air between provides very efficient insulation. But if the opposing charges build up sufficiently, they overcome this barrier. The negative charge at the base of the cloud seeks a path to the ground with initial flashes of energy called leader strokes.

"As one of these leader strokes gets close to the ground a

large positive charge, called a streamer stroke, builds up around the tree. It shoots up into the sky, connecting with the leader stroke some thirty to sixty feet above the ground. This conjunction of charges is merely foreplay. It creates a channel along which a second, more powerful flash can run. This second flash is called a return stroke. It's the one that contains the jolt.

"Sexy stuff, huh? If you took slow motion photographs of this electric ecstasy, you would see something extraordinary. The tree reaches up to the cloud just as the cloud reaches down to the tree, and when the two lovers meet, they pulse in hundreds of throbbing shivers per second until, fully depleted, they consume each other totally."

"Where was this kind of science when I went to school? I don't think I'll ever look at a cloud or a tree again without smiling," Larry said.

"Once we're finished here, you probably won't look at anything ever again without smiling," Zeus responded. "But I digress.

"Science paints a thin coat of reason over the force of attraction—or, to use a more comprehensive word, Love. All Creation is electric in nature. It arises from the infinite sea of Love, seeking to explore the infinite through form, motion, sound, color, or experience. Creation *always* seeks to know itself. It simultaneously calls and answers.

"Trees are tuned to universal energies in a most remarkable way. They reach to the sky in constant dialogue with the Great Unfoldment. In a sense they act as antennas, drawing cosmic Consciousness into themselves just as they transmit their essence into All That Is.

"Do you now grasp the deeper reason behind the pyramids, the standing stones, and even cairns placed in the middle of medicine wheels, like this one?"

"Wow," Larry exclaimed. "They act as antennas, drawing down additional streams of energies."

"Go on," said Zeus. "When these structures point to a specific star or some other astronomical event, what else takes place?"

"You've got to be kidding! You mean they can actually draw in the energy of the stars they align with?"

"Now you're cookin', pardner. This is one super-nifty, ginger-peachy-keen place we're in. Buckle your seat belt, we're in for the ride of your life. Ready?"

In all persons, all creatures,
The self is the innermost essence.
And it is identical with Brahman:
Our real self is not different
From the ultimate reality called God.

— THE UPANISHADS

CHAPTER 5

Parting the Curtains of Reality

Zeus had Larry sit on the same flat rock he had occupied the day before and positioned himself once again on the opposite side of the medicine wheel. Looking across at Larry, he explained, "It is always proper to honor your hosts—you know, when in Rome, and all that. As you have probably surmised, this is no ordinary place. It was used for powerful ceremony over many centuries, and it has a life of its own. By 'life' I mean a palpable form of Consciousness as real, in its way, as you or I. This is a true power spot—a vortex of energy spirals up from where the center cairn sits.

"The presence of this exquisite wheel indicates that we are welcome. However, we must bless this site by paying tribute to Gathering Cloud, his ancestors, and all the great keepers of wisdom for whom he speaks. We'll need their help on our journey—these beings and many others. Though ascension is a prize attainable only by those who break free of the herd, it needs support from those who have gone before—just as those who follow will require your assistance."

Zeus looked skyward, half speaking, half chanting: "Honor the sacred. Honor the Earth—our Mother. Honor the Elders. Honor all with whom we share the Earth: four-leggeds, two-leggeds, winged ones, swimmers, crawlers, plant and rock people. Walk in balance and beauty." As this ancient American

Indian prayer ended, a gray haze slowly enveloped the four-legged and two-legged sharing the sacred space. It was granted: Their two minds were as one.

"Larry," Zeus's voice suddenly took on a distant tone as if another intelligence was speaking through him, "soon it will be time to remember. You will gain much insight and will frequently shift the point from which you view. Who can say where this adventure will take you or what you will see along the way? Welcome to the portal that opens to the trail that points the way to the nameless path leading to the Unknowable Mystery."

Then, without missing a beat, Zeus shifted gears, as if mocking his own solemnity. "But before we begin we'll need to clear the legal stuff I mentioned a few minutes ago. You know, the usual disclaimers. All perfectly routine, I assure you."

Larry was clearly baffled. "Stop looking so bewildered," Zeus said. "Even though this is the fine-print stuff, it's pretty fascinating, and it'll make your remaining time in the illusion much, much easier. Here is page one, lesson one in *Understanding Consciousness for Dummies*: What do you get when you push a full-grown elephant through a strainer with twenty-six holes?"

"What?"

"Ah, the What-What bird imitation again. How inspiring. Do you need me to repeat the question?"

"We're exploring Consciousness, and you're doing elephant jokes."

"I assure you, Larry, this is no joke. What do you get?"

"It can't be done. The elephant wouldn't fit. And besides, he'd break the strainer," Larry replied.

"*Oi vai iz mir.* I'm dealing here with an elephant *maiven!* Get out of the box, man. Let's suppose the strainer with twenty-six holes is larger than the elephant and is an integral part of some immovable object. Let's also suppose the elephant is being pushed by an irresistible force. Use your full imagination here. Turn on the sound, your sense of smell, as well as touch and sight. You can leave out the taste part, if you like. What do you get now?"

"Twenty-six strands of gooey, smelly, slimy elephant spaghetti. Yuck! And what's with this Yiddish bit? You're not Jewish!"

"I like Yiddish. It's rich with gutsy emotion. *Es gefelt mir.* It tickles me. And where is it written you've got to be Jewish to speak Yiddish—or Catholic to speak Latin? I'll tell you where: nowhere. That's where. So don't be such a *foigel,* Mr. Wise-Guy, and stay with the pachydermic conundrum. However, I find your answer to be . . . how shall I put it? . . . sensuously descriptive. Pithy, I might add. To the point. Actually, I quite like it.

"How similar, then, is your elephant spaghetti to the original animal?"

Larry laughed, captivated by Zeus's irreverence. "Not close at all. In fact, if I didn't know it started out as an elephant, I doubt I would recognize the goo coming through the strainer."

"Aha! *Argumentum ab auctoritate*—spoken with the authority of one who has witnessed the event firsthand. It is exactly as you say. The elephant has been totally transformed into the barest resemblance of its former self.

"And so it is with words. The illusion we are now experiencing compels us to use cumbersome vocal constructs to communicate complex concepts by squeezing them through the twenty-six letters of your alphabet in predetermined sound patterns. What comes out is as close to the original as your elephant spaghetti is to the original animal.

"In other words, if it can be put into words—either spoken or written—do not consider it truth. The discussion we are about to have can, at best, be no more than a gross approximation of what either of us truly wants to transmit. That, *mon cher Laurence,* is caveat number one.

"Caveat number two is even more important. Over the next couple of days you will tap into a vast sea of Consciousness of which I am but a small part. Those of us who participate in this circle are no more, and certainly no less, than you. We simply join you as fellow travelers in service to the One Infinite Creator. What we share is given in love from love. The information each of us imparts, like the words we use, should never be given the weight of truth. It is transient and simply expresses our observations along the way."

"Whoa, there," Larry interjected. "More voices are going to join us?"

"Yes and no," Zeus replied cryptically. "These 'voices,' as you call them, are always present, so they don't really join us. Actually, it's you who tunes your Consciousness to join them. As the saying goes, 'When the student is ready, the teacher appears.'

"Your adventure has already begun. Several teachers have already visited you—Wind Spirit, the great eagle who blessed your journey; Gathering Cloud, who opened the door to the realm of the sacred wisdom; and of course, moi. But we are only a few of the players about to grace your stage. Each brings beautiful gifts. However, do not be dazzled by their brilliance or their powers of persuasion. I suggest you take everything said in this sacred place with a grain of salt and, without judging it, place it on a shelf somewhere in the back of your mind. If the concept is meant for you, it will eventually percolate into your Consciousness in a new form. If you then find it useful, it's yours. If not, you're free to reject it.

"We are about to explore the nature of Consciousness—an infinitely dimensioned, featureless, frictionless ice pond represented visually by a three-dimensional, twisted torus vanishing into the fourth dimension and beyond. It is like an inwardly twisting onion, with every part of its surface abutting every other part so that no matter how deep into the onion you travel, you are always on the outside looking in."

Larry looked completely baffled.

"Sorry," Zeus said. "That's the best I can do with words. Once you get there, you'll see how tricky it is, trying to explain elusive concepts with static terms. For now, don't worry about it. All I am trying to say is no matter how deep you go, no matter how many experiences you've had, how many epiphanies and life-altering realizations, you're still on the surface. Don't think you've accomplished anything of note. Just keep going deeper."

With that, Zeus began to utter a low, resonating tone that reverberated around the rock walls of their enclosure, completely filling the space. After a few minutes, the sound started to build upon itself. Complex patterns of tones and overtones emerged. Other voices seemed to join Zeus's, building to a pounding crescendo that made the rocks vibrate. Larry sat in frozen fascination, his own body resonating with the sound. He was being played like a violin in the hands of a virtuoso. He was being ripped apart. Part of him, enveloped in fear and led by his rational mind, fought for survival, desperately hanging on, while another, deeper part struggled to break free.

Suddenly, like a rubber band pulled beyond its ability to stretch, he snapped. He was floating some three feet above his body. "Ah, there you are," said Zeus. "Welcome to time/space."

"Wow! That was something else. Is it always such a struggle? What was that sound thing? What's time/space? Where am I, and why can I see my body down there?"

"Easy, big feller, one at a time. Far too important stuff to lump together. Briefly, the answers are no, Om, the flip side of space/time, and you're bilocating."

"What?"

"*What? What? . . . What? What? . . . What? What?*" A high, shrill voice echoing Larry's last spoken syllable abruptly invaded their space.

"Congratulations, man. I thought you could, but I didn't think it would be this soon. Well, done!" Zeus said. "Ol' What-What's here. Hi, guy!"

"*What? What? . . . What? What?*"

"Best ignore him for now. He's invisible and besides all he can say is 'w-h-a-t,'" said Zeus, spelling out the word. "Not very stimulating conversation, if you ask me. I'm told he taught grammar at a proper English academy in a previous life. Now he likes to hang around making certain everything is perfectly clear to everyone.

"I've grown to respect this strange bird. He has the gift of seeing into the heart/mind of a person and can instantly spot incongruity—a blockage in energy flow indicating inner conflict. Now that he's come, he'll not only monitor our sessions but will become part of your inner knowing. After you leave this place to reenter the S/T continuum—don't ask, I'll get to that in a few moments—you'll have the same ability. In your world it can be a heavy burden. You'll soon realize that hardly anyone is congruent with anything they hear, read, or even say. Except, of course, when they talk to infants or pets or plants, or when they are deeply in love. . . . Strange place, the illusion.

"But never mind. On to your questions. No, it will never be this difficult to break through again. Once you have consciously entered this expanded level of Awareness, part of you anchors here. When it senses your desire to reconnect, like the streamer stroke of lightning, it configures the path for your return stroke and you're back in a flash—pun very intended."

Larry groaned, feigning a deep-seated pain.

"Ah, pearls before swine," Zeus said. "Once you open to the possibilities of the flip side, you'll understand why we consider the lowly pun the highest form of humor. But yet again I digress. As to your second query, that 'sound thing,' as you so delicately chose to call it, is the Om, an onomatopoeic Sanskrit word approximating the sound of Creation itself.

"Every part of Creation is a harmonic manifestation of the infinite potential of Love. Love flows from intent through concept into light, sound, and form. Each part of Creation appears discrete, yet it belongs to a continuous circle of Consciousness. And each part reflects the intrinsic aspects of all the others. Just as each human has a unique fingerprint, so every part of Creation has its own sound, a distinct pitch and timbre—sometimes audible to the outer, physical ear, sometimes just to the inner."

Sensing Larry's confusion, Zeus said, "Think of the last time you were in an elevator."

Larry nodded.

"Okay," Zeus continued. "Do you remember the sound as it moved up or down?"

"Like a motor whirring. A sort of drone?"

"Yes, that's it. Next time you're in an elevator listen very closely, then start toning, trying to match the sound. When you get it exactly right, you'll set up a resonance, a lovely mini version of what we did here. You'll start hearing overtones and harmonics, and then, if you allow it, something else will happen. Something wonderful and mystical. You will meet the being of the elevator!"

"What?" said Larry.

"*What? What? . . . What? What?*" said the invisible bird.

Zeus laughed. "Larry, we're talking about the essence of God. In fact, every question you ever ask is about the essence of

God. You see, God is not what your sacred texts say it is. It is not a form, created in human image, flung out into the heavens to be worshiped and feared. Far from it.

"God is not even a noun. God is not even the primal cause of all. . . . It is far more than that. Even trying to name it, by calling it God or the Creator or Allah or Krishna or whatever, is no more than a curious bit of misdirection. If you insist on attempting to name the All That Is, a verb might serve better, for God is implicit in every facet of the infinitely unfolding diamond of Creation.

"God is the alpha and omega. The ultimate unresolvable paradox. The Great Mystery. Everything you see, hear, taste, touch, smell, see, think, conceive of is God. God is not *in* all things. God *is* all things. All is Consciousness. All is God.

"It is sometimes said that God is Love and therefore Love is all that is. While this is technically accurate, it only starts to make sense on the other side of the Veil. Trying to grasp its significance within the illusion is akin to attempting to trap a ray of light in your cupped hand and carry it home to illuminate your house."

Larry was stone silent. The What-What bird was not.

"Let it go for now," Zeus continued. "Let's focus on your third question, regarding time/space. This is tricky stuff, so try not to listen with your mind. Let the resonance of what I say move through you and shift you into a new place of viewing.

"Your illusion of space/time is the mirror image of the flip side, my pet name for the other side of the Veil. The illusion you and your fellow humans are experiencing was created to be a stage where you can study the extraordinary gifts of duality. To you, it seems that space is the constant and time streams through, producing a linear continuum of past, present, and future. On the flip side, we experience it in reverse: time appears to stand still while space is fluid. Time/space. Past, present, and future merge in a multidimensional soup of probabilities in which every possible moment or event directly abuts every other. It's like compressing the infinite into the instant while at the same moment exploding the instant into the infinite. It's what your scientists thought they were explaining with their theory of the Big Bang.

"And now for your last question: why you seem to be in two places at the same time. As I said earlier, you're bilocating. That means you simultaneously occupy two points of view. This multiple state of being is actually far more prevalent than you think. Only right now your conscious Awareness is present in both states, so you can view your physical body from a point well above it."

Larry, eyes closed, wore a slight bemused smile. The What-What bird was surprisingly silent.

Zeus continued, "You're doing great. Stay in the 'in-between' where the mind doesn't rule and try not to make sense out of what I'm saying. The perception of reality from the flip side is as incomprehensible to you as your perception is to us. That's why we need you as part of this effort. We can't accomplish our objectives without you. But we can't begin without your agreement and consent."

"What do you mean by that?" Larry asked, opening his eyes and attempting to focus on Zeus. However, a gray mist had materialized between them, like a London fog, all but obscuring the dog from view.

"I'll answer briefly, for now," Zeus said. "Patchuliti's just arrived, so I need to keep it short. By 'we' I refer to a collective that looks like a host of characters but is really a cohesive flow of intelligence—like many facets on a single diamond. As to the need for your agreement, keep in mind that the Prime Mandate of Creation—senior even to Love itself—is Free Will. Free Will is Creation's ultimate gift. It allows the infinite expression that you see as the Universe. Love serves no purpose whatsoever without the Free Will to express it and cocreate with it.

"Over the past fifty years there has been a gradual energetic buildup in the heavens, if you will, causing a corresponding tension in Earth energies—much as negative charge builds at the base of thunderheads, except the charge in this case is an increase in pure Awareness. The cosmic bride is being prepared to receive her lover. This process has accelerated significantly over the past eighteen months, until now it's at the point of explosion. Within your illusion, it's perceived as a quickening of time. But what's actually taking place is quite different. Time is not moving faster; it only appears that way because your past is receding at an accelerating rate.

"As you approach the point of transition between space/time and time/space, you increasingly release your old patterning, letting yourself be more present in the now. In theory, this should be a wondrous experience. In practice, it's turning out to be quite difficult. What's taking place all around the world at this time is due to the fear of letting go. People are agitated, committing apparently irrational acts. There is a marked rebirth of fundamentalism and extremism in all areas of your societies, not just in your myriad religious sects.

"The leader stroke has already been sent. Unlike lightning, which is confined to the physics of space/time, this leader stroke exists outside time's constricts. It's simply present—a portal of pure, potential Awareness, inviting each being on the planet to respond. It patiently awaits your streamer stroke. And that requires your Free Will, for it's the ultimate act of surrender. It cannot happen unless your yearning is strong enough to achieve terminal velocity, breaking you free of the gravitational field made up of the egoic self's beliefs. There is no consensus here. No earthbound support group. This step into the Void can only be taken by an individual willing to separate from the herd.

"You, and many like you, are being offered the opportunity to take that step. Each one individually. However, the collective impact of your actions is exponential. You are one of those who will show the way, making the path easier for those who elect to follow. But it won't occur unless you choose it."

I have a capacity in my soul
For taking in God entirely.
I am as sure as I live
That nothing is so near to me as God.
God is nearer to me than I am to myself;
My existence depends
On the nearness and the presence of God.

— MEISTER ECKHART

CHAPTER 6

The Heavens Respond

Larry sat very still, soaking up Zeus's words. The only sounds came from the flapping wings of a small black crow that flew into the circle, alighting on top of the center cairn.

Zeus broke the silence. "Hi, Patchy. Allow me to make the introductions. Larry, please meet Patchuliti, the legendary crow of the Spirit People. He speaks for all the Great Black Birds, from the Raven of the Salish and Kootenai to the Crow of the Arapaho and Cheyenne."

The best Larry could offer in response was an awkward nod. He was still struggling with the question of what it would take for anyone to willingly break away from the comfort of his or her beliefs. Everything was happening too quickly, like being force-fed successive courses of very rich foods with hardly a moment between bites. This, of course, was exactly what Zeus intended.

"Patchuliti is the gatekeeper of dreams and altered states," Zeus continued without missing a single beat. "He searches the psyche and selects the visions to be played on the screen of your inner mind. He is one of the left-handed guardians, the keepers of sacred law who know some of the arcane mysteries of Creation. He can give you the courage to enter the darkness of the Void, home of all that is not yet in form.

"There is powerful medicine here. You are about to undergo a process similar to the vision quests sought by spiritual warriors in cultures all over the world. You won't need peyote, ayahuasca, mushrooms, or any other mind-altering substance. These can sometimes help transport you into the Void, but they do so at a cost. You carry their signature with you. It muddies your Awareness, as if you were enclosed in thin plastic sheeting, and you sacrifice clarity and permanence. And if the chemical is too prevalent, Patchuliti, who often plays the clever trickster, may sense the impurity and decide to intervene, sending visions from the darker spheres of your subconscious. It's better to greet this magnificent bird with the innocence of a child and enter his domain through ceremony and breath.

"Patchy, the humanoid sitting on the rock there, with his bottom jaw touching his knee, is Larry. He's part of the vanguard that's working to shift the Consciousness of this planet. Considering the dazed expression on his face, I'd say we have a job and a half ahead of us!"

Patchuliti's eyes began to glow, then to emit streams of light that burst into tiny stars, like a July Fourth sparkler. Larry watched, mesmerized, as the crow grew larger and larger. His great wings opened and extended to twenty feet across, completely blocking the light of the sun. Darkness fell on Larry, and as his eyes slowly closed he fell into a deep trance.

"Excellent work, Patchy. Even better than I could have wished. Let's see what he sees."

Zeus did not move. He gazed intently inward, probing Larry's mind. After a while he slowly raised his head and spoke, "Larry, it appears you are ready to begin. Please tell us where you are and what's happening. Take your time; we want you to be as detailed as possible."

Larry's mouth twitched slightly. When he began speaking, it was in a hoarse, rumbling voice that seemed to come from somewhere outside his body. "I am in a very dark place. I am straddling the back of some animal. I can feel the fur and there's a high-pitched squeal coming from its mouth. There's an unpleasant dankness and a rank odor all about me. The animal—I think it's a giant mole—is lumbering toward a light in the distance.

"We're getting closer now, and I'm beginning to see more details around me. We're moving through a tunnel—like a mine shaft. The walls are rough rock and so is the ceiling. It *is* a mole! I'm sitting on the back of a *giant mole!* I can see his beady eyes now, and the short, pointed snout. He's still making those squeaking sounds. He seems to know he's taking me some place."

"Very good, Larry," said Zeus. "Tell us about the light. What does it look like?"

"We're getting closer. It isn't very bright—it looks like a very dim light bulb dangling from the ceiling. My God! That's exactly what it is! I can see the writing on the bottom. It's a fifteen-watt bare bulb hanging from the end of an electric cord. How weird!

"Wait. We're still moving . . . a little faster now, moving toward another light. It's getting closer. . . . It's another dim bulb, exactly like the first one. All parts of the tunnel I can see look much the same. Nothing seems to be changing except our speed. . . . We're going faster and faster, moving past the dangling bulbs in seconds, instead of minutes.

"There's a very bright light ahead; much brighter than any of the bulbs. It almost hurts my eyes to look at it. It's getting closer and closer. We're going so fast now we seem to be flying. . . . The fur is changing to feathers . . . and the mole . . . has become an eagle! We're flying! The light is coming from the end of the tunnel. We're soaring out into the sky. I'm looking back and I can see the tunnel, a tiny opening in the face of a sheer cliff.

"The brilliant light is coming from the sun! Wow, what a sense of freedom . . . expansion! It seems like I've broken through. Wait, hold it a second. I can hear a voice. There isn't any sound, but it's clear as a bell."

"And what is the voice telling you?" Zeus asked.

"It's saying, 'Behold the sun. You are at the beginning of a new tunnel now. Keep flying.'"

"Wonderful! Wonderful!" said Zeus. "This is what we discussed earlier. The path is all about the exploration of Consciousness. It's the Infinite Cosmic Onion. No matter how deep you go—how many tunnels you navigate—you're still on the surface. Keep flying!

"Patchy has given you a powerful vision, a great gift. For now you know—in a place deeper than the mind can travel—that there will never be a destination where you have not already arrived. The joy and magic are in the journey. As the *Interdimensional Survival Manual,* that great book of incarnational wisdom, says:

> *Of what value is the bee that returns to the hive without first visiting many flowers?*

"Some day you will rejoin the great cosmic Consciousness with full Awareness, and from there you will revisit the treasures you accumulated during your time behind the Veil. It's up to you to make as many of the experiences you have here as juicy as you can."

Larry slowly reoriented to his physical surroundings. The great crow was gone, and the pea-soup fog had been replaced by a transparent shimmering, like heat waves coming off hot desert sand. He found himself gaping at Zeus. "My God," Larry said, "That was so real. What just happened?"

Zeus paused, allowing Larry time to regroup before answering. "Pushing what just happened through the twenty-six holes of the strainer is going to be a bit of a challenge. Let's see if this makes any sense to you.

"Patchy, as you experienced firsthand, can evoke mind-altering states by simple induction. No need for chemicals or anything external. He's the guardian of the transition point between space/time and time/space, and he shifted you into the flip side with full Awareness. This means his gift to you is permanently etched into your being. It's an immutable portal, allowing you free access to the time/space continuum."

Zeus fully expected the What-What chorus to explode into song. There was only silence. "Not bad. I must be doing better than I thought. Is all this starting to sink in?"

"I guess so," Larry said. "A couple of questions, though."

Zeus laughed, "Only a couple. Even I can't believe I did that well."

"Okay, more than just a couple. For one, please explain what's going on. How come you're able to talk to me? How come all these birds and Indians appear?"

Zeus paused for a long moment, working out where best to begin. "How did last Tuesday's events make you feel?"

"You know how I felt. You were there almost every moment, from the horror of watching it all unfold live on television to the gut-wrenching aftermath. I was stupefied for three days."

"Yes, I do know. I asked so you can appreciate what it means when I say millions of people all over the world reacted much the same way. That event prompted the greatest focusing of human Awareness in the history of this planet. Consider, moreover, the extent of its influence. Outside of ground zero and the other points of impact, where else did the events of 9/11 strike?"

"Everywhere," Larry said. "Across the country. Around the world. They've affected the entire planet. Nothing will ever be the same again."

"And why is that?" Zeus asked.

"Because it has shocked us into confronting our mortality. It's made us feel violated and vulnerable. It's left us outraged and angry. 9/11 has galvanized the world into action; it's made clear the path we need to follow."

"And which path is that?"

"Why are you asking such ridiculous questions?" Larry said, frustrated at Zeus's apparent inability to see how he and the rest of civilized humanity obviously felt. "9/11 has shown the world that terrorism is a cancer that must be surgically eradicated. It's bringing everyone together in a common cause. Isn't that a good thing?"

"'Good' and 'bad' are such relative terms," Zeus said, "that I find them difficult to use with any precision. Perhaps you will view the extraordinary events of 9/11 from a different perspective after we complete our work here in Joshua Tree.

"Be that as it may, let's continue. Bear with me, as this next part is a bit tricky. Using your new gift from Patchy, I invite you to shift out of this illusion to a point a few million miles away, from where you can view planet Earth."

"*What? What? . . . What? What?*" The unmistakable trill pierced the air, making both Larry and Zeus wince.

"Okay, I'll backtrack a bit. We're dealing here with the nature of truth. The problem is that Truth—with a capital T—doesn't exist as such. Truth is a mutable commodity, shifting and sliding along, depending solely on the point from which one views. What's that expression you like to use? Oh yes, 'You can't see the forest for the trees.' Let's use that as an example. Imagine you've got your nose pressed into the bark of a tree. If I asked you what you perceive, you'd deliver a dissertation on the nature of bark. Step away a bit, and your Awareness expands to include the entire tree. Step into a hot air balloon and drift high enough, and your Awareness takes in the entire forest."

"*What? What? . . . What? What?*"

"*Oi vey*," said Zeus, looking up to the sky as if seeking divine guidance. "Okay, let's try this on for size. Allow me to paraphrase a delightful Jainist parable which speaks of six blind men being led to an elephant—before we pushed it through the strainer, smarty. Don't forget, I know what you're thinking. Anyway, the six spread out in all directions. One grabs the elephant's tail and exclaims, 'This elephant is shaped just like a snake, long and thin.' 'Oh no,' another says, his arms wrapped around the elephant's front leg, 'you're wrong. An elephant is shaped exactly like a tree—and just as rough!' 'Nonsense,' says a third, 'elephants are hard and pointy.' He was holding a tusk. Each of the blind men, in turn, shared his point of view. One was touching the elephant's side, another the end of its trunk. The last of the group was playing with one of the great beast's floppy ears. They argued among themselves, each saying his version was right. And soon, as has so often happened in your histories, they came to blows. Their actions were as befuddled as their eyesight.

"Who was telling the truth? All of them and none of them. You see, there is no truth; there's only perception. Being stuck is believing that only what *we* see is real. People within the illusion can never fully agree because each tends to identify so strongly with his or her own singular point of view. That's the nature of infinity—no matter how similar two objects or concepts or thoughts appear, by the very laws of Creation each is unique. As I said earlier, all coalesced Creation, in any form—physical, emotional, mental, spiritual, conceptual—is Consciousness. Each form is a distinctive facet on the infinite diamond—which, as I also said earlier, is the One Supreme Infinite Creator unfolding endlessly.

"We'll deal with some startling ramifications of this insight later. For now, would you agree that what you perceive is a function of where you're looking from?"

"Yes, I can go along with that," Larry answered.

"Great, let's move on, then. You already know how you, along with the vast majority of people, viewed the aftermath of 9/11 from the perspective of your egoic self—the part contained completely within the illusion. Let's see what happens when you witness the same events from a different point of view.

"Close your eyes, use your imagination, and be guided by your inner sight. Don't let your rational mind hold you back. Imagine being transported to a spot near the center of the Milky Way galaxy, and let me know when you're there."

After a couple of minutes, Larry nodded slowly.

"Okay, tell me what you see."

"I can see billions and billions of stars. In some places I can see vast swirls of color. I'm being caressed by wave after wave of beautiful, soundless music. It's like an incredible cosmic ballet."

"Very good. Now look back towards your solar system. Zoom in, if you wish, as if you had a giant telescope."

"I can see it now," Larry said. "There's the sun and Mercury and Venus and Earth! Wow, they look so small and helpless, floating in space."

"Excellent. Now focus only on planet Earth. Move beyond seeing with your eyes. What do you perceive?"

"The Earth is alive! She's . . . a gloriously beautiful, conscious being . . . full of love. When I look at her, my heart swells up so much I want to cry. Her continents, oceans, and atmosphere are gouged and sullied, yet she's singing. She's sending out ripples of light that wash over the sun, the other planets, the entire galaxy, and beyond. She's magnificent!"

"Yes, she is," said Zeus. "Magnificent beyond words. She's admired for her selfless service and well-loved. Now, can you find 9/11?"

"Not exactly," Larry answered. "Pinning down time seems almost impossible. Events appear to be moving in and out of each other, as if they're both discrete and simultaneous. That doesn't make any sense, does it?"

"Forget the words," Zeus responded. "Now you can appreciate our difficulty trying to convey information in precise terms for beings on your side of the Veil. There is no exactitude, only probabilities. No verisimilitude, only perceptions. You see, for us, like you, it's all in the 'tudes."

"The what?"

"*What? What? . . . What? What?*" The bird's screeching echoed Larry's confusion.

"Oh, the 'tudes? I'm bringing in a guest expert to delve into the 'tudes for you. For now, stay with your vision of planet Earth and the events surrounding 9/11. It's virtually impossible for those outside of the influence of Veil to pinpoint an exact moment in time. However, can you get a sense of the planet's essence before the event and compare it with how she appears now?"

"Yes. I never knew such a viewpoint existed: I can actually 'see' with my heart, and it makes everything a lot clearer than when I look through my eyes. I can see Earth before and after 9/11 simultaneously. There doesn't seem to be a big difference. It seems like she's still refining her vibrations, like an instrument playing a series of ascending notes. When she finally reaches some ultra-high note, she's going to pass out of this illusion and move into a new dimension."

"Interesting that you describe her journey in musical terms. Very perceptive," Zeus said. "You're quite right. Earth is leaving the third density and has almost completed her transit into the fourth. You'll learn more about this process in a while. The beings on Earth's surface were always intended to make this glorious journey into the next paradigm with her. Unfortunately, the probability is no longer very high . . . which speaks directly to why you and I are here now."

"You know, this is a pretty historic moment," Zeus quipped. "The last time animals stepped in to help humans deflect disaster was what you call the Great Flood, when they were sent in visions to save Noah's butt. What a joke, your stories! Humans believe it was Noah who saved the animals. What utter tripe! Humans are currently eradicating other species at the rate of one every twenty-five minutes or so. Yet millions and millions still survive. Work it backwards and consider how many species were alive at the time of the Flood. Noah would have needed an ark the size of Ecuador. No way, José.

"But, back to the Earth just before 9/11. . . . Let's say you had the job of delivering a State of the Planet address to some high council—like your American president's yearly State of the Union speech. What would you have to report?"

"From what I can determine, it doesn't look too good. We're in big trouble, aren't we?"

"In one sense, Larry, you are. In fact, from that perspective, the situation is so dire that it might already be too late. A lot depends on what you—and a few others like you—do in the next few years. However, I choose to see it differently. I like the challenge of creating against the odds. The shift in your collective

Consciousness has already achieved much. I have no doubt that the impossible is more than doable, if you collectively will to make it so.

"For your report to the Council you will need to be armed with far more information than you have now. Just relax and release your mind. You, my friend, are about to access the planetary mainframe—known to some as the Akashic records."

Zeus caused Larry to enter a deep trancelike state. His human master was fused directly into the vast archive containing the Earth's story, from its birth as a fiery ball through the unfolding of human history. Every thought, word, deed, and sensation—by man, animal, plant, and element—ever occurring on the planet has been recorded there in detail, alongside an extensive catalog of probable scenarios of future events. The impact of this sea of information was close to overwhelming. Larry's body shuddered, then began to tremble, his shoulders heaving with the weight of the knowledge downloaded into his being. Tears filled his eyes as he was transported into the Council's presence.

We see but dimly through the mists and vapors;
Amid these earthly damps
What seem to us but sad, funeral tapers
May be heaven's distant lamps.

— HENRY WADSWORTH LONGFELLOW

CHAPTER 7

The State of Planet Earth

L arry was once again enveloped by an impenetrable mist. Although he could not see the Council, he was certain of their presence, imaging them in his mind's eye: nine Great Beings sitting in large, padded chairs arranged in a semicircle on a raised platform.

Still in trance, hardwired into the incomprehensibly vast storehouse of arcane data concerning the planet, he felt like a small puff of gas trying to fill an impossibly large container. When he finally spoke, Larry's voice assumed a tone of urgency reflecting the enormity of the occasion. "Most esteemed members of the Council, it is with profound sorrow that I address you this day. Considering the cataclysmic state of affairs and the need for immediate, remedial action, I will attempt to keep my report brief and as free of emotional content as possible. The latter, I might add, will not be an easy task.

"I am currently linked directly to the Akashic records—a transcript of every thought, word, and deed as well as emotional reaction of every being that has lived on Earth from its very seeding some 4.6 billion years ago.

"You are well aware that this planet is at the very end of the current and final great cycle and that she is already shifting into the fourth density. You are also aware that human Consciousness has not evolved as expected. While great strides have been made in the sciences and arts throughout human history, there has also been a deliberate, clandestine effort to divide and compartmentalize humankind. What began as a need to circumscribe and thereby protect families soon spread to clans and tribes, then to countries, systems of belief, and ethical and moral codes of conduct. People began to sort themselves by skin color and geographic locale. Separation became commonplace and desirable.

"Leaders at all levels wielded fear as their weapon of choice. They fanned the fires of mistrust and hatred. People believed they lived in a universe of limited resources. If they didn't hoard, they would not have enough for the lean years. The result was a widening spiral of destruction and imbalance, in which a small percentage of the population overproduced and overconsumed while the vast majority barely survived.

"Most recently, the greatest value has been placed on whatever reinforces people's resistance to reality. Sex, drugs, and rock and roll have become the holy trinity of affluent societies. Entertainers are paid more than teachers. Sports personalities, supermodels, and business tycoons are elevated to Olympian heights. Magazines, like significant portions of the leading societies' economies, are devoted to what people eat, where they travel, how they decorate their homes, what they wear to opening-night soirees. Popular papers in supermarkets carry sordid gossip about affairs, arrests, child molestation, and innuendo.

"The human race is in abject denial, seeking any anesthetic at any price. Instead of expressing at the higher levels of our being, we seem to have regressed into our reptilian brain. We have all but destroyed the planet in our attempt to survive at our neighbors' expense. And hardly anyone seems to care.

"The following is an outline of the state of the planet immediately preceding the recent events of 9/11. I am sad to report that with precious few exceptions, the life-threatening conditions

I am about to list were not deemed important enough to merit a headline in a major newspaper or mention on the six o'clock news. In the months preceding the attacks on New York City and the Pentagon, none of these prompted the cancellation of a single baseball game, beauty pageant, or entertainment award spectacle. No school was closed. No flag flew at half-mast. Other than those immediately affected by a specific trauma, few even noticed.

"Some 1.2 billion people around the world live on less than a dollar per day. Thirty thousand children die each day of starvation.

"As I speak, 11 million Africans have already died of AIDS. This disease has reduced the life expectancy in Southern Africa from sixty years of age to only thirty-nine.

"War, in one form or another, has been the major activity of nearly every nation on the face of the earth for the past three hundred years. And millions of people continue to meet their deaths because of it. Yet there is little sentiment for peaceful resolution, and the rule of force not only prevails but is greatly admired. History always records the victorious as righteous, invoking the authority of God to vindicate and justify their acts.

"The so-called Cold War between Russia and the United States ended years ago, yet the USA spends more on weaponry than the next fifteen countries combined, while millions within its own borders are homeless or live below the poverty level. It now appears that the US military budget will increase even more. The poverty and homelessness will probably not be addressed, since doing so offers no political advantage.

"At present some two dozen countries have the wherewithal to set off an atomic device—some so small that they can be carried in a backpack. Yet instead of encouraging restraint—and despite more than fifty years of research—the United States now claims it must resume underground testing to insure the efficacy of its arsenal, despite the extreme danger to the planet's ecological balance.

"Perhaps one condition stands out as a global metaphor for aberrant human behavior. At present, 110 million land mines lie in the ground worldwide—some on every continent. To clear them all would cost more than 30 billion US dollars—and at the current rate of removal, would take 1,100 years. An additional 240 million unplanted mines lie in the arsenals of about a hundred nations. Among the ninety countries that have unexploded ordnances buried in their lands, seventy-three—most of whom are at peace, not war—reported casualties from these weapons in the past year alone. Twenty-six thousand people are killed or injured by land mines every year. That's seventy people per day—one person every twenty-one minutes. Since 1975, more than a million people have been killed or maimed by mines. Three hundred thousand children have been severely disabled. Yet many countries still refuse to sign the prohibition treaties, and many who do sign continue to use these weapons anyway.

"Countries are bankrupt, unable to repay international lending institutions. Some nations are experiencing rampant inflation while their better-heeled trading partners flirt with recession. Economics is driven, for the most part, by personal greed and short-term goals. Corruption, duplicity, coercion, and globalization are proving more effective instruments of self-interest than armies.

"There is a marked resurgence in religious fundamentalism. Extremists and literalists have become more vocal and visible on all fronts. Each sect seems to have spawned a righteous majority that sits in judgment over their more liberal fellow believers while fomenting hatred and violence against those who do not share their dogma. Terms like "ethnic cleansing" are now mainstream. People have become pawns in an international game of escalating violence.

"The rainforest is being destroyed at the rate of 214,000 acres per day. That's an area larger than New York City gone every twenty-four hours. Besides losing this ecological treasure, we are forfeiting countless endemic plants that could have provided natural cures for the growing number of diseases affecting an increasing proportion of the Earth's population.

"Species are dying off a thousand times faster than their natural rate. By examining fossil records and studying ecosystem destruction, some scientists estimate that as many as 137 species disappear from the Earth each day, an astounding fifty thousand species vanishing every year.

"Scientists are finally admitting that their ecologist brethren may have been right all along. There is now conclusive evidence that the planet's biosphere may be on the brink of collapse. One relatively minor event—a flood or drought, a prolonged rain storm or large fire—could tip the balance forever.

"These conditions have been known for quite some time. Yet the drain on the environment, instead of being moderated, has been stepped up dramatically. Easily accessed resources are dwindling. Even so, over the last thirty years the mining of coal has jumped from 2.2 billion metric tons per annum to 3.8 billion; natural gas extraction has nearly tripled, going from 34 trillion cubic feet per year to 95 trillion; oil extraction has increased from 46 million barrels per day to 78 million. These energy sources pollute at every stage, causing irreversible damage to the planet's ecosystem: spills and fires happen during extraction, shipping, and storing; toxic byproducts are generated during refinement; pollutants are introduced into the atmosphere as these fuels are burned.

"Delegates from various countries meet and articulate beautifully worded, caring pledges promising relief. But their deeds belie their words: Since 1970, human carbon emissions have increased by more than 60 percent, going from 3.9 million metric tons per year to 6.4 million. The global vehicle population has swelled from 246 to 730 million. Air traffic has increased by a factor of six. The human population has escalated by more than 2 billion people—that's over 60 percent in a little more than thirty years! To keep up with the skyrocketing demand for paper products—now exceeding 200 million metric tons per year—we have doubled the rate at which we chop down forests. Using sonar, satellite imaging, bigger nets, and more sophisticated boats, we pull almost twice as much fish from the seas.

"We use increasingly powerful chemicals to coax growth from the soil so we produce 2.25 times as much wheat, 2.5 times as much corn, 2.2 times as much rice, almost twice as much sugar, almost four times as many soybeans as we did thirty years ago. But at what cost? These fertilizers and herbicides leech into our waterways and converge in the ocean as a death shroud, destroying coral reefs, poisoning fish, and defacing the beauty of our shorelines. Acid rain, ozone depletion, and other toxic consequences deform and mutate life forms in many parts of the world.

"The Akashic records show that if the current state of affairs continues, it will not be long before the soil is depleted of minerals and can no longer produce viable food; before the oceans can no longer feed us; before there are not enough forests to convert our carbon dioxide waste to oxygen.

"In short, as of the tenth of September, 2001, the world was in dire straits, apparently accelerating along a fast track to self-destruction.

"Then came the events of this past Tuesday. Four commercial airliners, commandeered by terrorists, stopped the world dead in its tracks. The stark reality of their attack, broadcast live by the international press, managed to shock a populace completely inured to all the other events threatening its very existence.

"For the remainder of this week, everything in America ground to a halt. Sports, entertainment, work were suspended. Attitudes changed; people found new ways to express concern for their fellow humans. There was a genuine outpouring of heartfelt love. People gave blood, money, their time, comfort. For a brief while, people actually debated the circumstances that might have spawned the unthinkable.

"But from what the future records reveal, all this may prove to be a brief awakening, and excepting an unlikely sudden shift in Consciousness, the majority of humanity will eagerly return to their somnambulistic existence. Over the next few weeks, leaders will step in to channel the spontaneous heartfelt reaction in more controlled directions. Flags will be printed by the tens of millions to be displayed on every rooftop, door, car window, T-shirt, and lapel. The enemy will be named, the world mobilized, and the battle lines clearly drawn. Every nation, every man, woman, and child, will be called upon to declare sides. A powerful, devastating response, carefully planned, will be surgically administered.

"National pride will flourish. New heroes will be declared. At interfaith ceremonies, mullahs and rabbis and priests will speak of the nobility of religion and the universal love for peace that their faiths proclaim. The individual voice will be replaced by a Greek chorus lamenting fate as people gather at thoughtfully orchestrated candle-lighting ceremonies, prayer vigils, and fund-raising concerts.

"We will be urged to return to normal, to our pre-9/11 existence. We will be told not to give in to the enemy and to display our patriotism by spending and playing more. The collective focus of the world will be shifted to a long-neglected part of the

globe populated by desperate people living on the brink of existence, too weary, weak, and disenfranchised to be concerned
with more than making it to the next day. It will be no surprise
when they become the victims of their own deluded leaders, who
are joined at the hip with the agents of chaos.

"I would like to report that we are beginning to awaken. I
would like to say we are led by wise visionaries who have risen
beyond the myopic perspectives of special interests—even the
grand ones held by nations and alliances. I would like to tell you
there is a bright light clearly visible at the end of this long, dark
tunnel. But I can't."

Larry paused for a long moment. For the first time he
grasped the full import of the message he was delivering, and he
was visibly shaken. The flow of information was disrupted, and
he slowly began to disconnect from the Akashic database. "We
are in deep trouble, and we need help."

The powerful voice that spoke through Larry receded and he
felt alone and perplexed. The softness of his tone reflected his
creeping self-doubt. "I'm not sure I understand what I've been
looking at. I can see that the actual events transcribed in the
Akashic records are rarely the same as the way they're written in
human histories. And there appear to be hidden files or restricted
areas within the records beyond my reach. Is there a reason? Is
there something buried here that could make sense of it all?
There seems to be an underlying pattern—a hidden agenda—but
I can't quite make out."

Larry looked up, fully expecting to see the members of the
Council before him. The mist had lifted completely; he was back
on the rock next to the medicine wheel in Joshua Tree. Zeus's
eyes were intently focused on his own.

"Interesting stuff, ain't it?" Zeus asked. "As to those last few
questions: Yes, certain files in the Akashic records are unavail-

able to you. Yes, that information would help you make sense of a great deal. And yes, there is an underlying pattern, a frame-work—or hidden agenda, as you called it—on which history is woven. There is a reason why this information has been deliber-ately secreted within the Akasha; however, now is not the time to explore it further."

It took Larry several minutes to completely reenter his body. He had heard Zeus's words and indeed found himself unable to probe deeper. Solving the mystery of the hidden files would have to wait for another time.

"Okay, then, who exactly is the Council, and where did they go?" Larry asked.

"You certainly don't ask easy questions," Zeus chuckled. "I saw your image of them as nine beings sitting on a raised plat-form. Interesting, what the human mind creates to fill in the blanks. The 'nine' part is accurate. The Council is made up of nine discrete. . . ." Zeus looked lost for a moment. "Here's where language falls short. The name I used, 'High Council,' is a bit misleading. It suggests the Nine might be some sort of cosmic commission that makes decisions regarding the conditions of forms of intelligence and their biospheres. That is not what the Council is about. Moreover, they are not 'beings,' in the strictest sense of the word."

"*What? What? . . . What? What?*" The high-pitched shriek was right on cue. Zeus couldn't help but laugh.

"The Council, sometimes called the Council of Nine or more simply, 'the Nine,' is named for its constituent members, the nine expressed aspects or principles of Creation—part of the Universe's sacred geometry. Collectively, they form the matrix on which subjective realities manifest. The Nine, together with the three unexpressed and as yet unknown aspects of Creation, make up the Illimitable Dodecahedron—twelve infinitely large twelve-sided geometric shapes defining an identical dodecahedral shape at their center. This inner, infinite space, from which the twelve radiate, is the domain of the Great Unknowable Mystery.

"Forgive the vagueness, but this is the closest that words can come to describing the true nature of the Council."

"But if they are so . . . omniscient, why did they need my report?" Larry asked.

"Obviously, you said nothing they didn't already know. Your report's purpose was not to tell them but to allow you to verbalize your own insights so you could bring them back with you as you reentered the illusion. Already, your words have created an echo accessible to all on your planet.

"It's not surprising that you don't appreciate the implications of your own statements. You were in a deep trance. However, your account calls into question the very core of the entrenched belief systems that underpin your planet's political and religious structures. You, my friend, have set a fox loose in the hen house of complacency. You have opened portals to unplumbed avenues of exploration. You have added new spice to the stew!

"The law of Free Will requires that the impetus for change comes from your side of the Veil. Although others, in higher densities, may wish to stir the pot and raise the level of Awareness on this planet, to interfere like that without express permission and a call from within your illusion is as impossible as it would be for you in your present form to walk through that boulder over there.

"You also added a subtle overlay of emotion to what you transmitted. Emotions are integral to communication within your space/time illusion but nearly incomprehensible on the other side of the Veil. Since you will be a key player in helping your human race through its transition, your reactions—on all levels—are of vital importance."

"I'm not sure I follow you," Larry said. "I was obviously saying something to someone, but now you tell me they weren't really there. I know I had access to a wealth of information I never knew before. I was even able to see into the probable future.

"Wow, was I channeling? Is communing with the Nine the same as talking to a disembodied intelligence, like Lazarus or Abraham, or God for that matter?"

"No and yes," Zeus responded. "Remember what I said earlier: All questions, whatever their depth or subject matter, inquire into an aspect of God. God, as you are gradually realizing, is not a Creator sitting off somewhere causing the Universe to unfold. God *is* the Universe. There is nothing real or imagined, nothing expressed or potential, that is not God. If God is all things, then all things are God, and by extension, all is One."

"Zeus, you're messing with my mind," Larry said. "You're suggesting that you and I—not to mention everything around us—are God. If that's so, then we are One—even though I can clearly see we're not. Besides, if all the channeled beings are One, how come the information coming through is so diverse?"

"Aha!" Zeus exclaimed. "You have stumbled upon one of the more slippery paradoxes of Creation. For the harder you try to understand how you can become One with All That Is, the more distance you create between it and you."

"So how do I close the distance between us?"

"Understand that it isn't there," Zeus replied with obvious amusement.

"Then you *are* saying that God and I are One?"

"Not one, not two," Zeus said, enigmatically.

"Huh?"

"Leave the mind behind on this one, kiddo," Zeus chided, "it will only get in the way. Consider the sun and its light, the ocean and the wave, the singer and his song—not one, not two. Whatever you do, Larry, please don't try to make sense of this. Just let it splash you like a gentle rain. For once in your life, simply be an innocent child and let yourself get wet.

"As to the specifics of your question, in the strictest sense, all channeled entities are the same, in that they're all aspects of the One. There's a data bank for the entire Universe, analogous to the Akashic records. Given your need to grasp and name, we can call it the heart/mind of God—the HMG, for short. Consider it the central hub. It connects all things; it animates them; it allows, facilitates, loves, experiences, integrates, interpenetrates, embraces—even a mile-long list of verbs can't begin to capture the fullness of what it does.

"One might even say the heart/mind of God *is* the One—the very source of Consciousness itself, without which there would be no Creation. All Consciousness draws freely from the HMG and contributes to it, as well. In theory, you and I can access this infinite knowledge any time. In practice, it doesn't work that way. The information is stored as patterns of Light/Love energy in varying levels of intensity. Much of the data are so brilliant that neither of us could view them. Raising one's Consciousness increases access to the HMG, until, at some indeterminate point, it becomes expansive and pervasive enough to encompass the entire bank. Then it merges with the source.

"The One is composed of infinite parts, or points of view—of which you and I are prime examples. Like components of one great bouillabaisse, we are One but we are also individuated, each contributing a unique twist or taste. Because I can access information beyond the Veil that marks the outer boundary of your illusion, I—like Lazarus or Abraham—can countenance a slightly higher level of light intensity within the HMG. So I, and they, appear to have greater understanding. However, the information within the HMG is not stored in words. It is, as I said, made up of Love/Light energy rather than organized cohesive concepts."

"Now you're really making this difficult to follow," Larry said. "A moment ago you used the term 'Light/Love'; now you are saying 'Love/Light.' Aren't they the same?"

"Yes and no," Zeus said. "They interpenetrate each other just as 'teach/learn' and 'learn/teach' or 'space/time' and 'time/space' do. The placement of each word creates a subtle but important distinction between the two.

"Thanks, by the way, for that question. It underscores an important point. Even though much that we'll be discussing transcends the mind's ability to follow, it must nevertheless completely understand the words it hears. Please interrupt any time the meaning of a term isn't crystal clear. Don't depend on What-What to show up; you can monitor your own comprehension. If you allow me to continue past a term you don't understand, everything that follows will be foggy and will fall away—like trying to build a skyscraper on a foundation of sand."

"Got it," Larry replied. "From here on I'll ask about the words. But God knows, I'll never get out of the starting gate if I have to grasp the meaning as well."

"Don't be too hard on yourself, Larry. You're doing just fine. This will all come into focus as a few more pieces are added to the puzzle. Now, where were we? Ah, yes! You wanted to know why channeled material varies so much, since it all comes from the same source.

"When beings hanging out in the time/space continuum connect with someone within your illusion, they act as transducers, feeding information into the recipient's mind/belief/thought construct. Thus, a channeled entity assumes a form and signature that's pleasing and comfortable to the channeler.

"That's why the Virgin Mary appeared to Bernadette Soubirous at the grotto in Lourdes and to Margaret Mary Alacoque in Burgundy. It's also the reason why aspects of the Infinite Intelligence came to Jane Roberts as Seth, to Esther Hicks as Abraham, to Carla L. Rueckert as Ra, and to Neale Donald Walsch as God. It also explains why I, and others you have yet to meet, may come to you as aspects of your inner self or some of the more irreverent characters in your life, like your fellow members of the PDQ Society."

At first, Larry was taken aback at Zeus's reference to his monthly poker and drinking buddies. Then he began to laugh. "Nothing here makes sense. I'm probably going to wake up and find I've never really left L.A. Since there are no rules, I might as well suspend rationality and enjoy the ride."

"Clever boy," Zeus responded. "Now you're getting the hang of it. If you try to grasp any of this with your rational mind, you'll probably slip off the face of the earth. Just ease off the reins and go with the flow.

"For all the apparent differences, all channeled information is drawn from the same pool of knowledge. Part of the diversity has to do with the disembodied entity's light quotient, which directly affects its ability to penetrate levels of Awareness. But the biggest factors are the expectations and personal biases of the channeler.

"As to the Council of Nine, that's a different kettle of fish altogether. Notice that they never once spoke to you, never asked a question, never made a comment? They can't. The dimensional difference between you and the Council is so vast, it cannot be bridged in direct communication. In the rare instance when they perceive a need to interact directly, the Nine use a highly evolved being as an intermediary, shuttling between them and the channel.

"In your case, the Nine consented to the creation of an energetic matrix enabling you to freely pierce the Veil and access the Akashic records. Then, with your agreement, they assisted you to open a portal into higher Consciousness on behalf of this planet. Incidentally, you did one helluva job, there. My guess is the Council was suitably impressed. I sure was."

"Thanks," Larry responded, "but a lot of it seems pretty depressing. I never knew we were so close to extinction. Given the actual state of affairs and our leaders' unwillingness to address it, I don't think we've got much of a chance, do you?"

"Oh, lighten up already. This is a piece of cake. It's all a question of tuning your 'tudes. Once you get the hang of it, the rest will quickly fall into place. You've done some good work here. Don't weaken on me, kiddo. It's now time to begin one of the most important lessons of your training.

"Ready?"

Your vision will become clear
Only when you look into your heart . . .
Who looks outside, dreams.
Who looks inside, awakens.

— CARL GUSTAV JUNG

CHAPTER 8

Rocky's Rap

Larry had to laugh at Zeus's extraordinary unpredictability. That dog could turn a straight line into a Gordian knot and total disaster into cotton candy. Reality was permanently knocked into a cocked hat, and reason walked obediently at heel.

Out of the corner of an eye, Larry glimpsed a shadow slipping through the openings between boulders. Zeus apparently saw it too. "Top o' the day to 'ya, my good man," said Zeus in an Irish brogue. "And where've you been hiding this fine mornin'? Been telling the lad here all about you and the important teachings to come from the master himself. Get out from the shadows now and show yourself!"

An unexpected clatter of rocks directly behind Larry and Zeus made them both whirl about just in time to see a brightly decorated animal emerge from among the boulders. The visitor was absolutely delighted at fooling the pair so completely. His broad grin and sparkling eyes were captivatingly contagious, obliterating any remaining tension in Larry from his experience with the Nine and the dire circumstances challenging the planet.

A two-and-a-half-foot-tall ring-tailed raccoon stood before them, balancing easily on his hind legs. His right front paw was wrapped around a cane. He sported a straw boater on his head and wore a richly embroidered brocade vest. The orange bow tie strapped around his neck tilted very much to the left.

"Rocky, you never cease to amaze. Your timing, as always, is perfect. What an entrance! What theater! And what's with that outfit?"

"You like it?" Rocky asked. "Just a little thing I threw together when I saw how heavy things were getting with the Nine stuff. Thought your boy here could use a little change of pace.

"Oh, hi there," Rocky said, turning from Zeus to Larry. "I'm Rocky Rap-Coon, and it's my job to teach you to *tune* your *'tudes*. You must be Larry, the great planetary savior. Pleasure to meet you. Glad to be of service." Rocky made a small bow and touched his cane to his straw hat.

Larry was at a complete loss for words. Zeus came to the rescue. "He's got a touch of the grippe. Can't seem to hold onto anything." The two thought this uproariously funny.

"Maybe he's *waiting for God's toe*!" Rocky suggested.

"I think the entire foot's more like it. Twelve inches of measured rule to spare the rod in the hand of God. For as our *Interdimensional Survival Manual* clearly states,

> **Nowhere is it written that the Universe must deal from the top of the deck.**

"Ah so, little cricket. You quote my favorite *ism* from the great *I-S-M* text. But is it not also written that 'The greatest journey begins with the same foot that steps unknowingly into the steaming droppings of the *mattaboy?*'"

"What's a *mattaboy?*" asked Zeus, ever the perfect straight man.

"Nothin's the matta wit' me," Rocky responded. "What'sa matta wit' you?" Both howled with laughter. Larry looked at them in total disbelief. How could these apparently illumined teachers act like complete clowns?

"I heard that," Zeus said. "You hear that, Rocky?"

"Clear as day. The boy don't know nothin' 'bout 'tudes. Best we start real quick."

"I couldn't agree more," Zeus said. "Larry, listen closely. This is not only important, it's the key to the rest of your journey."

Rocky entered the medicine wheel from the east and gave a comical bow to each of the four directions. He then did a mock Indian hop dance, kicking some of the carefully placed rocks out of alignment, and jumped to the top of the center cairn, where he teetered on one foot, extending his cane for balance. He winked at Zeus, then glanced casually at Larry, who gaped at the raccoon's irreverence. Rocky, now in complete command, turned his full attention to his new student. "You gotta tune up your 'tudes, man. But before we begin, you might want to close your mouth. Don't want all this precious info leaking out onto the ground, do we?"

Larry nodded dumbly and did as he was told.

"There's a good boy. Now listen carefully. You're about to receive pearls distilled from eons of experience, the quintessential wisdom culled from the collective experience of galaxies, the juice of the goose!" Rocky made sure his hat was securely in place. "Here's the rap:

> It's the Étude of Attitude 'bout Gratitude makes for
>   Plentitude.
> Don't matter where you've run, gotta come back
>   from afar.
> Who cares whatcha' done? What counts is
>   whatcha' are.
> Gotta have the Fortitude hangin' thru the Rectitude
>   if yo' wants to get the Magnitude!

Check out yo' inna Verisimilitude, refine yo'
    Exactitude in the stillness of yo' Solitude.
Gotta stop the constant chatter, find the soul in all
    you see.
Move on past the world of matter, look into the
    Eyes of Infinity.
Give yo'self some Latitude, amp up yo' Aptitude if
    yo' wants to reach the Beatitude!
The way's been opened to take you higher
Once you've leaped into the consuming fire
To rise anew in brilliant flashes
Like the Phoenix born from burning ashes.
Yo' wanna transcend mere Platitude?
Move past yo' ideas of Gratitude,
Master the art of Desuetude,
And embrace the world of OMNITUDE!

"Well done, Rocky. Bravo! Bravo!" said Zeus, executing a complete back flip like one of those trained circus dogs. "Rappin' Rocky-style always moves my soul."

"My God, Zeus," said Larry, "where did you ever learn to do a flip?"

"Didn't you get any part of the message, man? It's not 'bout what I've done, it's about who I am! Lots of people travel the world staying in five-star hotels. I bet they can barely tell the difference between one country and the next. Ask them what they've experienced and they'll tell you about the food or museums or the golf they played.

"Life's an adventure, man. It's a gift. Don't be the bee so focused on returning to the hive that it skips all the flowers on the way. Live life to the max, on the edge. Take the biggest bite of the apple you can . . . or, I promise you, you'll wish you had.

"The whole answer—everything you ever wanted to know about anything—is contained in Rocky's message, and I bet you didn't get the half of it."

"Zeus, you can't be serious. Get the meaning of life from a rappin' raccoon? Give me a break."

"Okay," Zeus responded, "I'll give you a little break. The rest you'll have to figure out on your own. Ready?"

"Yeah, sure. . . ."

"Don't be such a wise-ass. Your cup's so full, I don't think there's room in there for Rocky's wisdom. But let's try some on for size anyway. For starters, let's look at the first line: 'It's the Étude of Attitude 'bout Gratitude makes for Plentitude.' What does that mean to you?"

"Étude is study, so I guess it means that the contemplation of my perception about thankfulness determines how much I get out of life," said Larry, quite pleased with himself.

"Brilliant, wonderful, insightful," said Zeus, "if all we wanted was the gift wrapping. Go deeper, man. Tell me what's *inside* the box!"

"I don't understand," Larry said.

"No, you don't, yet. Cut yourself some slack; there's a lot more to be done. Now let's try another line. What did Rocky mean when he said to 'look into the Eyes of Infinity?'" Zeus smiled a conspiratorial grin toward the little raccoon, who was enjoying the proceedings from his new vantage point, sitting atop one of the smaller cairns at the medicine wheel's periphery, with his chin and hands resting comfortably on his cane.

Larry wisely chose to think carefully before answering. "Now, that's a very interesting image. For me, it suggests that the eyes are the window to the soul and that I should surrender into the eyes of eternity, or God, and lose myself in the swell of Creation."

"Good luck," said Zeus, "tell me how it all works out." Larry was obviously miffed. Zeus was obviously delighted. The lesson was going exceedingly well. "By the way, that was a trick question. But the entire illusion is little more than smoke and mirrors, so almost all questions, perforce, are a matter of *leger de main*. Don't be so easily fooled that you fail to look beyond the obvious to find the blatant—hidden, as always, in plain view. This one's on me. Treasure it, for it's one of the most important keys for your journey. So listen up, trooper."

Larry chuckled at the way Zeus assumed different voices. His little dog was turning out to be totally unpredictable, shifting from one character to another at will.

"The secret," Zeus continued, "is to see the literal significance of messages, the way small children do naturally. When you filter them through preconceived images of reality, you create bridges of assumption that carry you *over* the river of meaning.

"*Over the river* . . . what a metaphor!" exclaimed Zeus, obviously well pleased with himself. "A little shaky perhaps, but not too stirring, if I may borrow a phrase from Double-O Seven!

"Forgive the digression; I just couldn't help myself. Let's continue, if we may. Consider once more the line: 'look into the Eyes of Infinity.' Be a simple child, Larry. What does the line say?"

Larry paused. Time passed. Nothing happened.

"I'm sorry, did you forget the question?" Zeus teased.

"No, I just don't get it."

"Okay. Sound out the words and be literal. They tell you to look into the Eyes, that is, the I's, within the word 'infinity.' Sound out the word. How many I's are there?"

Larry did as he was asked. "In-fi-ni-ty. Three."

Zeus looked triumphant. "That's it, by Jove, you got it." Zeus grinned at Rocky, who was quietly twirling his cane, a knowing smile betraying his amusement. "This time, my good man, I think you've really got it!"

"Got what?" said Larry.

"*It*, of course! The three I's in "infinity" symbolize the three I's of the self: the egoic I, the soul I, and the God I. This is the key to the eternal trinity of Creation hidden in the depths of infinity. Follow this great path and you will find yourself on a veritable eighteen-lane superhighway to ascension. It's the yellow brick road. It's the trail of the grail. It's the great teacher clearly marking the way home. Once you grasp the significance of your threefold nature, you'll be able to transcend this plane of existence and roam freely among the stars."

Larry looked confused. The What-What bird definitely concurred.

"Who doesn't like a good mystery?" asked Zeus.

"I assume that's a rhetorical question?" Larry responded.

"You see? There you go assuming again. It isn't a rhetorical question at all. In fact, it's an extremely profound question. Many people on this planet don't like mysteries at all. They prefer their world neat and orderly, with as few surprises as possible. They belong to clubs, churches, associations—anything that will give them an identity and create order. They would rather steer clear of mysteries or anything else that might rock their boat.

"But some people thrive on mysteries. You, my good friend, are one of them. If you weren't, you wouldn't have invited yourself into our realm of Consciousness. We are all pilgrims on a wonderful journey to nowhere. We are devotees of the Great Mystery. We seek knowledge of the deepest I's of infinity. We seek to merge once again with the All That Is."

Larry still looked confused. What-What agreed.

"Ah, confusion reigns," Zeus said. "Where to begin? . . .

What's a mother to do?

"Ah! Voilà! Eureka! Of course! Enough of this theory stuff; it's time for some field work. You, my good man, are about to explore the realm of the I's firsthand. It's time for you to go out into nature and meet some cool-dude teachers.

"Take some water and wander out among the rocks and trees. You will see something you didn't notice before: a great white buffalo standing guard at the entrance to this sacred area. Request permission to enter further into his domain and ask that the edges of your I's be softened so you can merge with the Consciousness surrounding you."

Sensing Larry's puzzlement, Zeus added, "For now, please don't ask any more questions. We have already used far too many words. They only ensnare us in tangles of significances— mere puffs of smoke that distract, then dissipate, leaving nothing but a residue of confusion and bewilderment. Go. Shoo. *Au revoir. Ciao. Hasta la vista,* baby. You will return bearing a great treasure, and I will be waiting for you."

CHAPTER 9

The Dialogue Circle

L arry left the medicine wheel with his thoughts reeling. The more he tried to understand what he was experiencing, the more it slipped beyond his mind's grasp as improbable. He wondered about his sanity—whether he might lose it all together. Picking his way through the pathless terrain in a daze, he half expected to be greeted by a talking white buffalo offering him the sacred talisman of Xanadu.

Eventually his mind, exhausted from its thwarted attempts at trespassing, simply stopped. For the first time since he'd arrived at Joshua Tree, Larry began to appreciate the place's magnificence. The rocks were strewn about carelessly like marbles left by a giant child. They formed breathtaking designs of light and shadow against a backdrop of perfect blue. Here and there a twisty Joshua tree had taken root, its gnarled limbs reaching unpredictably up and out in all directions.

Feeling lighter, he moved intuitively through the landscape, letting the rocks direct him. His inner voice heard them calling him to move here, then there, up and over. He joyfully let his body follow. The ridge above him was outlined by several junipers, their rich green foliage in stark contrast to the whites and beiges of the surrounding boulders. As Larry scanned the jagged mosaic his eyes locked onto a solitary, stock-still figure silhouetted perfectly against the sky, like a general surveying the battleground below.

Larry froze, hardly breathing, mesmerized by the most magnificent animal he had ever seen—a giant white buffalo. For the next ten minutes, neither of them moved a muscle—Larry, because of numinous awe; the buffalo, because he was made of solid granite.

Eventually, the animal morphed, flickering between life and stone until, in Larry's mind, it settled on the latter. As the buffalo granted him permission to enter it spoke one word: *espavo*.

Although Larry's mind did not understand, his heart did. He continued on, guided only by a soft inner voice. Making his way between large boulders, picking his way up and down rock-strewn hillsides, he walked until he knew he had found it—the place of his next adventure.

He sat for a while in the shade of a juniper, taking an occasional sip from his water bottle. He pondered the last twenty-four hours of his life and the way reality—at least as he had known it—was rapidly slipping through his fingers. Again, his heart embraced what his mind could not. Somehow he knew the rest of the journey would be an affair of the heart. Together they would go to strange and wondrous places, meet extraordinary, unpredictable beings, experience delights beyond the ken of reason. Yes, Larry and his heart would travel to realms well past the horizon of the mind, and it would be a marriage lasting for all eternity.

"Sounds good to me," said no one in particular.

"*What? What?*" said the ubiquitous bird.

"Huh?" said Larry. "Who said that?"

"I did, of course." The words seemed to come from the fifteen-foot tree that was shielding Larry from the sun's intense afternoon rays. "Do you think I'm just here to provide some shade?"

"You can talk?" said Larry. "Though why should I be surprised about that? Around here, it seems everything can talk."

"Everything can, and does," the juniper replied. "You've just never listened before. I gather you're here to find a treasure of great value?"

"So I'm told."

"Well, then, you've come to the right place. Yes indeedy, you sure have! But first, if we're going to have true discourse, you should be completely at ease. Why don't you look around and select a comfortable rock to sit on?"

Resolutely determining to keep reason at bay, Larry surveyed the scene. The sun angled from the left, splitting the bowl-shaped area, scooped out of the hillside, into half shadow, half sun. The talking juniper was rooted right at the line of demarcation, some of its lower limbs already in shadow. The boulders ranged in size from giant twelve-footers down to ones he could pick up if he wanted to. There were a few scrub plants he couldn't name and a lizard with blotches of color along its back playing among the smaller rocks.

"Actually, I kind of like it right here, it feels good." Larry was already seated in the middle of the bowl on a medium-sized boulder. "By the way, if we're going to be talking, perhaps I should introduce myself. I'm Larry Randers. Who, might I ask, are you?"

"Hello, Larry. I know who you are. Zeus told us to expect you. *Espavo.* As to my name, I don't know that I've ever had one other than *Juniperus californica,* which has always sounded a bit impersonal. It would be nice, I think, to have one of my own. Perhaps you'd be kind enough to name me."

Larry was nonplussed. Junie—the first name that popped into his head—sounded so flippant. But what else do you call a talking juniper? His mind raced in all directions searching for political correctness but finding only cul-de-sacs.

The juniper laughed. "'Junie' will do just fine. It's got a nice ring to it. Kind of reminds me of my own."

"Your own what?" said Larry.

"*What? What?*" echoed the bird.

"Why, rings, of course. I get a new one each year," said the tree. "It's my way of recommitting to myself. Most of us trees do it, you know. It keeps us conscious of who we are and why we're here.

"By the way, you're sitting in the perfect spot. I'm glad you decided to stay there and didn't feel compelled to move simply because you were given the option. That's an important lesson. Well done! As to the other question you've been silently mulling over: *Espavo* is a word from long, long ago within this illusion. It was used for both 'hello' and 'goodbye,' the way many people now use *namaste*. Just as the Sanskrit word at a deeper level means 'I bow to the divine in you,' *espavo* also has a more profound meaning: 'Thank you for taking your power.' Its vibrational matrix helps people remember. It helps reconnect them to their rightful place in the Universe.

"You are about to journey into that state of recollection. But first, there are several people you must meet. Without their consent and assistance, I'm afraid you won't be able to travel any further."

Larry felt a wave of resentment that slowly built to indignation, then anger. What kind of craziness was this? What ever happened to Free Will? Who was so mighty, so powerful, so bloody important that they had to be appeased before he could move on? "And who, might I ask, are these omnipotent, omniscient gatekeepers? And what, exactly, is their price?"

"Quite a performance, I'd say. Ah, the range of human emotion—so broad, so sudden, so wonderfully unpredictable. How can mere sounds, shaped into significance by the mind, cause such an immediate, knee-jerk response?"

"All I asked was who is this powerhouse group and what am I expected to do to earn the right of passage," said Larry, wishing he could have do-overs on what he'd said.

"Indeed," Junie replied, keeping any judgments completely to herself. "I understand you've met Rocky, one of the galaxy's most profound teachers, and that he performed his rap song enjoining you to look into the I's of infinity. Well, Larry, that's exactly what we're about to do. The three I's—ego, soul, and God—are part of the infinite continuum of I's. There can be no soul without God—and no ego, or lower self, without soul.

"Imagine yourself as a being expressing itself through all three aspects of the ego/soul/God continuum simultaneously. Try viewing them not in a vertical hierarchy, with God sitting above soul and soul above ego, but as a mélange—a stew, if you will— of three elements, each emitting its own range of color, sound, and energetic signature. Their ratio of activation—or the taste of your particular stew—is simply a function of Awareness. The more your Awareness expands in the egoic realm, the more you can access the sphere of the soul. And the more expansion in the realm of the soul, the closer you are to God, to remerging with All That Is.

"Awareness is like a hot air balloon; it can only rise freely once all the tethers are untied. Then it finds its own way, responding more to the air currents than to the will of its passengers or the observers on the ground. Our job is to meet the people who are keeping your balloon firmly anchored to this reality and see what it will take for them to let you ascend."

"You still haven't answered my question," Larry said. "Who are these people? And what do they want?"

"These people, Larry, are *you*. Each one is a different part of you, a subpersonality, holding tightly to a singular point from which it views. As to the price they will exact to release the tethers, I'm not able to say."

"*What? What? . . . What? What?*" The bird spoke before Larry had a chance. Junie chuckled softly.

"It really isn't all that complicated. The egoic complex of third-density beings—humans, to you—on your side of the Veil is the sum of its parts. These parts are the many voices in your head that have been directing your life—essentially without your knowledge, and certainly without your conscious consent. They tell you how to react, what to do, and when to do it. Your 'inner outburst,' to coin a phrase—the swell of negative emotion when you believed someone had the power to determine your fate—is an excellent example. As soon as you felt threatened, one of your parts—let's call it your Warrior—stepped forward to defend.

"Larry, you have a host of characters in your employ; all humans do. In fact, you could call these subpersonalities the defining characteristic of human beings. They make up your persona. The extraordinary range and diversity of your emotional scale is essentially what separates you from all other life forms on this planet. You and your fellow humans add spice to the cosmic Consciousness, and we appreciate this beyond our ability to express it. Each of you can be compared to a great orchestra with thousands of talented musicians.

"Your particular array of voices is what makes you unique, what defines how you interact with the world. All emotions are experienced through them. All thought, all belief takes place within them. Let's meet some of them, shall we?"

Larry nodded in assent. "You mean all the voices in my head are actually parts of me?"

"That's exactly what I mean. For example, let's take a brief flyover of your marriage and subsequent breakup with Marianne."

"Ouch," Larry said.

"Struck a nerve, have we? Good. We'll have some juicy material to work with. Let's go back to when you first met her. What attracted you the most?"

Larry closed his eyes. A small smile played across his face. "She was beautiful, incredibly intelligent, and very sexy. No, it was more than that. I liked her drive, her wit, her ambition. It felt great being with her—going on picnics, the movies, making love. It's like the two of us were perfect together."

"Okay, then what happened? Why did you split up?"

"Interesting question," Larry answered. "I often wonder about it myself. I guess the directions each of us chose in life simply pulled us apart. She got more involved in her job, writing articles and several books that made it to the *New York Times* bestseller list. Both of us began to travel. Marianne's success took her on the promotion circuit, doing the rounds of radio, television, and magazine features. My partnership at Cresswell, Timmons meant getting more involved with some top-level international clients. At the end, we were speaking to each other on the phone more often than in person. We still loved each other but were no longer in love."

"How did you feel about that?" Junie asked.

"Wow, talk about voices! Over the past two years I've felt a thousand different things. Part of me was angry, resenting Mari's choosing her career over our relationship. Another part was sad, feeling I'd lost my lover and best friend. Another part made me feel like I'd failed completely, that it was my fault, that I wasn't good enough so she left."

Larry sat in silence for a while, and Junie made no move to interrupt. "You know, there's actually a part of me that's relieved. I have this gnawing sense that I need to be doing something entirely different with my life, and if I was still married to her, I wouldn't be able to do it. I sense that being here with you and Zeus is part of that."

"Excellent, Larry," Junie said. "You've got a great grasp of what I meant when I said your psyche is composed of many parts. If, as I said, your egoic complex is like an orchestra, each of your voices is a different instrument. When you listen to the same note played on a violin and an oboe, how can you tell the instruments apart?"

"That's easy," Larry answered. "Each makes a different sound. They have distinctive timbres."

"And so it is with the voices residing in your head. Each one speaks with a unique tone or vibrational quality that is its identifying signature. In your brief recap of your relationship with Marianne, you've identified several of these inner voices, some adult, some childlike. For example, one of your child voices was sad and lonely, feeling unwanted and abandoned. The other child was stamping its feet in anger, blaming Marianne for considering her needs above its own.

"Then you introduced the voice of the Critic, who feels that no matter what you do, it never measures up. The Critic always finds fault. Just like What-What, it cannot do otherwise; that's all it knows. One of your voices sounded almost cosmic in nature, holding the overview of the greater plan. If you listen carefully to the subtleties beyond the meaning of the words, you can distinguish each voice's energetic pattern, much as you distinguish a violin from a cello or an oboe from a French horn, even if they play the same passage.

"Communication within the egoic matrix is quite complex. You assume, when someone speaks, that the voice is coming from them. In fact, it rarely does."

"*What? What? . . . What? What?*" The shrill cry, echoing among the boulders, made Junie laugh.

"Am I going too fast, Larry?"

"No. It all made sense until you said that the person whose mouth is moving isn't the person speaking."

"I see. Let me try to arrange the twenty-six letters of your alphabet more effectively. In other words, let me try to put it in other words." Junie broke into a fit of giggling at her own play on words. Larry, still weathering the emotional aftermath of reviewing the pain of Marianne, had difficulty seeing the humor of anything.

"Let me back up a bit," Junie said, once she had recovered. "All humans are made up of a host of voices or subpersonalities. A handful of these play major roles and dominate the individual's personality—let's call these the primaries. The many other voices play subordinate roles—some active, some disowned or suppressed. The primaries are usually formed in early childhood. They're the ones that worked best to get the surrounding adults to feed or hold the infant or fulfill its other needs, since it cannot fend for itself.

"A primary personality can emerge from the patterning of any one of the subpersonalities—for example, the Pleaser, who gets attention by gurgling and smiling; or the Crier, who complains and demands; or the Sickly Child, who discovers that chronic illness brings the care it needs. Once formed, the primaries generally stay in charge until the day the person dies. If you could view vignettes from a person's life, spaced, say, three years apart, you'd see that precious little changes except their size, the clothes they wear, and their external circumstances."

"I know," said Larry. "One of my favorite tricks at important meetings is to visualize all the people at the table sitting at little desks in their third grade classes. It kind of defuses the tension for me, levels the playing field."

"Very clever," said Junie. "Instinctively you know there is more to those people than what they choose to project, and you use this knowledge to advantage. You see, at the egoic level precise communication is virtually impossible. A person almost always speaks through whatever subpersonality is front and center in the moment. The listener, too, hears through the filters of its active subpersonality.

"For example, from what I understand about your relationship with Marianne, I'd bet there were times when she seemed like a reprimanding mother and you played the hurt child."

"Yes. But not always," Larry added defensively.

"Of course not always. The two of you no doubt had worked out a well-orchestrated dance with many variations. Sometimes you played the role of judgmental father, and, from what you've led me to believe, Marianne would act like a rebellious daughter."

"You've got that one right," Larry asserted.

"So when Marianne spoke, who was actually talking? And when you listened and reacted, which one of your parts was pushing your buttons? You see, the mouth may move and the words may come out, but that doesn't mean either party even knows who's in charge."

"But if I'm not any of my parts, then who am I?" Larry asked.

"Always remember your 'tudes and look into the I's of infinity," Junie answered. "You are the sum of your parts and much, much more. At the egoic level, you are every one of the instruments in your orchestra as well as an important character you haven't met yet—the Conductor, your Aware Ego. In a very real sense, your orchestra has been playing on its own while your Conductor is bound, gagged, and stuffed into the bottom of the Conductor's platform. Their sound may be pleasant enough to get by, but after a while it gets repetitious. Your life assumes a patterning about as diverse and adventurous as flowered wallpaper.

"The Conductor doesn't play an instrument himself. Instead—when he's on the platform and in control—he directs the symphony, determining which instrument should play which passage. Every one of your personalities is vital. The trick is never to erase, bury, or change any of them, even the Critic—just as you would never go and bash a cello simply because it played out of turn. Rather, embrace all the voices, blessing them for their gifts. Appreciate that each one perceives from only a narrow point of view, and that you created each one to cope with certain circumstances. If some of them seem obstructive or counterproductive, keep in mind one of your illusion's operative axioms: 'Every problem arises as the solution to a previous problem.'"

"Then, how do I untie myself and get back onto the platform with my baton in hand?" Larry asked.

"If I may borrow one of Zeus's favorite expressions, 'piece of cake.' Let's play a game that will introduce you to some of your parts, including your Conductor. To start, you'll want to find a place where your hurt child would like to sit. Look around this little basin and move to the spot that feels right."

Larry briefly surveyed the area and chose one of the little boulders off to the right. He sat at its base and placed his arms around it, holding it like a teddy bear. It still held the warmth of the afternoon sun and felt comforting.

"Hello," Junie said in a soft, gentle voice, as if talking to a five-year-old child.

"Hello," came the timid reply.

The two talked for quite a while. A story emerged that fascinated them both. The child's voice, it turned out, was coming from "Lallie," a little boy of three who was very frightened. He was terrified by almost everything in Larry's life—the breakup with Marianne, going to faraway places in noisy planes, all the responsibility Larry was assuming at work, and now, the crazy things that were happening in Joshua Tree. Lallie adored Zeus, on the other hand. But he liked him more when he didn't talk. Junie directed the process so that Lallie voiced all these concerns to Larry, speaking about his older alter-ego in the third person and pointing to where Larry had sat earlier as if Larry was still there. One of Lallie's more poignant comments was, "I don't think Larry even knows I'm here anymore. Since Mari left, he seems sad and busy with a lot of things, so there's no time for me. We don't even go out for ice cream or pizza or anything."

After Lallie had finished, Junie thanked him, assuring him that Larry had heard every word. She then asked Larry to move to a new position, one appropriate for a personality she called his Pusher. This time Larry chose a much larger boulder on the opposite, shadier side of the enclosure. He climbed to the top and sat upright, looking squarely at Junie.

Junie spoke to this subpersonality in an assertive tone. "Hello, I understand you're the one who makes sure Larry gets things done."

The Pusher needed little prompting. It was quite used to being in charge and felt comfortable playing its instrument loud and clear. This was the voice responsible for all of Larry's successes. Without its constant insistence, it claimed, Larry would fall back into his natural "chill" state, drive a beat-up Honda Civic instead of the Lexus, and work for the public defender's office or some nondescript civil rights organization instead of the prestigious firm that employed him now. The voice had opinions about virtually everything in Larry's life—from the breakup with Marianne to the absurdity of coddling a three-year-old emotional cripple to the woo-woo nonsense he was being fed by the "Animal League."

At Junie's request, Larry returned to his original seat and did his best to clear his mind. She reviewed both characters Larry had just met, recounting salient points of each conversation. She then asked Larry to do what seemed to him an extraordinary thing.

"Larry, tune into the energy of Lallie and let me know when you've got it."

Larry closed his eyes and recalled the precious three-year-old. "Okay, I've got it."

"Good. Now draw that energy into you and really duplicate its feeling in your body." Larry nodded, eyes still closed. "Fine. Now send Lallie's energy out completely." Larry did so and nodded once more. After repeating this procedure several times, Junie had Larry do the same with the energy of the Pusher. "Can you feel the difference?"

"Very much so," Larry answered. "Lallie is soft and tentative, while the Pusher is present and commanding. They're almost like opposites."

"That's exactly what they are," Junie said, "opposites." She had Larry alternate the two energies, then mix them together, and finally release them both and just remain as the Aware Ego, separate from either persona. "The egoic world is determined by what you just experienced—the tension of opposites. And the perspective you seek—the Conductor's—is your Aware Ego, the part of you that can hold opposing subpersonalities in tension while residing in neither of them.

"Each of your myriad parts represents a unique point from which you view. Obviously, in any situation some will be in agreement and others may disagree as to the best course of action. As we continue, you'll discover many such dichotomies in your psyche."

Larry's lessons continued. He met several of the key players in his life drama, including some familiar ones—the Capable Executive, the Playful Rebel, the Lover, the Adventurer, the Beach Bum. He also dialogued with several he'd not known of before, such as his Witness/Protector. The sole function of this aspect was to keep him safe. Like a chaperone, it was ready to intervene if Larry seemed to be getting in over his head. As it turned out, this character held the lion's share of the power to give the consent to which Junie had alluded. It would ultimately decide whether or not Larry would continue his journey.

With the Witness/Protector's permission, Junie introduced Larry to several disowned personalities. "You're about to meet a few characters you may not like at first," she said, "but believe me, they're all parts of you. In fact, there's nothing you can conceive of that isn't included in your inner repertoire. You may be aware of some and keep them suppressed because your primary personalities consider them repugnant; others may be dormant, waiting in the wings.

"Let's go back to the report you delivered to the Council of Nine."

"How could you possibly know about that?" Larry asked.

"We all know, Larry. In the higher densities, individuals are linked together energetically such that their minds form a collective Consciousness that belongs to both the group and the individual. Since Zeus is part of our group—our social memory complex—we are all aware of everything that happens in his immediate environment, just as he and the others are fully tuned into everything happening here. Do you understand?"

Larry nodded vaguely, trying to process the enormity of what he had just heard. It occurred to him that he was like a toddler in diapers trying to grasp Einstein's theory of relativity.

Junie chuckled, "Don't let it worry you. It will all come together in time. You can think of our group's social memory complex as an analog of your pool of subpersonalities. The first step in elevating Awareness out of the third-density illusion into the fourth density is to embrace the entire complement of your subpersonalities—your personal social memory complex. Even with my capacity to distort time, you couldn't possibly meet them all during this session. We need to be selective. The point is for you to learn how to activate your Aware Ego and use the 'tension of opposites' principle to elevate the point from which you view from your egoic I to your soul I and God I.

"Don't try to understand these words with your mind. Be like a stone in the middle of a gurgling brook. Let the water move past, polishing you, while you simply hold your position. It will all make more sense as you continue this exercise.

"Now, returning to your report to the Council of Nine, you alluded to several planetary conditions brought about by leaders wielding fear to fan the fires of mistrust and hatred. Can you remember what went through your body as you delivered that part of your address?"

"Yes, there were quite a few examples of some pretty dumb behavior. I can recall feelings ranging from incredible sorrow to rage. Part of me wanted to cry; another part wanted to strike out like the Red Queen and lop off someone's head. And one voice felt so ashamed of what we're doing to ourselves that it wanted to hide."

"Thank you," Junie said, "you appear to be in touch with several voices that collectively sit in judgment over the conditions you reported. I'd like to meet the parts of you that are the prime cause for the warfare and ecological devastation you enumerated."

"What! Are you nuts?"

"No, Larry, I certainly don't think so. Did I say or do anything to lead you to believe I am?"

"No. That's not what I meant. I . . . totally disagree with what is happening. I want no part of any of it. In fact, it makes me sick to even think about it!"

"Is that so?" Junie asked, "Okay, let's have some fun, shall we? Can you envision a part of you that thinks there are too many rules, hates organization, and is the main reason your Playful Rebel first came into being?"

"You bet I can."

"Great. Where would that character like to sit?" Larry chose a place not far from the position his Witness/Protector had selected earlier. "Tell me what you think of Larry," Junie said.

What followed was a diatribe fit for a sailor. Besides having a dim view of the "woosie-wimp," as he chose to call Larry, the persona that surfaced took on the government, college fraternities, all religions, and the "dick-heads who are screwing up" his favorite planet. He hated most being told what he couldn't do. It was he, not the Warrior, who had caused Larry's earlier "inner outburst." "Who the hell is anyone to tell me what I can or can't do? I'm sick of all the NO signs posted by some bird-brained bureaucrat. All you see nowadays are circles with diagonal lines telling you what you shouldn't be doing. NO Bike Riding, NO

Littering, NO Skateboarding, NO Smoking, NO Walking on the Grass, NO Food or Drinks Inside, NO Personal Checks, NO Parking, NO Loitering, NO Bare Feet, NO Trespassing, NO Dumping, NO Alcoholic Beverages, NO Fishing, NO Soliciting, NO Pets, NO Admittance, NO Breathing, NO Living!

"We're all victims of the greatest chapter-and-verse rip-off of all time: Exodus, chapter twenty, verse numero uno, where some bearded joker in a robe scampers down from a mountaintop carrying two pieces of rock and tells us GOD spoke to him and GOD said, 'Let me give you guys a list of NO-NO's.' We bought into that gibberish and two things happened: the sign industry was born and our individuality died.

"What kind of jerk needs to be told not to kill his neighbor or shack up with the guy's wife or lie about him or steal his goat? That kind of thinking robs us of any shred of dignity we might scrape up and reduces us to subhumans. Then there's the stuff where GOD admits he's about as mature as a spoiled nine-year-old and will knock the crap out of people for three generations if you piss him off 'cause he's the jealous type.

"You want to know where 'NO' gets you? I'll tell you: Do NOT think of a pink elephant. Got it? Okay, what color is the elephant? What stupidity, basing a world model on prohibition rather than possibilities! You spend all your time in avoidance and political correctness, believing what you're told to believe and doing what you're told to do so you can collect as many gold stars and medals and commendations and awards and certificates as you can before your time runs out. And when you finally buy the farm and look back, you find you've left no footprints in the sand. Not even one."

Larry was stunned to hear these words come out of his own mouth. "Who the hell was that?"

"That," Junie said, "was one of your disowned voices. I'm

using some energetic overlays to allow you easier access to your darker side. Normally, some of these parts would be so cleverly buried that it could take months of digging just to find out where they've been secreted. This was just a sample, so brace yourself, Sweet Pea, there's more to come."

As the exercise progressed, Larry encountered a considerable number of his suppressed parts. He was stunned. All the people he detested most—the terrorist, the polluter, the crooked politician, the rapist, the scam artist, the corporate raider, the pimp, the spreader of AIDS, the skin head, the fundamentalist, extremists on all sides of all issues—were alive and well inside of him, playing their instruments in horrific, subaudible counterpoint to the persona he revealed to himself and the world.

Larry began to view the powerful, seething cauldron cached within the shadow side of his inner world with rapt fascination. The focused rage and destructive intensity these subpersonalities contained were awesome. He was beginning to understand how closely he, like every other human on the planet, was flirting with the edge. No wonder so many politicians, evangelists, and other prominent role models got caught crossing the line.

"These hidden parts," Junie explained, "covertly animate your 'good' side. When you move to the light to escape the dark, you simply spin, like a hamster on a wheel. Falter for just one second, and the dark side emerges. Humans on this planet succumb to temporary insanity many times each day. Fortunately, most of it dissipates in the mind as unspoken thoughts. Occasionally a spurt of energy is so powerful that it breaks through the ingrained defenses. Road rage is a common example. Fathers being beaten to death over an argument at hockey practice, soccer fans mauling each other, mothers drowning their children are more extreme expressions.

"Once you learn to embrace both the light and the dark within you, holding them in tension, then—and only then—can you create a platform solid enough to allow you to ascend consciously. When you avoid the disowned parts, you actually empower them and so keep your Conductor in bondage.

"You are quite right that humans live dangerously close to the thin line separating them from their dark side. Perhaps this is why they insulate themselves beneath layers of dogma, laws, regulations, standards, and ethical codes. A society in denial of its shadow is inherently unstable; it's on perilous ground. The San Andreas Fault running just a few miles from where we sit is not much different; it's absorbing the energy of two vast tectonic plates in motion, the tension slowly building until it can no longer be contained. Perhaps when you appreciate the extraordinary implications of this condition, you'll be able to go deeper, as Zeus continually directs. Then you will discover that every dilemma included in your report to the Council is merely the consequence of a far more insidious problem."

What a curious phenomenon it is
That you can get men to die for the liberty of the world
Who will not make the little sacrifice
That is needed to free themselves
From their own individual bondage.

— BRUCE BARTON

CHAPTER 10

The Ultimate Proposition

Larry sat in thought, his head spinning. Junie's words had opened up a completely new perspective on history. The world was little more than a vast edifice of pseudogeometry built on false axioms. The very pillars that supported societies and systems of belief lay crumbled at his feet. "That explains so much," Larry said. "All the wars throughout history . . . the Crusades . . . the Inquisition . . . the Salem witch hunts . . . the McCarthy hearings . . . the constant ethnic bickering. Bloody conflicts alive for decades, flaring for a while, then lying low, smoldering, like underground fires."

Larry paused for a long while as a map of the world gradually formed in his mind. One by one, portions of the map were engulfed by a blood-red ooze that bubbled up from beneath the surface of the outlined territories. He slowly pronounced the name of each country as its color changed. "Northern Ireland, Spain, Kashmir, Sri Lanka, the Philippines, Indonesia, Israel, Palestine, Cyprus, Iraq, Macedonia, Bosnia, Kosovo, Afghanistan, Kurdistan, Azerbaijan, Tajikistan, Russia, Chechnya, Serbia, Colombia, Ecuador, Albania, Algeria, Tunisia, Ethiopia, Eritrea, Egypt, Mauritania, Zimbabwe, Côte d'Ivoire, Rwanda, Somalia, Kenya, Tanzania, Nigeria, Sudan, Burundi, the Congo, South Africa, East Timor, Tibet, India, Pakistan, Bangladesh. . . . My God, does the list ever end?

"It seems like the dark side has always been well entrenched. And we—who claim to wear white hats as we sit in judgment and dispense retribution in the name of God and decency and democracy—are we any different?"

"You always ask interesting questions, Larry. I'll let you work that one out for yourself. Just keep in mind that, at the egoic level, righteous indignation is the most powerful and damaging force of all. Both sides draw on it to feed their frenzy. The illusion you experience is dualistic in nature; polarity is the basis of its existence. So where's the gain in deciding someone is right in an ideological dispute? Polarity and peace, like two solid objects in your world, cannot occupy the same place at the same time. The current state of affairs is the only possible outcome."

"Then how do we get out of this mess?" Larry asked.

Junie chuckled at the seriousness of Larry's tone, "An inspiring inscription printed on a T-shirt—one of your more expressive art forms—says, 'Fighting for peace is like fucking for virginity.' The problems you've outlined are momentous. They're also so hopelessly entangled that they can no longer be resolved at the level at which they were created. Every conceivable solution has been attempted on political, diplomatic, economic, social, military, religious, and humanitarian fronts. Yet the situation only grows more critical. Remarkably, despite the obvious failure of all previous efforts, the collective response is to throw even more gasoline on the blaze, hoping that the sheer fury of effort will drown the fire.

"If you expect to lead the world to greener pastures, you might consider a different approach."

"I'm definitely open to suggestions," Larry said.

"Good. Let's open up another avenue of exploration. A world in tension is no more than a planet-sized expression of the same phenomenon in microcosm—you know, 'as above, so below.' Nations are at war because their ideologies conflict. Ideologies draw fuel from the fear engendered by the gulf separating the haves from the have-nots. This fear drives individuals into protective factions—gangs, cults, and paranoia. The paranoia springs from growing up in unstable families, where children are subject to abuse or—even worse—neglect. And what do you suppose is the underlying cause of the breakdown in modern families?"

"I don't know."

"Of course you do. Just go deeper. Follow the trail to the lowest common denominator."

"The individual?"

"Not *the* individual, Larry, *an* individual—*you.* For this planet to progress beyond the energetic cesspool created by its collective unconscious, *you* have to move past your concept of 'us and them.' Problems created by separation are not resolved by more separation. It's time to move in the opposite direction and embrace unity. Humans unfortunately think they can look to others for their own completion. They wish for perfect relationships, failing to realize that neither party can possibly give more to another than it first gives to itself.

"With this fact in mind, I'd like to introduce you to another region of your inner world. The powerful parts of yourself who dwell there are the ones you'll need most for the next stage of your journey. But before we invite them in, tell me, what strikes you as the most remarkable common quality of the parts comprising your shadow?"

The encounter with his dark side was still fresh in Larry's mind. The answer was not difficult. "Three things, actually: their destructive nature, their ability to focus on an objective with absolute certainty, and—maybe the most impressive—their sheer power."

"Excellent answer," Junie said. "Imagine what would happen if you allowed them free rein."

"My God," Larry gasped. "I'd be in jail—or dead—within a week."

Junie laughed at his vehemence. "Don't worry, I'm not suggesting you do it. I just wanted to underscore what you said. If you can move past the view of your shadow parts as negative, you will see them for what they really are: vast reserves of untapped energy. Once you embrace them and reclaim them, they will willingly share their assets. Just imagine the possibilities!"

"No way, José! Forget about it. Those bad dudes stay under lock and key. I make no pact with the devil."

"Listen to that," Junie said. "Such intensity. Good. I'd like to meet the part of you who just appeared." She asked Larry to choose a spot from which it would like to speak. Without a moment's hesitation, he went right to where his Witness/Protector had sat earlier. "Ah, welcome back. I see you have some strong views on this matter."

"First of all, I'm not *back,* because I never left. There's no way I'd leave Larry alone for a minute. And what's this crap about asking Larry to cozy up to his dark side?"

"Thank you for reminding me of the important role you play in Larry's life. What do you think might happen if Larry embraced some of his shadow?"

The Witness/Protector personality took over Larry's body completely. It glared defiantly at Junie as if challenging her for control of Larry's psyche. "You don't make my job easier by opening up this can of worms. When his Playful Rebel called Larry a 'woosie-wimp,' it wasn't far off the mark. Larry's got a lot of wonderful qualities, but I don't think managing a herd of wild, angry horses is one of them. He'd get sliced and diced so completely, you wouldn't be able to reassemble the pieces. When it comes to his disowned parts, we're best off letting sleeping dogs lie."

Junie thanked the Witness/Protector for its input and its intense loyalty to Larry. She then had Larry move back to his Aware Ego's position and experience the powerful, shielding energy of the Witness/Protector from there. Following Junie's instruction, Larry moved the energy of this dominant, primary part of himself into his Aware Ego, then away. Within a few minutes he fully identified its signature so that he would be able to recognize its presence whenever it appeared. It became clear to him that this voice, in the absence of an active Aware Ego, was the prime arbiter of many of his preferences and avoidances. "Larry, how do you think your Witness/Protector keeps your shadow side in abeyance?"

"It jumps in whenever I get too close?"

"Yes, it does do that!" Junie said "But I'm asking about something else. Given their sheer collective power, what does your Witness/Protector have to do to keep them from breaking free and overwhelming you?"

"I don't know. But it sure must be a full-time job."

"That it is. Because you have not yet found a safe way to own these personalities, your Witness/Protector must be on guard even when you sleep. This is exhausting and expensive work."

"What do you mean by 'expensive'?" Larry asked.

"Interesting question. It requires us to delve briefly into the nature of your existence. Let's keep it simple and say that at the very core of your being, you consist of particles of Awareness. Awareness is subject to the laws of the illusion in which it resides, and thus these particles are subject to the filters of viewpoint. The more you move toward the soul and God levels of your I's, the more Awareness particles you regain. The lower you go in the egoic realm, the less Awareness you have to work with. That's why so many people on your planet appear to be living day to day without purpose, as if they're sound asleep.

"If you accept reality as it appears on your side of the Veil, your Awareness must bow to the constraints of space and time. The phenomenon this causes is the root of much of the mischief and anguish on the Earth."

"*What? What? . . . What? What?*" It was inevitable, Junie thought. Both she and Larry burst out in laughter.

"Thanks, What-What," she said, "let me try to do better. Sometimes using words is like trying to empty the ocean with a thimble."

"*What? What? . . . What? What?*"

"Oops! I've just done it again," Junie said. "I think I understand the source of your confusion. What do you know about the Veil?"

Larry was stuck for an answer. Junie was absolutely right—Zeus had talked about the Veil but not explained it, leaving him to guess its nature.

"I see," Junie laughed. "It seems I've struck another tender spot. The Veil is no more than a barrier that filters out particles of Awareness so that those who choose to experience the lower densities can do so fully. It's like your comic-book hero Superman deciding to live on Earth without his super powers so he can fully experience the human condition. When beings incarnate on this planet from the higher dimensions, they simply check a major part of their Awareness at the entrance, before entering through the Veil."

"I think I get it," Larry said. "It's the lower levels of Awareness that cause people to behave so destructively. But I still don't understand what that has to do with my Witness/Protector and it's role in keeping me safe."

"Let me explain." Junie said. "I was alluding to the mechanism humans use to avoid pain and suffering. Let's say someone suffers a major traumatic event."

"Like being sexually abused as a child?" Larry asked.

"That will work as an example. In fact, because it's on the increase, child abuse has become a major metaphor for your planet's condition. What do children usually do with their memories of abuse?"

"They bury them somewhere so they don't have to deal with it."

"Yes," Junie said. "However, only a few victims succeed in hiding the incident so deeply that they cannot access it. Most bury it partially. They keep the memories out of their Consciousness by sublimating them into feelings of shame, guilt, isolation, powerlessness, and so on. They may even blame themselves for the abuse. This constant avoidance and denial is precisely what I was referring. How do you suppose it's possible to keep something unavailable to the conscious mind twenty-four/seven?"

"I don't know," Larry responded. "It seems almost paradoxical, like trying not to think of a pink elephant. If you are aware of something, how can you pretend to be unaware?"

"Imagine a cork bobbing on the surface of the ocean. Let's say the cork is the trauma, the surface is your conscious mind, and the water beneath the surface is your unconscious. If you wanted to hide the cork in the depths, what would you do?"

"I'd tie a heavy weight to it," Larry said.

"Exactly. It's Awareness particles that make up the weight. The child has to tie enough particles to the unwanted thought so it stays deeply buried in the unconscious. The more painful or shameful the incident, the more Awareness is required. The child's Witness/Protector doesn't want a random trigger, like a news story or a movie, to bring the unwanted thought to the surface, so it heaps on more than enough layers of Awareness particles.

"As a person's life continues, more and more particles are spent keeping unwanted memories and potentially dangerous subpersonalities at bay. It's a costly undertaking because every unit of Awareness used means one less unit available for the ongoing process of conscious exploration.

"This mechanism is in play at all levels of human society—from individual infants to blocs of nations. Given this extraordinary expenditure of your collective Awareness, is it surprising that so many decisions—personal as well as global—are destructive?"

"My God," Larry said. "It's a wonder we can operate at all!"

"Now look into the way this process plays out for you," Junie urged, "and tell me what you see."

Larry sat silently with his eyes closed for several minutes as he reflected on the new perspectives this wise juniper had shown him. When he was ready, he lifted his head and turned toward Junie. "What I see is a whole new way of seeing what I see. I'm defined not so much by what I've consciously chosen to be but what I've unconsciously chosen *not* to be. I'm the offspring of avoidance. I settle for anything that doesn't rock the boat or get me into hot water. But by not owning my full potential, I'm sacrificing the spice of my life."

"Don't stop there, Larry. Relate this new insight to your disowned parts. Tell me how they might react to this treatment and what your Witness/Protector needs to do to keep them contained."

"No wonder they're pissed! I'd be too, if I were imprisoned like that. I can see them pressing harder and harder against the lid—like Pandora's box—trying to get out, and my Witness/Protector having to use more and more Awareness particles to keep them locked away. If it relaxed, even for a second, they would break loose and cause havoc."

"Interesting that you chose the metaphor of Pandora's box," Junie said. "There are riches in that myth worth exploring in light of our work here. Why don't you go deeper and connect with the reason your subconscious chose that particular phrase? I'll assist you by providing an energetic overlay again."

Junie directed Larry to select a new location for this exercise. When he had settled into a comfortable position with his back supported by the gentle curve of a boulder, she plunged him into a deep, altered state where he could see several layers of reality beyond the usual third-density perspective. When he spoke his voice seemed trancelike, as if coming from far away.

"According to this ancient Greek story, before humans had fire they lived an idyllic life, free from heavy labor, sickness, and evil—not unlike life in the biblical Garden of Eden. Then the Titan Prometheus gifted humankind with fire. At a deeper level, 'fire' refers to passion, an intense hunger for experience, expression, and experimentation. However, Zeus, king of the gods, felt that fire should have remained a power for immortals only and that humans would misuse it.

"Zeus confronted Prometheus and told him that as a price for fire he would bestow them with another gift that would enchant their hearts, minds, and bodies. He directed Hephaestus to mix earth and water and shape it into a maiden whose face resembled that of a goddess. Athena was commanded to teach this creature skills and weaving; Apollo, to confer the skill of music; Aphrodite, to infuse her with breathtaking beauty, unbridled sensuality, and the arts of sparking conversation and divine grace. Hermes was directed to imbue her mind with a treacherous nature. Hermes was instructed to add lies, flattery, and disloyalty in the depts of her heart. It was Hermes who named her 'Pandora,' an elusive word that can mean 'she is the giver of all gifts,' 'she who was given all gifts,' and also 'the gift of all the gods.'

"The gods did their work well. Zeus sent Pandora, endowed with every imaginable charm, including curiosity and deceit, to Epimetheus, Prometheus's simple brother, to be his wife. Thus the first woman was introduced into the paradise of man. And before she departed, Zeus gave her a box that he forbade her to open. Counting on her curiosity, the crafty god packed the box with all the unexpressed shadow voices destined to destroy the seemingly idyllic civilization.

"Of course the inevitable happened. One fateful day, Pandora cracked open the lid, unleashing all the ills that have plagued the world since. As soon as she realized what she had done, she slammed the lid closed, keeping only one voice, Hope, inside the box.

"The simplistic interpretation of this myth would have us believe that the world is a sinful, evil place and that we cling only to Hope, awaiting a better life in the hereafter. Other facile explanations caution us not to go against the injunctions of angry, vengeful gods, or suggest that women were sent by the heavens to bring men down. However, the myth has a deeper, more powerful message. Pandora's box contained the virtual template of the Grand Third-Density Experiment—the matrix of the illusion that we, on this side of the Veil, call reality. When she opened it, men were allowed—for the first time—free access to their shadow. Thus were born duality and the tension between opposites. This is what allowed the Consciousness game to begin.

"Pandora let loose the means for humankind, now infused with the fire of passion, to experience the full spectrum of emotions that shattered man's paradisiacal lethargy. In time, man will learn to hold separate the great opposing forces of duality and, succumbing to neither, transcend this density and rise to the level of the gods. Pandora brought with her the sacred wood with which to build the fire that consumes the Phoenix. She is the destruction and death that must precede rebirth."

Larry slowly emerged from his trancelike state and faced Junie with an impish grin. "Without her gifts, a Paradise entropies over time into a 'pair of dice,' and as you know. . . ."

Junie fell into laughter and joined Larry in completing the sentence with Einstein's famous rebuke, "God doesn't play dice with the Universe!"

"Well done, Larry. And what have you just learned from this myth?"

"For one thing," Larry quipped, "it's evident that anyone can bend and twist a myth into whatever interpretation validates his agenda."

"Very funny," Junie said. "Get serious."

"Actually, I wasn't trying to be cute—entirely. Images conveyed through language—no matter how precise—are open to endless interpretation. For a theologian, the myth validates his belief in original sin. A psychologist might say the story reinforces the patriarchal belief that women are merely objects of beauty to be coveted and used. A child, focusing on the obvious, might tell you Pandora was a bad lady who caused a lot of trouble because she didn't do what she was told. Sometimes I wonder if all the symbolism just gets in the way of a good yarn?

"I've never much liked the common interpretation—that humankind is blessed because Hope remained in Pandora's box. Logically, if Hope is still trapped inside, we can't access it. Hope is presented as the great balancer—the ultimate gift to offset life's tragedies. What utter nonsense! Hope is what my Playful Rebel would certainly call a 'woosie-wish' made by a gelded castrato crooning to a tone-deaf God. Asking people to hope separates them from their power and their innate exquisite nature.

"Wow, listen to me," Larry said, surprised by his own vehemence. "This must be another disowned part of my self I'm allowing to emerge."

"Indeed," Junie said. "And what more do you know about your disowned parts in the light of Pandora's myth?"

"I'm beginning to see that my shadow voices are integral parts of me. And I see that not having access to them is like playing a Beethoven symphony without percussion or brass. They hold most of my power, including the ability to focus with real intensity of purpose. They also hold the seeds of destructiveness. This—the potential to inflict death and chaos—is what I think I resisted most. But now I see that even destruction has a place in my orchestra. Given the choice, I'd opt for the post-Pandora era every time.

"What happens next?"

"You must ask your Witness/Protector for permission to proceed," Junie said. "He's your gatekeeper for this part of the journey. Please return to his place among the boulders."

Junie waited for the energetic signature of Larry's Witness/Protector to emerge completely before beginning. "Thank you for being here again. As you can see, much has transpired in the short time since we last spoke. Larry seems to have significantly shifted the point from which he views and is requesting your permission to carry on."

This time the Witness/Protector was noticeably less hostile. It seemed to take comfort that its authority was not threatened and that it was being consulted. "I understand. I was present during the Pandora analysis and was impressed with Larry's perceptions—they certainly reached a deeper level of Awareness than I've noted previously. However, they were done with the help of powerful energetic overlays. How do I know whether these insights came from him or you?"

"I assure you, the insights were purely Larry's," Junie said. "The energetic overlay was no more than an artful device to part the Veil so Larry could contact the parts of himself that embody higher states of knowing. I understand your concern, but rest assured that, unlike psychedelics and other mind-altering substances, overlays are quite safe. They're also permanent. Larry can access those parts of himself whenever he chooses.

"Now, with your permission, I'd like to introduce him to some subpersonalities hidden on the side of his psyche opposite the shadow. They have been waiting in the wings until Larry was ready to invite them to join his orchestra."

The Witness/Protector agreed—with the caveat that it could intervene whenever it felt Larry was getting into dangerous waters.

Junie had her pupil return to the place of the Aware Ego before continuing. "We're about to meet the cavalry. These are the guys in the white hats, who are more than a match for the power and intensity of your dark side. Find a place representing the part that assisted you in penetrating the deeper meaning of the Pandora myth."

Instinctively, Larry chose a spot on the bowl's sunnier side with an overview of the entire setting. He climbed atop one of the largest boulders and sat motionlessly, eyes in soft focus, looking in the general direction of Junie.

"Welcome and thank you for coming. Who are you?"

The voice spoke with soft precision. "I am Larry's higher Consciousness, his expanded, aware presence. I hold the overview of his essential nature and purpose. It would not be inaccurate to call me Larry's Higher Self."

"Well, what about me?" a little voice brazenly interrupted. "What am I, chopped liver?"

The unexpected voice startled Larry. Junie took it all in stride. "Hi there. Exactly who are you?"

"Why, Larry's Body Elemental, obviously!" replied the voice.

Junie welcomed the Body Elemental into the circle, and at her request Larry shifted a few feet to the right, selecting a somewhat smaller rock to accommodate this new personality, who was clearly not shy. "I'm a major player in Larry's life, but until this very moment he didn't even know I existed! I'm glad he's finally shed enough of his armor so we can meet."

The Body Elemental turned out to be androgynous, though it held a distinctly female orientation. Her name, she said, was Kiyoura, which meant "beautiful song of the sky." Larry asked if he could call her "Kichi"—a name she absolutely adored. She worked together with Larry's Higher Self, she said, to carry the vital life force, or pranic energy, from the God-source, the I AM Presence, down through an invisible gold cord into every cell of Larry's body. This duo continually monitored and regulated Larry's mind/body/emotion/spirit complex. They also facilitated the development of spiritual wisdom by advising, counseling, and teaching when Larry requested their help—which, she commented, was not as often as it could be.

Kichi knew the entire blueprint of Larry's physical structure right down to its DNA and RNA. She was the master librarian, able to locate every memory stored anywhere within his cells. With her help—providing he asked, of course—any of this information could be instantly retrieved, brought forth into Consciousness, and healed.

Kichi was prepared to be Larry's staunchest companion as he proceeded through successively expanding layers of Awareness, she said, but bound to honor the Law of Free Will, she could not interfere with Larry's egoic dictates. She explained several ways Larry could access her, including focusing his inner knowing, meditating, and using the muscle-testing techniques of applied kinesiology. For the last, all he had to do was hold the thumb and little finger of each hand together and interlink the two circles. Then, using a moderate amount of pressure to keep his two left digits together, he was to try pulling the right-hand loop out of the left-hand one. He could use this technique in conjunction with any "yes/no" question. If his right hand broke away easily, the answer was no; if the two loops remained strong, the answer was yes. If he connected with her via this muscle-testing technique, he should ask, "Kichi, are you there?" Not only should the finger circle remain strong, but he should also experience the "giggly sensation" that is her signature. Just before leaving, Kichi chided Larry like a good Jewish mother: "So now that you have my number, I don't expect you to be such a stranger. Would it kill you to call once in a while, just to say hello and see how I'm feeling?" Her accent, to Larry's amusement, was perfect.

At Junie's behest, Larry returned to the higher boulder to accommodate the voice of his higher Consciousness. "Sorry about the interruption," Junie said. "She was quite something, wasn't she?"

The unmistakable elegance of the Higher Self's energetic signature was fully present. "Kiyoura is always a delight. Although she loves to be playful and a little mischievous, she is a tireless worker and totally devoted to Larry. She was being modest. She is far more than a librarian able to access data. Kiyoura was also part the design, engineering, and programming team that built the library, Larry's physical body. Don't treat this fact lightly. If asked, she can assist Larry in assuaging unwanted thoughts or physical conditions. He would do well to take her advice and call upon her often."

"I'm certain Larry has absorbed every word." Junie said. "Why hasn't he used her wisdom before now?"

"The simplistic answer is that he did not consciously know of her existence—or mine—until a few moments ago. However, I suspect you are asking a deeper question: 'What kept him from knowing before now?' The answer lies in Rocky's injunction to look into the I's of infinity. As long as Larry chose to remain in the egoic I, he unconsciously blocked both Kiyoura and me.

"It is, as she so wisely suggested, a matter of Free Will. Beings within the illusion are allowed to experiment in whatever manner they choose. For the most part, they elect to restrict the points from which they view to those within the lowest aspect of the ego/soul/God continuum. Paradoxically, this appears to confer a sense of power and security, reinforcing the fantasy that they are in charge. Unfortunately, they rarely examine the obvious question: 'In charge of what?'

"In seeking solutions to the mystery of life—not to mention personal relationships and the broader issues of war, ecology, overpopulation, and disease—humans create for themselves a quandary that recalls the words of Einstein you referred to earlier: 'No problem can be solved from the same level of Consciousness that created it.' When seeking understandings or attempting to resolve conundrums, it is always beneficial to elevate the point from which one views—in other words, to shift from the lower-self I into the one of the higher perspectives on the infinite continuum of I's. However, this requires the ego to relinquish control—the one act it fears most.

"Isn't it interesting, the number of times the myth of the Phoenix has appeared in Larry's life? Hasn't it been a consistently recurring signpost along his current avenue of exploration? Nothing in the universe is random, as Dr. Einstein so correctly indicated. When words or symbols, messages, feelings, or people present themselves again and again, one profits by taking notice and giving them deeper examination. We will revisit the Phoenix allegory once Larry has absorbed certain insights into impediments that he—and many of his fellow Light Workers—have encountered during their incarnations within the space/time continuum."

"Thank you," Junie said. "You clearly speak from a perspective well beyond the illusion of the third density. How would you describe your relationship to Larry?"

"A simple question, though the answer is nearly impossible to express through the sound complexes you call words. That said, I will endeavor to be as clear as possible.

"Like the other voices Larry has been meeting, I am a part of him. Some of us live within Larry's persona in what he might call present time. Others, like myself, transcend the limitations of this illusion and are not bound by linear time. You might say I am Larry's future self, having already experienced the lessons he is now learning. I've come to assist him on his journey into the Great Mystery."

"Will this be a difficult process for Larry?" Junie's tone was concerned, almost motherly.

"Let me begin by assuring Larry that the road to higher Awareness is not nearly as daunting as it is made out to be. From my perspective, it is an instantaneous event requiring only the decision to make it so, reinforced by full application of the three components of manifestation: intention, attention, and love. In worldly terms, the process is comparable to climbing a ladder. It requires the intention to do so and attention on the activity at hand, and one must trust in the grace of Love sufficiently to release the rung where you are presently.

"This last requirement, letting go of the current rung, or belief system, appears to be more challenging than those at my level of Awareness could have imagined. To appreciate this more fully, I will provide Larry with one of the golden keys with which to unlock the portals through the Veil. Consider how the vast sea of information constantly suffusing each entity is processed through the four conduits available to each point along the I-continuum: belief, thought, knowing, and faith.

"The lower egoic level is driven primarily by belief; thought is used only to rearrange one's presuppositions in new permutations. This is the realm of judgment, where a concept—like the rung of a ladder—is held to desperately as truth. Many in the illusion would argue that belief underpins moral, ethical, and political structures. In reality, belief has proved to be the most difficult obstacle to higher Awareness and is the denominator common to most ills on the planet today. Rather than encouraging individual exploration and innovation, belief draws the believer closer to a predetermined group mentality.

"Consider a simple illustration. A man has lost his car keys. He panics as he envisions himself missing an important engagement. Racking his brain, he searches every drawer in the house, and at the last possible moment, finds the keys in his coat pocket. What is the very first thing he does when he finds them?"

Larry's Higher Self paused for a long moment, letting his question swirl in rhetorical eddies. "Typically, third-density beings offer answers related to their psychological or religious beliefs. For example, 'He gave thanks,' implying the assistance of a higher power. Or, 'He felt immediate relief knowing he would not miss his appointment.' Or, 'He berated himself for forgetting that he'd put them in his pocket.' However, none of these answers matches the pure simplicity of the question. Such responses would all be afterthoughts—secondary reactions to the emotional content of the event.

"The answer is hidden so cleverly in plain view that it is nearly always overlooked. The very first thing the man did when he found the keys was to *stop looking*. This illustrates the lamentable legacy of religious doctrine. When one is given answers as if they carry the imprimatur of the Word of God, what incentive is there to look further?

"As one ventures higher in the egoic realm, one is freer to use thought to probe the intellect and the environment. This is the domain of curiosity, of the arts and scientific exploration. Even so, at this level of the I's, belief still predominates and thought is ultimately influenced by it. An amusing example is the way scientists define life. From our perspective, they suffer from CMS, chonic myopic syndrome—'chonic' referring to the acronym for carbon-hydrogen-oxygen-nitrogen, CHON. That is, in their view, if it isn't organic, it isn't alive. Based on limits they themselves have set, the scientists then proffer a list of conditions that define 'life' as the ability to be cellular, to metabolize, to tend toward homeostasis, to respond to stimuli, and to reproduce.

"Larry should recognize this situation as a variation on the parable of the missing keys. By creating a set of self-limiting definitions, the scientists miss the obvious. Their definition of life in fact delineates one tiny example of the diverse expressions of intelligent Awareness found throughout the Universe.

"Consider another demonstration of narrow thinking: Human beings throughout their history have believed the human form was created in God's image. In reality, it is just the opposite. Humans have created their deity in human image, then cast him onto a throne in the heavens, imbued him with the psychogenic panoply of human histrionics, and proceeded to cower before him.

"Scientists searching the galaxies for intelligent life practice the same manner of thinking. They, too, look for other forms of themselves while missing the essence of their own Consciousness —too close for their eyes or intellect to perceive. No telescope, no matter how powerful, can reveal what they seek if it is pointed in the wrong direction.

"Having experienced the events of these two days, can Larry possibly doubt the immeasurable intelligence contained in plants and animals, not to mention every other form of matter and thought throughout the many Universes?"

The Higher Self allowed its question to remain hanging—a small tear in the Veil inviting later exploration. "This brings us to the domain of soul Awareness, which offers a markedly broader perspective than the egoic level. Here one experiences at the level of knowing. Knowing in this sense differs from intellectual activities such as perceiving, understanding, grasping, comprehending, and the like. It is closely allied with intuition and is the subtle force behind hunches, premonitions, and gut feelings. Larry has used this mechanism often without realizing it. In fact, if he scanned through his life dispassionately, he would see how often this kind of knowing has shaped his actions—from the dissolution of his marriage to his acquisition of Zeus to the uncanny way he was led to this spot so we could have this dialogue.

"Knowing is a powerful tool. However, it comes at a price. To reach the rung of knowing, one must let go of the rung of belief. If Larry wishes to do this, Kiyoura and I can assist him."

Junie could see Larry was mesmerized by this previously unknown part of himself. She wisely said nothing, allowing his Higher Self free rein, fully aware of the importance of the connection being fashioned between disparate bands of the I-continuum.

"The last element we'll explore is faith. Faith operates at all levels of the I's as the force impelling every portion of the intelligent Awareness to seek reunion with the One Infinite Creator. Faith is analogous to the ocean's attraction to the moon, which causes the tides. Each domain responds to this call in its own way. At the egoic level, religion directs that faith be expressed as faith *in* something—in a system of belief, an entity, or divine teachings. In the realm of the soul, faith is simply a spiritual pursuit along the infinite path. It is not bounded by the egoic need to name, measure, and understand.

"Both religion and spirituality allow exploration of the deeper mysteries. Religion might be termed the outer path, spirituality the inner. Both paths require surrender. The outer path, based on belief, dictates 'giving oneself' to the Lord or the guru or the dogma as an act of faith. Faith here means trusting, without supporting evidence, that the Word written in the holy book or spoken by the cleric or master reflects the ultimate truth, the Word of God or the Universe. 'My will is Thy will, and Thy will be done' is a prime example of the individual's surrender to the collective self of a particular belief system.

"The inner path also demands surrender in the absence of material substantiation. However, this act of faith cannot originate in the mind or ego. It can only come from an inner knowing that no matter how chaotic a situation may seem, everything in Creation is exactly as it should be. Perfection pervades All That Is, and *everything*—including the seeker—is part of that perfection. This faith is symbolized by the Fool in the tarot, who blithely steps off the cliff, unaware that the hand of God awaits to steady and guide his next step.

"Surrender on the inner path is akin to death. It is represented in mythology as the Phoenix, which is also the noble Bennu of the Egyptians, the shimmering Feng of the Chinese, and the Thunderbird of Native America. The Phoenix story speaks of a great, magical bird so rare that only one of its kind exists at a time. This sacred bird, being linked to the cycles of Creation, has a fixed lifespan, the length of which varies greatly from culture to culture, though five hundred years would be typical.

"When the Phoenix feels the end of its cycle is at hand, it builds its own funeral pyre of aromatic wood, which it sprinkles with rare spices and exotic herbs. The pyre bursts into flames, and the bird is entirely consumed. After the embers have cooled, a new, reborn Phoenix rises from the ashes, embalms the remains of its predecessor in an egg of myrrh, and places it on the altar of the sun god.

"Like the Phoenix, Larry has now reached the end of his present cycle. He, too, is being presented with the ultimate choice. His decision can be guided not by the Trojan horse of reason but only by faith. The proposition being offered is simple: Surrender everything he believes and he will receive absolutely nothing in return. Should he elect to accept this offer, I promise he will have the better of the bargain."

With these words, Larry's Higher Self fell silent.

CHAPTER 11

Making the Decision

Larry sat stock still, his shallow breath barely moving his chest. He was visibly shaken, hardly trusting his own witness that he'd just had an encounter with his Higher Self. His mind screamed. Every instinct urged him to bolt and run. Not knowing what to do, he turned to Junie for advice, half believing that she was no more than a figment of his overactive imagination.

But Junie turned out to be very real indeed. Her presence had an immediate calming effect on Larry, and after some words of reassurance, she had him return to the place of his Aware Ego. "Breathe," she said. "Take a few deep breaths and come back to earth. It appears you've got a major decision to make."

"But what does all this mean? This can't possibly be happening." When Junie failed to respond to his insistent questions, Larry's fear grew. "Say something, Junie; this is scary stuff! What do you think I should do?"

"Larry, I've done all I can," Junie said. "The rest is up to you. You have everything you need to make the right choice. Now you must give yourself the space to allow it to happen. Your lesson here with me is over, and it is time to go. I've enjoyed meeting you and will follow the rest of your journey with great interest. *Espavo*."

"Wait!" Larry exclaimed. "I want to tell you something." But Junie had withdrawn completely, and Larry found himself very much alone among a clutter of boulders playing court to a beautiful juniper tree. Its upper branches were barely catching the diminishing rays of the late afternoon sun. His heart knew a void that his mind could not fill. Walking despondently over to the tree, he hugged it tightly, as if begging Junie to return. He loved her and appreciated her priceless gifts and wanted her to know it. Suddenly, wave after wave of rapture struck him. His knees gave way and his body sank slowly to the ground, his heart fusing with the tree's essence. His beloved juniper seemed to send out tendrils of Consciousness connecting all the trees within a five-mile radius, then a hundred, a thousand, until every tree on Earth seemed joined in a vast, loving energetic grid welcoming Larry's presence. Nothing in the forty-one years of his life had remotely prepared him for the magnificence of this homecoming.

It was several minutes before Larry was able to right himself. His fingers reached out, gently tracing the intricate ridges and hollows of the rough bark. "I love you, Junie."

He arose and wandered aimlessly among the boulders that a few moments earlier had been seats for his personalities. A joyous tingle radiated from the pit of his stomach. "I know you," Larry said, laughing out loud. "Hi, Kichi, what's up?"

"Judging by the way you're glowing, I'd say you were. But such a *toomel* I'm hearing. Can you ask your mind to put a lid on all the *mishegas*, already?"

"That was unbelievable!" Larry blurted. "I felt Junie connect me to every tree on the planet. We were linked. Each of them was inside me and I merged with every one them—an absolute paradox. I lost my identity and fused into a great collective, yet I felt more purely *me* than I ever have before. And what's with this

Yiddish thing? My mind's blown quite enough already, thank you."

"Ah, the eternal question posed by linguists throughout the ages: does language form culture or does culture form language? Use a little *seychel* and you'll work it out—the chicken comes from the egg and the egg comes from the chicken, and in the end, all you have is a bird that escaped being an omelet. If you could tune into the worldwide consciousness web, you'd hear your fellow humans conversing in over six thousand languages. Think how dull this world would be if everyone spoke the same language!"

"Are you suggesting that I'm dull because I speak only English?" Larry asked somewhat defensively.

"Oy! Heaven forbid. I would never suggest any such thing. On the other hand," Kichi giggled, "in the face of such profound wisdom, who am I to argue?"

"Cut it out, Kichi. I'm trying to work out what just happened when Junie connected me to all the trees on the planet. Does any of that make any sense to you?"

"Does it ever," Kichi said, dropping all traces of her Yiddish accent. "You've just described my reality, being part of universal Consciousness. It felt like home to you because, in a very real sense, it is. Only a small fraction of you is in fact invested in this earthbound adventure. You knew, when you agreed to enter the Grand Experiment to assist at this crucial time, you would be stripped of the conscious knowledge of who you really are. Now you're being given the opportunity to remember."

"But the thought of giving up everything I believe—it's like committing some sort of mental suicide!"

Kichi found this comparison comical. "I don't think the Phoenix's flight into the ashes is motivated by ego. Do you?"

"I don't know. Absolutely nothing makes sense."

"Aha, now you've got it!"

"Oh stop it, Kichi, you're beginning to sound like Zeus. What have I got?"

"Just because the egoic mind disconnects from its source doesn't mean the rest of you does. Listen to yourself carefully—especially to those offhand, unconscious words that suddenly pop out. You'd be astonished at the wisdom you possess. What are the exact words you just used?"

"Absolutely nothing makes sense?"

"Go on," Kichi urged.

"Oh my God! *Absolutely nothing* makes sense! Of course!" Larry said, slapping his forehead as if to shake out cobwebs. "I remember now. The proposition: surrender everything I believe and I will receive absolutely nothing in return. Part of me actually said it makes sense to accept absolutely nothing. . . . Do you suppose I should take the deal?"

"No, Larry, I'm not supposing anything. Besides, the decision to 'take the deal,' as you so offhandedly called the most momentous choice of your current incarnation, is not mine to make. Nor can it be made by rational thought or for reasons appealing to your ego. At this fork in the road, only your heart can choose the path. But I will gladly help in any way you ask."

"Sorry, I didn't mean to be flippant. I guess I said it that way to cover up my fear."

"To hide it from *me?* Larry, you forget who I am. Nothing can be hidden from me. I'm aware of things concealed even from yourself, thoughts buried long before you took your first breath in this body. I'm aware of the rhythms of your pulses, the complex of chemical and electrical signals that keeps your physical form functioning. I know your innermost desires and aversions. It's I who, each night as you sleep, unravels the emotional entanglements your conflicting voices create. I am the spinner of your dreams. But most important, I am your conscious link to your Higher Self. It's through me that you can contact your own greater intelligence—should you wish."

Neither spoke for quite a while as Larry picked his way around boulders, looking for familiar landmarks pointing the way back to Zeus. He had no clue how to begin letting his heart decide and was trying to sort through the mass of information impressed upon him over the past few hours when Kichi unexpectedly broke the silence, "How does the Phoenix know when it's time to build the funeral pyre?"

"Hell, I don't know. It looks at the calendar and there it is, somewhere between Groundhog Day and President's Day—Phoenix Day!"

Kichi's total lack of response conveyed disapproval, and Larry apologized a second time for wisecracking. "Okay, I'll try that one again. Actually, that's a pretty fascinating question. For one thing, there is only one Phoenix alive at any time. For another, it lives for five hundred years before immolating itself. That means not only are there no other Phoenixes to talk to or learn from, but at the end of each cycle there is no one alive who has witnessed the cycle and knows the Phoenix will be reborn.

"Perhaps there is only *one* eternal Phoenix, complete within itself. Maybe there are no external references marking the passage of time. In that case, its cycle isn't tied to the rotation of the planets or the rise and fall of dynasties. It doesn't stage its exit to attract attention or make a statement." Larry soon realized his line of reasoning was taking him nowhere. He fell silent and disengaged his mind completely, allowing another part of his being to wrestle with the problem. Suddenly, his head shot up and he smiled. "I've got it. "There is no 'how.' The Phoenix just knows!"

"If that's so," Kichi said, "then how does the Phoenix deal with the fear of dying?"

"There isn't any fear. Fear belongs to the world of the egoic self; but if the Phoenix is eternal, it lives in the soul realm of knowing, where there is no fear."

"Then what, Larry, are *you* still pretending not to know?"

Larry stopped dead in his tracks. The directness of Kichi's last question stunned him. How perfectly her words unmasked the hidden battle raging in his psyche between the part that counseled him to let sleeping dogs lie and the part that urged him on. He felt the panic growing in his Vulnerable Child persona even as a far more powerful force welled within.

Larry dropped into deep thought. He was committed to forging on and would follow the trail wherever it led. "When I look into the I's of infinity, I see a multiplicity of me's existing at different points along the Awareness continuum, each having a different perspective on reality.

"For example, there's the egoic me, an orchestra of subpersonalities playing every instrument known to humanity—plus, I suspect, a few we've yet to discover. This is the part of me that can't 'know,' for by definition, it deals only in belief and thought. It feeds on duality. It knows nothing of true knowing, so it simply tries to understand, name, and explain everything.

"My soul me, on the other hand, has no need for belief since it deals in the domain of knowing. Whereas the egoic me identifies only with my singular presence within the illusion, my soul is linked to a huge collective pool of information—the One Mind—which extends way beyond my ability to comprehend from here.

"So when you ask what I'm pretending not to know, what you're really asking is who am I pretending not to be!"

"Bravo!" Kichi exclaimed. "An elegant display of *aikido*."

"What do you mean by that?" Larry asked.

"*Aikido* is a peaceful form of martial arts in which you assess the flow of energy in a situation first, before responding. Then you get maximum result with minimum effort.

"What do all successful matadors have in common?" With hardly a pause for breath, Kichi answered her own question. "They know how to stand to the side of a charging bull. In life this translates to keeping oneself out of the line of fire, taking nothing personally. When attacked, don't defend or justify; simply observe. That's precisely what you did just now, and I applaud you for it. Instead of allowing one of your subpersonalities to take over, as usual, you let your Aware Ego emerge. Then you executed a perfect veronica, distracting the bull with a slight motion of your cape while you held your ground. Well done."

Larry remained confused by Kichi's appreciation. "Then why am I still struggling with the decision?"

"Because you are trying to pick up a pomegranate seed with a single chopstick."

"*What? What?*" The bird chirped in, right on cue.

"Because you're going about it in the wrong way," Kichi said. "Stop trying to use your mind. It's useless here. This is solely *une affair de coeur*. You have to learn to love with your mind and think with your heart. Remember Junie's last gift to you."

"That was absolutely amazing," Larry said, dropping into recollection. "Truly an affair of the heart. Junie, all the trees on the planet, me . . . we were linked in a sea of love."

"Was your thinking mind involved?"

"No, not in the slightest."

"Then how did it happen?"

Larry stopped walking and sat on one of the nearby boulders, allowing *aikido* to guide him. He made no attempt to answer Kichi's question with his rational mind. Instead, closing his eyes, he went inward and reached out to Junie with strands of Consciousness, just as she had done earlier. The energetic tendrils extended from him not by purposeful thought but through flows of love radiating from his core. He offered a leader stroke of pure, unconditional love, Junie responded with a matching streamer stroke, and the two met once more in Rumi's field,

Out beyond ideas of wrongdoing and rightdoing. . . .
When the soul lies down in that grass,
The world is too full to talk about.
Ideas, language, even the phrase each other
Doesn't make any sense.

Kichi said nothing to disturb Larry's reverie. When he was finally centered again in his physical form, he spoke just one word. "Love."

"And so it is," Kichi responded. "You have just experienced the next rung on the ladder. That was the energy of the fourth density. There individuated Consciousness merges, duality and fear begin to fall away, and all life forms—not just the chonic entities recognized by your scientists—consciously join as one. You've just had a glimpse of what awaits humankind at the next level of existence.

"Something similar is currently taking place with young children all around the planet. You might want to ask your Higher Self about it.

"So, *boytchik, zay gezunt.* Be healthy, live long, and prosper, and above all, don't be such a stranger." With these playful words, Kichi exited as suddenly as she had come, leaving Larry alone under the single spotlight fixing his presence on the bare stage of his mind. He smiled. What a blessing to have such a wise, powerful, and outrageous ally!

Then, recalling his recent encounter with his Higher Self, he focused as closely as he could on its impeccable energy signature. Repeating the process that had connected him to Junie, he radiated a leader stroke of perfect love directed by his intention. There was no mistaking the moment his offering was accepted and the communication channel opened. It was explosive.

His Higher Self spoke soundlessly, yet every word and nuance was crystal clear. It said that for the last sixty years or so, many intelligent life forms had been allowed to incarnate on Earth from the higher densities. "These beings, of which you are one, agreed to take form on Earth at this critical time to assist the transition into the next paradigm. Each came in absolute love, intending only to be of service. Each also came fully knowing it must go through the Veil of Forgetting, separating its Consciousness from that of its Higher Self to create the illusion that it is fully human, subject to all the physical challenges and emotional vagaries of the space/time continuum.

"More than sixty million entities willingly accepted the assignment. What none of us appreciated, however, was the incredible skill with which the fabric of this Grand Experiment had been woven. The forces dragging Consciousness into the lower, egoic realms are so potent that more than 90 percent of these Wanderers—as they are called—have failed to reconnect with the higher aspects of their I's and fully believe they are merely third-density humans.

"Now that you are beginning to emerge from your own slumber, you will be able to spot your fellow Light Workers almost instantly. Like you, they are salmon swimming upstream out of season, true strangers in a strange land. Wanderers are often plagued by allergies and a gnawing feeling of malaise. As children they typically display vivid imaginations and have make-believe playmates. They often find themselves outside the core of social cliques and are more apt to be loners than joiners. They develop a curiosity that may well get them into hot water— questioning authority at every level, needing to understand before obeying. Wanderers tend to have a highly developed rebellious side, intuitively realizing that most of the rules they have to follow are arbitrary and make little sense.

"If they accept religion at all, they tend to gravitate toward Eastern philosophies, like Buddhism and Taoism, or the less orthodox versions of the classical religions into which they were born. They seem to know instinctively that, at some point, they will have to transcend their beliefs to fulfill the purpose for which they came."

"You've just described me to a T," Larry said. "What's the secret to awakening fully?"

"The answer is simple. To move past any restrictive construct—whether an idea, a relationship, or a full-blown illusion—all you need is Awareness. Degree of Awareness is what distinguishes one density from another. It is also what guides all intelligence along the journey back to the infinite One. Every experience, every thought, word, and deed, increases your Awareness. When you experience consciously, it increases more quickly."

"How do you suggest I experience consciously?" Larry asked.

"Hold one vital question in the forefront of your mind at all times," the Higher Self replied. "We of the sixth density postulate that this very question first spurred the One Supreme Infinite Creator into action. And we, along with every other aspect of Creation, continue to delve into its mysteries. With its help you will break through this illusion's bonds with surprising ease.

"The question is: 'Who am I?' It has a companion question: 'What is my purpose?' Whatever your circumstances, align your perception with these two questions and everything changes. All you are required to do is remain conscious.

"For example, should you find yourself in an argument with a friend, turn immediately to the first question, 'Who am I?' and add its variant, 'Who is he, or she?' If this question reveals that the energy of separation is present, you can be certain you are dealing at the level of the egoic I. Recall the many active subpersonalities each of you has. Identify the role each of you is playing. Are you a reprimanding parent, a faultfinding critic, or some other energetic form prompting an unconscious defensive posture in the other person?

"Then ask the second question, 'What is my purpose?' Do I really wish to cause pain? Is it my intention to drive a wedge between us? Why am I *really* sharing this information? Is there a better way to accomplish my true purpose? Then ask the variant, 'What is his, or her, purpose?'

"The heart of *aikido* is knowing the mind of the enemy. When you feel attacked, look past your adversary's outer trappings—no matter how well you feel you know him or her—and ask, 'Who are you?' and 'What is your purpose?' You'll find that the process diffuses the negative energies and allows you to experience consciously. If you actually ask the other person these questions out loud, you'll be amazed at the outcome.

"Asking yourself these questions many times a day, particularly when judgmental thoughts arise, pays large rewards in little time. Reflecting on them before falling asleep can evoke deep and powerful dreams. If you were to answer these two questions now, what would you say?"

"I don't really know," Larry answered. "These last few days have me in a bit of a spin—especially when you, Zeus, and the others keep alluding to me as some sort of planetary savior. What's all that supposed to mean? Is there something I'm not seeing?"

"Interesting," the Higher Self said. "You still haven't put two and two together. Given all you have just experienced, aren't you beginning to suspect that there's a level of reality that extends well past the horizons of this illusion?"

"Of course," Larry said. "What you and the others have been revealing seems entirely weird, yet it's also familiar. I feel like I'm being exploded from the inside out!"

"Relax, Larry. Your mind is of little help here. You won't find the answers you're looking for inside your head. Not everything is known, even for us at what you call a higher level of intelligence. That's why we continue to seek as we do. For us, it is a joy to explore the unfathomable realms of Creation, for we have learned that questions always outrank answers and each answer is but a stepping stone to the next question. Always bear in mind, as you acclimate to the role you came here to play, that the journey holds more value than the destination—for the journey contains the present moment, while the destination resides only in the future. Even when you arrive, you are merely in a new present moment and the destination dissolves into a new part of the journey. Larry, you will visit many places and have many adventures in the months to come. Try always to stay in the now.

"'Render unto Caesar the things which are Caesar's, and unto God the things that are God's.' This is sage advice, for it speaks of the illusion of time, the realm of the ego, and the domain of the soul. Give your lower self those things that enrich its sense of importance—beliefs and thoughts of past and future.

And give your soul what it yearns for—knowing in the now, sharing as one with all Creation.

"And so I ask, why do you hold yourself separate from me? Why do you hold to the rung of your lower self so tightly? Can you not see that I, for all my lofty appearance, am simply a part of you? Can either of us find fulfillment in separation? Perhaps it is now time to move past your old, constricted view of who you are.

"When I asked you to respond to the two questions, I was inviting you to explore the nature of your Consciousness and why you chose to incarnate on Earth at this time. Who *are* you, the essential you, when you peel away the labels and personas; the preferences, possessions, and accomplishments; the thoughts and beliefs—everything belonging to the egoic I?"

Sensing Larry's frustration in trying to break free of old patterns, the Higher Self said, "Let me put this another way: You just had a very meaningful interaction with Junie that has left an indelible impression on your psyche. Do you think your meeting was a random event; that you just happened to find her, one of thousands of trees in this park?

"I never thought of that," Larry said. "Come to think of it, Zeus just told me to look for the buffalo and wander out among the rocks and trees."

"Then how did you know how to find her?"

"I don't know."

"*This* you do know, Larry. It's time to stop settling for the easy way out. Search deeper and you will discover that she called you and you went to her. Don't you remember?"

"I'm not sure," Larry responded.

"Do you recall playing the game 'hot and cold' when you were a child? You are supposed to find something, and the clues are in the form of temperature readings. The farther away from the object you go, the colder it gets. As you get closer you are told you are getting warmer, then hotter, then burning hot when you are almost on top of it."

Larry nodded.

"That's pretty much how the mind finds solutions. It processes bits of information in various permutations and combinations until they fit into hypotheses that seem to work. When you think with your heart instead of your mind, you process information a completely different way. Go back to the point just after you left Zeus. Your tangle of thoughts simply gave way, and you let yourself be guided by the flow. As far as your conscious mind knew, you weren't headed toward anything in particular. Your inner knowing, or intuition, took over, however, and honed in on Junie's frequency. It brought you right where you were meant to be.

"Let your inner knowing guide you now. Go into your heart and let it speak to me about your essence. Allow it to reveal who you are and why you've entered this illusion at this particular time."

Larry remained silent a very long while. Wrapped in the safety of his Higher Self, he allowed himself to splinter into countless fragments. He felt his essence falling backwards into a black hole while his mind remained imprisoned in the illusion of its own making, appearing to recede past the vanishing point. When he finally spoke, it was with great difficulty, as if he was translating a message from a dimly remembered foreign language. "I am Consciousness, part of the indivisible whole, yet unique. . . . The whole is an infinitesimal part of me. . . . We are One. . . . I embody the wonderment that inspires Creation to unfold in Consciousness. . . . directing itself to probe every possibility in self-aware evolution."

"That's essentially correct," the Higher Self said. "You have just described an aspect of the matrix on which existence hangs. Now, build on that and follow your journey's path. Tell me what all this has to do with your presence on Earth at this time."

"I have come to serve," Larry said, still speaking as if in a dense fog.

"Continue."

"My God!" Larry suddenly exclaimed, jolted from his reverie. "We *are* One! It's exactly like Junie's trees. It's as if I've lost myself in an ocean of billions of other entities, while they have lost themselves in me. Each of us is distinct, capable of individual experience, yet we're inexorably linked. And you and I are part of each other. You are the part of me still residing in the higher density, and I am the part of you manifest within the illusion."

"Excellent," the Higher Self said, "that is precisely so. What you describe is a social memory complex: billions of points of Consciousness—non-chonic intelligent life forms—joined as one to plumb the depths of the Unknowable Mystery receding constantly before us.

"As our understanding of the Oneness, together with our Consciousness, becomes progressively refined, it is expressed as ever-purer forms of unconditional love. We expand our ability to enter these higher states of love by offering service to all our other selves who request it. This is our chosen path."

"That's it, that's it!" Larry said excitedly. "I am here to help midwife the shift. I . . . we . . . elected to incarnate on Earth to assist those who wish to move on to the next density."

"It appears you now know who you are and why you're here. That leaves only your reply to my earlier proposition."

"There can be only one reply," Larry answered. "My earlier fear was fed by ignorance. I didn't appreciate that all change requires surrender. The old must die to make way for the new. I confused who I really am with the point from which I was viewing. I believed that I and my egoic self were a merged entity through which the entire Universe found expression. It seems silly now, but it seemed real enough only a few moments ago.

"When you asked me to surrender everything I believe and receive absolutely nothing in return, it frightened me. Now I realize that I am surrendering only my old points of view. In exchange, I receive the absolute freedom of not being chained to any one viewpoint. I am then free to explore them all. By accepting the proposition, I truly have nothing . . . which in fact means I have everything."

CHAPTER 12

The Consummating Experience

"Well done. I am truly proud of you!" The familiar voice came from Larry's left. He turned and saw his beloved Zeus sitting on a medium-sized boulder, catching the last rays of the afternoon sun. "It appears you have mastered the *espavo* paradox and have returned with the greatest treasure of all—nothing!"

"My God, Zeus," Larry said, "how long have you been sitting here? What paradox?"

"Oh, long enough, I suppose. Besides, if you remember, I don't exactly have to be here in order to be here, if you know what I mean." Even What-What understood Zeus's offhand reminder that he was in constant telepathic contact with his master, as were the other beings who had chosen to link consciously to their adventures in Joshua Tree.

"Time's a-wasting, my good man, and the day is fast disappearing. Perhaps it would be wise, before taking another step on our epic journey toward liberating the inhabitants of this glorious planet, to consider a little sustenance for ourselves. Don't know about you, buddy, but I could eat a horse—figuratively speaking, of course."

Larry laughed, rubbing Zeus just below his hindquarter so the dog's right leg twitched in a comic, scratching motion. The two, walking in silence, made good time back to the car. Zeus led the way.

As Larry backed slowly out of the parking space, Zeus curled into a comfortable ball tucked into the recesses of the SUV's soft leather bucket seat. "Go back to the main road and hang a right," Zeus said. "There's someone else you need to meet before we feed our faces. We'll have to hurry or we'll miss out. We can discuss some of your endless questions en route, if you like.

"Let me see," Zeus said, quickly scanning Larry's consciousness, "what loose ends beg resolution? Ah yes, the special kiddies Kichi mentioned and the *espavo* paradox. *Espavo*, as you might remember—when you finally break free of the fog bank you're in—means 'thank you for taking your power.' This extraordinary word counsels you to treasure your power and not barter it for false security. People too readily relinquish their power to any two-bit authority figure peddling a solution to a perceived problem. Government agencies, doctrines of belief, codependent relationships, educational and financial systems, committees, bylaws, statutes, nations—almost any worldly institution you can name exists solely because people have invested it with their power, rationalizing that they're doing it for the common good.

"The collective mosaic you human types have constructed nearly always disenfranchises the individual in favor of the group's perceived needs. What is absolutely amazing is that you all buy into it. Invariably, as you have just discovered, instead of being nurtured by the whole, you are made to compete for crumbs. You live in a world of vying factions that has caused a stunning imbalance in the use of global resources. As you are fond of saying, 'The rich get richer and the poor get prison for doing exactly the same things.'

"If the poor got fair exchange for the power they hand over, they would at least have something to show for it. But the hucksters are too clever to give them a square deal, so instead they swap the entire island for twenty-four dollars worth of trinkets. So in exchange for their souls' birthright, humans receive the bread and circus of hope and dogma. 'We have the power; you have the Super Bowl and the promise of a better tomorrow.' What a deal!

"It is written:

> *Free Will, the ultimate gift of the gods, can only be exercised once it has been surrendered.*

"This cosmic axiom, taken directly from the 'Must Read' section of the *Interdimensional Survival Manual,* is commonly misinterpreted by the lower-self I as, 'My will is Thy will, and Thy will be done.' No. True Free Will—free of preference, judgment, predilection, or other biases of the ego—can only be exercised in the realm of the soul. This is not the stuff practiced on the lower rungs of the ladder.

"This commentary on Free Will, the Prime Mandate of Creation, is paralleled in the *espavo* paradox, which states: 'To truly claim one's power, one must first give it away.' That, my dear friend and comrade in arms, is what the Phoenix does every time it dies, and what you did just a few moments ago when you accepted the ultimate proposition. *Espavo!*"

Zeus's head suddenly turned toward Larry. "Slow down, you'll be making a right in about a quarter of a mile. You'll see a sign pointing the way to Keys View."

It took Larry nearly fifteen minutes to negotiate the well-paved, five-mile road ending at the famous lookout point. He was so wrapped up in his conversation with Zeus that he all but forgot he was behind the wheel. Zeus had begun to explain the other "loose end," and Larry was absolutely spellbound, astonished at the incredible events taking place right under his nose—and he, like almost everyone else on the planet, had never suspected a thing.

"There's a lot of interest in a special breed of children showing up all over the planet," Zeus was saying. "More and more kids are being born with an array of suprahuman talents, ranging from being able to restructure their DNA and cure themselves of HIV/AIDS to creating a new web of Consciousness surrounding the planet.

"On the surface, this seems extraordinary. In fact, it is quite ordinary—especially when you consider that every one of the tens of millions of Wanderers currently alive on this planet started out as kids themselves. Each of your fellow interdensity servers came with the same latent abilities these children display. The only difference is the quality of the Veil at the time of their arrival. When most of you entered this illusion, sometime during the past sixty years or so, the Veil of Forgetting was still operational, only just beginning to thin. So you were blocked from knowing who you really are and why you elected to incarnate here and now.

"Due to significant shifts in the energetic matrix of your planet as well as your solar system and galaxy—which we will explore in due course—the Veil's original structure is rapidly disintegrating. Many of the babies currently being born are slipping right past the extensive filtering and distortions engineered to strip elevated beings from their source of inner knowledge.

"There are many names for these *wunderkinder*—the Indigo Children, the Crystal Children, the Children of Oz. The names are unfortunate. They reinforce the illusion's compulsion toward separation by placing this particular group of planetary servers on a pedestal.

"I'll give you a working knowledge of what these kids have to offer. Just don't get caught up in the mystique. They are here now only because of the significant strides made by millions of others over the past decades, just as you are beginning to awaken now because you stand on the shoulders of those who came before."

Larry nodded, appreciating the warning. These gifted children are merely the Roger Bannisters of the new millennium, breaking the imaginary human barrier, inviting us all to follow into uncharted territories. "What about the kids who can restructure their DNA and cure themselves of AIDS?"

"Ah," Zeus responded, "the Children of AIDS. A remarkable bunch, really. These are entities who willingly incarnate into a body infected with HIV/AIDS. While most of these babies succumb, more and more of them are learning to alter their DNA, boosting their immune system sufficiently to eradicate all disease from their bodies."

"How is that possible?" Larry asked.

"DNA is actually a sophisticated form of innate intelligence, a self-correcting and self-advancing piece of software written by a cosmic genius. Structurally, human DNA contains four nucleic acids, which combine in sets of three to form sixty-four codons, akin to the sixty-four hexagrams of the *I Ching*. The Veil's programming deliberately deactivates forty-four of these codons to prevent participants in the Grand Experiment from straying too easily beyond the illusion's walls. However, now that the Veil is rapidly dissolving, what do you suppose continues to keep the dormant codons shut down?"

Larry shrugged, silently encouraging Zeus to continue.

"Habit. People simply assume that because something could not be done yesterday, it still can't be done today. In fact, most humans have invested so heavily in their old beliefs that they would rather die than let go. That's why these kids are here—to demonstrate that altering the DNA programming is literally child's play.

"It's working. Scientists *are* beginning to take notice in a new way. They find it remarkable that DNA is subject to what they term spontaneous genetic mutation. To their amazement, they are forced to accept that DNA can alter itself at any time. Major mutation does *not* have to occur, as they originally believed, at conception. Can you imagine what this does to the theory of evolution?"

Larry burst out laughing, and Zeus, following Larry's train of thought, soon joined in.

"That's so funny," Larry said. "The battle between creationists and evolutionists has been raging for years. Science and God duking it out, each claiming the moral high ground and condemning the other as a heretic, spurning either faith or truth. The new information unveiled—pun intended—by the children, changes everything."

"And so it does," Zeus agreed. "Given the choice between 'a: creation' or 'b: evolution,' why not choose 'c: none, or both, of the above?' Creation itself is divinely intelligent. Like DNA, it is an autocorrecting and autoadvancing Consciousness that directs itself. Viewed from the arena of science, this process appears to be natural selection; from the perspective of religion, it looks like the unfolding of the Mind of God.

"Since God *is* all things, each species is directed by its own innate curiosity to explore the limitless potential of its experience. Since the environment is composed of the same God Consciousness, there is constant feedback evaluating the potential and richness of any particular mutating experiment. As a result, both the environment and the species in question mutate—just for the pure fun of it! So you see, the entire Universe is simply God expressing itself through the olio of creative, naturally selective evolution."

"Then maybe we should call it 'crevolution,'" Larry said.

Zeus chortled. "Ever wonder what makes people take themselves so seriously?" he asked, more as a rhetorical remark than a question. "Just listen to either side of this impassioned debate and the answer becomes alarmingly clear. Nothing breeds arrogance more than ignorance! Each side gets half a point for showing us one aspect of the elephant and loses five points for dismissing all other viewpoints. Both sides have painted themselves into such a corner, they've left no wiggle room to reconcile these amazing children with their old beliefs. How can either of them deal with the reality that an increasing number of adults are beginning to mimic the AIDS children's ability to resist disease? How does either religion or science explain away the hundredth monkey?

"Perhaps the most celebrated special kid in the past forty years has been Uri Geller. He entered the illusion in 1946 with the primary purpose of piquing science's curiosity. His ability to bend metal—even under rigorously controlled conditions—was researched intensively for years. Uri would go on national television and bend spoons in front of the cameras. Following virtually every appearance, TV stations would be flooded with phone calls from parents reporting their kids just performed the same trick with the family silverware.

"Somehow, scientists missed the point entirely. Well, they're not missing it now. Thousands of children are being born every day with Uri's abilities and more. It may have been easy to dam up a trickle, but this is turning into a veritable deluge. China recently admitted to having a hundred thousand of these youngsters in special schools to further develop their paranormal skills.

Do you think, for a second, that every other country isn't vitally interested in corralling these children's talents for its own special interests?

"Researchers, to their absolute astonishment, are finding that so-called normal kids can easily develop these unusual abilities when they're exposed to the new breed of children. These super-tricks include the ability to 'see' with their hands or feet while blindfolded, read the future like an open picture book, and psychically tune into a photograph and 'read' the life stories of all the people involved, including the photographer. Something is happening that cannot be named or controlled, and it's freaking out the establishment, big time.

"The sixty-four-thousand-dollar question is: What opportunity does this impressive influx of super-children offer?"

"For one thing," Larry said, "they show us that it can be done. And they certainly make us reexamine our perceived limitations. The game is suddenly much, much larger than we ever imagined it. They give us a sense that there is light at the end of this tunnel and that, if we could grasp the meaning behind the phenomena, we might be able to use it to catapult ourselves into the next paradigm."

"It's good to have you on the team, Larry. You've come a long way since Patchy first showed you the light. As you suggest, treasures lurk in the shadows of the parlor tricks they show us. As I alluded earlier, these children tend to stand out. In the past they were the collective poster kids of the 'Ritalin generation.' How else would you expect your highly structured, well-entrenched society to deal with its misfits?

"This too is beginning to change. As these children continue to incarnate by the millions, they are markedly changing the flavor of the stew. You've probably noticed a different approach to parenting starting to emerge. Somehow, these youngsters have activated a latent knowing within their mothers and fathers, causing them to wake up to the fact that they have birthed the progenitors of the next paradigm. Many of these adults now appreciate that their gift to humanity will come through their children.

"But this is far from universally true. Most of these children have chosen to incarnate in difficult conditions of war, pestilence, and starvation. Yet even these kids have quietly trumped both their circumstances and those who would abuse their gifts. What's little publicized is that many of these new arrivals have keen telepathic abilities secreted within their paranormal arsenal. Whatever they appear to be doing in the outward 'normal' world, they have created a private supraworld in which many of them have already connected."

"Like Junie and the trees?" Larry asked.

"Exactly like Junie and the trees, and exactly like the social memory complex your Higher Self described. These children have formed a complete lattice of love around your planet as a portal into the next density. Over the next few years they will be increasing the amplitude of radiant love energy within this grid to act as a lightninglike leader stroke, inviting every single being on this planet to respond. Our job, in the little time we have left here, is to help as many as possible become aware of this opportunity and, should they ask, assist any way we can with their process of ascension.

"The outcome will be determined entirely by how people choose to perceive the messages these wonderful children bring. If they're dazzled by the outer display of exceptional abilities and simply want to attain the same aptitudes for themselves, then they—like the scientists, who seek only to measure, dissect, and analyze—will remain stuck on the lower rungs of the egoic I. If, on the other hand, they listen with their hearts and 'feel' the rapturous music played in the cracks between the keys, they will see past the wrapping paper to the true gift inside."

Zeus's discourse on the super-kids and the road ended simultaneously. The two found themselves at a circular parking lot right at the edge of a steep escarpment nearly one mile above the valley floor. They had arrived at Keys View, overlooking the entire Coachella Valley—arguably one of the world's more remarkable vistas. Larry pulled into one of the lined parking spaces and turned off the engine as he asked one last question about the children. "Do they have a particular message that lets people know why they're here?"

"Until recently, no," Zeus responded. "They simply appeared as isolated anomalies, freaks of nature. As they grew in number, each sent out energetic dendrites to the others, gradually fashioning a psychic, neurological mesh that over the years has sheathed the entire planet. Now that this network is complete, the children are beginning to speak. Their message is as open and innocent as they are: 'Come join us. We are waiting for you.' When asked how, they advise us to return to our own childhood, when we created any playtime reality we chose simply by imagining it. They ask us to conduct our lives as if we were already conduits anchoring the transforming light of unconditional love on Earth."

"Is it as easy as they make it out to be?" Larry asked.

"Yes," Zeus replied. "Once you 'get it' and make the shift, it happens in an instant. However, as you can appreciate, getting it is not an intellectual process. The soil must be prepared and the plant tended before there is a harvest. The kids are doing their job; now we have to do ours.

"Come on. I want you to meet someone, and we don't have much time. Grab the flashlight from the glove compartment," said Zeus, mysterious as ever. The two got out of the car, and Larry started toward the concrete path leading up to the famed Keys View lookout. "No, no, no," said Zeus. "We walk the path less traveled. Follow me, for I have a dream and I shall lead you to the promised land."

With that, Zeus walked off in the opposite direction, picking his way along a steep switchback trail winding its way some four hundred feet up to Inspiration Peak. Larry followed as best he could, torn between his desire to keep pace with his little dog and his need to pause occasionally to allow his pulse to stop imitating a demented woodpecker.

This time, the destination was more than reward for the pain of the journey, proving, to Larry's amusement, that even the inviolate admonishments of his beloved dog have exceptions. The panorama from this elevated promontory dwarfed the earlier view. Standing on the rocky outcrop at the summit, Larry towered over the man-made tourists' viewing area on the other side of the parking lot. From where he stood, he felt he could see the entire Universe. Directly before him loomed the majestic presence of Mount San Jacinto, jutting more than two miles straight up from the desert floor. Looking down, he could see the sprawl of the city strip weaving through the entire Coachella Valley, from Palm Springs to Thermal and Mecca. To the right he could see the grayish pall of early evening smog congregating at the crest of Banning Pass, somehow knowing it was not permitted to move any further east. In the opposite direction stretched the entire Salton Sea, a forty-by-fifteen-mile papaya-shaped inland lake formed in the early 1900s when poorly made irrigation dams gave way, allowing the Colorado River to flood local communities and farms for over a year. The surface of this accidental body of water lies some 228 feet below sea level, its bottom just a few feet higher than the lowest spot in Death Valley.

The last of the sun was just disappearing behind San Jacinto when Zeus disrupted the sanctity of Larry's reverie. "Ah, we're in time. Now you too will know how this place—a highly charged vortex of energy—earned its name. You are about to meet a supreme master. No one who partakes of the experience about to be presented to you ever emerges unchanged."

Zeus's words both perplexed and excited Larry. Despite the many cars in the parking lot, the two had the entire mountaintop to themselves, save for the occasional Joshua tree, yucca, or cactus dotting the stark landscape. It seemed the show had just begun; Larry's attention was riveted on the most impressive light display he had ever seen.

Blues gave way to every imaginable shade of purple, mauve, and lilac. Flickers of red and orange flames flared through vast portions of the sky, while brilliant strokes of yellows and gold marked the movement of angels swooping through the heavens. Larry screamed decibels of joy. It was a kaleidoscopic masterpiece choreographed to perfection, one luxurious swirl after another freshly flowing out of and redefining its predecessor. He was bearing witness to the Cosmic Dance of the Seven Veils in which the heavens reveal the secrets of the steps of enlightenment to the ancient Merkabah mystics. He was being bewitched by the irresistible charms of Salome, seduced by the tantalizing allure of Mohini, enchanted by the devastating beauty of Pandora.

Words, thoughts, concepts deserted him completely. He was helplessly, hopelessly, ecstatically in love. Every part of him eagerly surrendered, begging to be taken, consumed, totally devoured by the experience. On that September evening, on a lone mountaintop at the southern edge of the Mojave Desert, in the presence of his beloved dog, Larry died.

CHAPTER *13*

Cosmic Perspectives

Who can say what the Phoenix experiences at its demise? Even if this magnificent bird were given to speech, where would it find words adequate to the task? Death explored from the vantage point of the ego is such a scary prospect. Who among us, when the last moment comes, will rise eagerly to welcome and embrace the Grim Reaper or whatever other image our culture has imprinted into our psyches?

Our egoic self is not equipped to deal with death. The very thought of it is too . . . final. We are here for a while, make a few awkward markings in the sands, and then we're not here and life, whatever it is, is over. We're not even allowed to die with dignity, in full recognition of ourselves as infinite beings. Even those pretending to have spiritual awareness do little better than cast us into an envisaged heaven, surrounded by ascended masters, angels, attended by a retinue of deceased friends, family, and adoring pets.

Imagine projecting any of the common euphemisms for death onto one of humanity's beloved religious leaders. Jesus—or Buddha or Muhammad or Krishna—didn't die; he just

assumed room temperature
improved the gene pool
won the Darwin award

became living impaired
cashed in his chips
went to take a dirt nap
kicked the bucket
moved into upper management
began push'n up the daisies
shuffled off this mortal coil
went to sleep with the fishes
went to meet his maker
began hangin' with St. Peter
bought the farm
went to play rummy with Jimmy Hoffa
bit the big one

These colloquialisms aren't meant to be sacrilegious. They're just eloquent declarations of ignorance, expressed comically to assuage fear. Larry's death was considerably grander, far more magnificent than any of these flippant clichés. When one dies and comes face to face with All That Is, the thought of "sharing a cold one" hardly comes to mind.

There is no worldly comfort to be taken from Larry's experience, no promise of being taken into the Light, surrounded by the heavenly host, and provided with gossamer robes, six vestal virgins, and the key to the Eternal City. He simply fractured into 1,548,008,755,920 fractals which in turn disintegrated into immeasurable wave beams of immaculate light that ultimately consumed itself in Pure Unconditional Love. In short, he returned home.

Eons passed. Galaxies were birthed, spreading gangly limbs ever outward in far-flung spirals of light, sensing, probing, learning—ever learning. Then they, like the Phoenix, knowing the proper moment had come, retreated once more, back into the darkness of their cores, reinstating vast portions of Creation to utter silence. The bee returned once again to the hive, having visited many, many flowers. And so the Universe took yet another great breath as time twisted inward upon itself and space ceased to have dimension.

Zeus sat stock still that night watching the ultimate initiation of his beloved master. His highly sensitized empathic abilities allowed him to join Larry for the first few steps of the journey. After that, he could only wait. The last of the magnificent light show had disappeared behind the darkened peaks of the San Jacinto Mountains, and the only glow to be seen came from the hundreds of thousands of lights illuminating the Coachella Valley below and the knowing twinkle of the stars overhead. Larry's earlier thoughts proved prophetic: from where he had stood on the top of Inspiration Peak, he was indeed able to see the entire Universe.

There has been mention of a strange phenomenon in which people who have completed the task for which they came to Earth die consciously and leave their body in the care of another soul. These new arrivals—usually more evolved beings on a specific mission—are called walk-ins. They assume the departed entity's entire history, including family, friends, work, commitments, and everything else making up the complex mosaic of a human life. It takes a while, but eventually these elevated beings adjust to the Grand Experiment and bring a greater level of compassion, awareness, and love to this planet.

Like all concepts passed through the strainer's twenty-six holes, this explanation of walk-ins suffers much from the process. In the world of illusion, speech is conjugated into pronouns of separation. He is not she, we are not they, and certainly you are not I. The heart says, "We are all one"; the mind says, "Fiddlesticks!" The mind would argue that if one soul departs and another soul enters, there are clearly two souls. "Not so fast," says the heart. "If it is true that we are all one, then both souls must be the same." What a tangled mess! If only the brain/mind and heart/mind could see that, wondrously, they are two sides of the same coin!

Creation is not a constant. It is made up of Consciousness and thought held together by agreement—a current ebbing and flowing in endlessly varying cycles. The illusion, as we experience it, is similarly constructed. All matter and energy flicker in particle/waves oscillating at dazzling speed back and forth across the threshold of manifestation. Our thoughts are frames on a strip of motion picture film blended by the light of our Consciousness to create the streaming illusion of reality. In this respect, we do not actually exist. We are simply projections of our own thoughts, butterflies dreaming we are human beings.

Our lives flicker with every breath. We die thirty-four thousand times each day during the fleeting interval at the peak of each inhalation and exhalation. We die for an instant each time we sneeze, cough, yawn, or sigh. In French, orgasm is called *la petite mort*—the little death—honoring the process through which mind and body surrender completely to the ecstasy of sensation. Every night when we sleep we sit on the bank of the Great River, watching our Consciousness flow into the Eternal Sea. Each morning when we awake we are renewed, having integrated and processed the harvest of the previous day. We are not the same.

And so it was that whoever or whatever returned to inhabit Larry's mind/body/emotion/spirit earthly form was certainly not the same aspect of Consciousness that had climbed the four-hundred-foot rise a short while earlier. Both he and Zeus knew words were totally irrelevant and inappropriate. It is said, "Before enlightenment, chop wood, carry water; after enlightenment, chop wood, carry water." The new Larry simply turned on his flashlight and once again followed his beloved dog, retracing their steps down the mountain to the only car left in the parking lot.

I would rather live in a world
Where my life is surrounded by mystery
Than live in a world so small
That my mind could comprehend it.

— HENRY EMERSON FOSDICK

CHAPTER 14

The Other Side
of the Veil

Sunday morning more than lived up to the promise of its namesake, the sky a perfect sapphire frame for the brilliance of the sun. Mountains and trees were defined with crystal clarity. The rocks seemed alive, the early morning rays transmuting them into dazzling reflectors of light, as the two returned for their last visit to Joshua Tree.

"Want to talk about it?" Zeus asked.

"Not really. There's not much to say."

"Anyway, I'm glad you decided to return."

"For a while it was touch and go," Larry said. "I probably wouldn't have had a chance of returning if I hadn't heard my own voice calling me back. I had a vague sense of being in two places at the same time, separated by layers and layers of Consciousness yet connected by a long silver thread. The curious part of being in the Void isn't the stillness or the incredible sense of peace. It's more than that. There's a completeness, a perfection so absolute that it's virtually impossible to formulate thought or intent. I cannot imagine, given the totality of All That Is, whatever prompted the Creation to seek more. I know trying to explain it doesn't make sense. Words somehow aren't enough."

"Funny, that," Zeus commented. "How people love words! How they delight in rearranging the letters to symbolize thought, believing they know anything at all. Kinda' reminds me of a wonderful story."

Larry laughed. Everything reminded Zeus of a story. "Go for it, O great Doggie-San."

"Well, since you insist," Zeus said. "This story takes place thousands of years ago, before the destruction of the last temple in Jerusalem. It was on Yom Kippur, the most sacred day of the Jewish year, when the high priest entered the holy of holies and communed directly with his God. During this particular session with the Almighty, he prayed for divine guidance, for peace among the tribes, for forgiveness on behalf of all humankind for any sins committed during the previous year. He entreated with his heart, pleaded with his mind, and petitioned with all the fervor his soul could muster.

"The following day, in the privacy of his rooms, he thought about the eloquence of his prayer and once again reached to God. 'Please tell me, Ha-Shem, was my prayer well received?'

"'Yes,' came the answer, 'it was.'

"'And was it not the finest prayer you heard?' the rabbi asked.

"'No, my child it was not. Another in your synagogue delivered a prayer that moved me even more.'

"The rabbi was shocked. How was that possible? 'Who,' he asked, 'spoke a prayer more perfect than mine?'

"'Kefa,' came the reply.

"'But how is that possible?' the rabbi exclaimed. 'Kefa is the janitor. He keeps the synagogue clean and runs errands. He knows nothing of prayer.'

"'Yes, this is true. But Kefa knows he knows nothing of prayer, so when he wished to speak to me he simply said, 'Dear God, I am a simple man who knows nothing save that I love you. I do not know the proper prayers and dearly do not wish to offend you. So instead of speaking words, I will recite the alphabet. Please rearrange the letters in whatever manner pleases you most.'

"If you offered this option to God," Zeus asked Larry, "do you think he would be able to rearrange the letters to fully describe your experience?"

Larry spoke with a new voice neither of them had heard before. "What a loaded question! First of all, it implies that I agree there is an entity called God existing separately from humans. Second, it suggests that this God, who has permitted Free Will to be the driving force behind Creation's infinite diversity, would actually entertain dialogue that could abrogate this precious gift. It's a nice story, but I have trouble with the concept of relegating the Great Unknowable Mystery to the confines of an anthropomorphic pronoun like 'he' or 'she' or 'it.' Somehow, even trying to name God seems blasphemous."

Larry found his voice growing surprisingly intense. "How do you rationalize making an object-noun of God when you claim that the I AM THAT I AM is no less than the infinite sum total of the unfolding Creation? In fact, wasn't it you who intimated that separating humankind from God is the fatal flaw in the premise upon which Western religion is built?"

"Whoa there, buddy!" Zeus responded. "Interesting thought, but don't lay that one on my doorstep. I don't recall ever saying such a thing. But while you're on a roll, go for it. I'd like to hear more of your take on Western religion."

Larry looked puzzled. He was certain he had heard these ideas. If not from Zeus, then who? Why were new thoughts flooding his mind like a torrent unleashed by a broken dam? Where was this new voice in him coming from?

"That's an easy one," Zeus chided, eavesdropping on Larry's train of thought. "Change the point from which you view and you change what you see. The trouble with most people down here is they want everything they see to conform to the point from which they view, which—if you ask me—is a little ass about face."

"Thanks," Larry said. "I guess we both have to get used to the new me. What a trip! You're right, by the way—in case you need my validation—it's the unwillingness to let go that's humanity's main stumbling block. We get so entrenched in our beliefs, we'd rather defend and die than move past dogma and live.

"I suppose that's what's at the heart of my beef about religion. Anyone would admit there's a lot of good in scripture. However, that doesn't justify it as the foundation for such a huge building. Imagine what would happen if the underlying base of a skyscraper was only 98 percent. We'd get the same heap of conceptual rubble we find today all over the planet. There's no question that belief in the separation—or the fall—of humanity from God *is* the driving force that fosters blind adherence to religion. Help me out here, if you don't mind—I'll have to schedule memorizing the Bible for my next life. It's the part about wolves looking like sheep and trees growing bitter fruit."

Zeus laughed. "Be happy to, good buddy. You are no doubt referring to Matthew 7:15–20:

> Beware of false prophets, which come to you in sheep's clothing, but inwardly they are ravening wolves. Ye shall know them by their fruits. Do men gather grapes of thorns, or figs of thistles? Even so every good tree bringeth forth good fruit; but a corrupt tree bringeth forth evil fruit. A good tree cannot bring forth evil fruit, neither can a corrupt tree bring forth good fruit. Every tree that bringeth not forth good fruit is hewn down, and cast into the fire. Wherefore by their fruits ye shall know them."

"Damn you're good!" Larry exclaimed. "Is there anything you don't know?"

"Just a parlor trick," Zeus said. "Any kid will soon be able to do it, and—if I may paraphrase—greater works than these shall they do when they awaken to their true natures."

"That quote is exactly what I was trying to remember," Larry said. "Just consider the fruits that the collective trees of religion have borne. Throughout history, humankind has evoked the many names of God to rape and pillage, kill and maim, subjugate and ravage—generation after generation drowning in their own blood."

Larry's voice reached a pontifical pitch. "Read any mainstream newspaper, listen to any newscast—the overwhelming recurring theme deals with the evil fruit of the tree of belief: terrorists, massacres, mothers killing children, husbands killing wives, children killing classmates, peasants with chain saws killing forests, toxic runoffs killing lakes and oceans, multinational corporations killing smaller competitors. Now read the sacred texts. Aren't they full of words like "battle," "kill," "judgment," "hatred," "revenge," "fear," "jealousy"? Don't the ancient myths speak of wars and enslavement, good versus evil, black versus white, my God versus yours? They have elevated separation to an art form."

"Quite an indictment," said Zeus. "Sounds like you're fixin' to butt horns with the whole world. What would you say to those who claim none of the writings are to be taken literally, that they are merely metaphors, stories rich with inner meaning?"

"To them I would say," responded Larry, not losing his stride for a moment, 'then so is the alphabet a metaphor, containing within its bosom answers to all the challenges your mind can frame. We've already seen how a myth can be shaped to validate whatever conclusion you're backing. What I'm questioning is the assumed authority of the written word. How does one argue when 'God' speaks? If the entire Universe is God, then any voice, any event, any thought is an aspect of that God. When I have a thought, it comes from God. When I speak, it is God speaking. When I see you, or a tree or the sky, I see God. If I truly *see* this and know it with all my heart and soul, then no one need ever fear me, for I can do no harm."

This last phrase poured out of Larry with a vehemence that took his own breath away. He was beginning to revel in his new voice—part of him imagining himself preaching from a soapbox in London's Hyde Park. In his mind's eye, he envisioned throngs of people hanging onto each syllable, each transformative concept triggering waves of epiphany.

Zeus could only chuckle. "Ain't nothing more of a pain in the butt than a born-again believer."

But if Larry heard the remark, it had no dampening effect on his discourse. He was on a roll. "Yet the so-called holy texts beseech believers to kill in the name of their God. In some passages, God promises revenge and retribution upon the believers' enemies. This cannot be the same God I know. No part of me feels compelled to fear God. Why should I prostrate before God's altar when I worship him with my entire life? Every beat of my heart, every breath I take, every thought, every word and deed is begotten in the name of God, for God.

"Every bird, every tree, every flower is His prophet. How words pale to insignificance in the face of *their* glory! Why live in the shadow of interpretation when the sun illuminates every atom of my being? Must I listen to the sounds of yesterday's trumpets when each moment the celestial symphony resonates anew in my own Consciousness?

"I say, forget the wisdom of the past. If you must quote, then quote from the depths of your own heart. If when you look into that sacred space you find nothing, then remain silent. In that silence you will make room for the Great Mystery to arrive. If your heart is already filled with preconceived belief, then it will surely pass you by."

"Very impressive!" Zeus said. "That must have been one helluva trip into the cosmos you took last night. I'd like to package some of your passion and sprinkle it all over this little planet. It'd sure make our job a lot easier. But, if you don't mind a suggestion, you might want to lighten up a bit and give folks some space to maneuver.

"Getting back to my question, I know language can't explain your journey into the Void. But if you put aside your supposition that God doesn't use words to talk to us mortal beings—supposing, for the sake of argument, he could—would he be able to rearrange the letters of the alphabet to fully describe your experience, as he did for Kefa's prayer?"

"Okay, okay," Larry responded. "I get the message." The fervor in Larry's voice began to ebb. "If I allow that God is a noun and imbue him with the three O's—omnipotence, omnipresence, and omniscience—as all true believers do, then by definition he can do anything, make silk purses out of sows' ears, construct skyscrapers out of dental floss. After all, he *is* God! So I guess he would have the words to explain the nature of exploding Consciousness—at least to himself."

"Clever answer. You're suggesting that even if he could stuff your indescribable, mystical adventure into Never-Never Land through the strainer's twenty-six holes, who else could possibly understand?

"Intellectuals revere the mind," Zeus continued. "Their quest to understand in terms they already accept keeps them locked within the prison of reason, able to comprehend and accept only what will pass through the twenty-six holes. They would rather measure, analyze, and hypothesize about the properties of water than take one sip. When it comes to love, would you rather be the anthropologist writing volumes about how various indigenous tribes have practiced it throughout history or the one having the ecstatic experience? Or consider the different perspectives of Schrödinger's hypothetical pussycat and the scientist who's wondering how it's doing."

"*What? What? . . . What? What?*" The invisible bird voiced Larry's confusion.

"Erwin Schrödinger. You know, the Viennese physicist who shared the 1933 Nobel prize with Paul Dirac for his contribution to the development of quantum mechanics. It seems both he and Einstein were arguing against the premise that the wave and particle properties of subatomic bits are complementary. Heisenberg's uncertainty principle, on the other hand, proposes that the more precisely a particle's position is determined, the less precisely its momentum is known in this instant, and vice versa. In other words, you cannot know the position and the momentum of a particle simultaneously because when you measure one, you randomize the other. It is this uncertainty that lies at the heart of quantum mechanics as well as the rest of the Universe beyond the illusion's domain.

"The mere thought that Creation could be infused with a large dose of probability, rather than the certainty of a conscious Creator, drove poor Schrödinger absolutely batty—or in his case, catty! He posited his famous cat paradox to ridicule the whole affair. In case you want to actually carry out this imaginary experiment—which I highly discourage—here are the ingredients you'll need: one cat, one sturdy box, one radioactive atom, one bottle of poisonous gas—cyanide will do just fine—one Geiger counter, one hammer.

"First, set up the Geiger counter inside the box so it can monitor the state of the decaying atom. Second, put the hammer and bottle of poisonous gas inside the box and rig them up so the hammer, when it receives a signal from the Geiger counter, will break the bottle of gas. Third, insert the cat and the radioactive atom in the box. Fourth, close the box and wait.

"Radioactive particles have a certain probability of spontaneous nuclear decay—which means that over any period of time, the atom may or may not emit an alpha particle to trigger the Geiger detector to release the hammer to break the bottle to kill the cat.

"There's no way to see inside the closed box, so no one knows whether the cat is alive or dead until the lid is opened. According to Schrödinger, the cat's condition is simply a function of whether or not a radioactive decay has occurred. Case closed.

"However, Heisenberg, and other eminent physicists such as Niels Bohr, argued that since observation is needed to determine whether or not the atom has decayed, it's this act of observation that determines the state of the cat. Case reopened.

"Common sense, championed by Schrödinger and Einstein, bucked heads with the quantum 'heresy' espoused by the Bohr camp. Bohr and Co. suggested a superposition of mutually exclusive, simultaneous realities in which the cat was both alive and dead. At one point, in total frustration with Einstein's obstinance, Bohr reputedly made a profound remark to his learned colleague: 'You are not thinking. You are merely being logical!'"

"What an amazing statement!" Larry said. "It's a nice way of saying 'you can't get there from here.' Bohr and Einstein were talking about two different though interpenetrating worlds and were trying to bridge the gap with language and logic. 'Quantum physics and the Newtonian model meet at dawn to settle a matter of honor.' How was the dispute finally resolved?"

"It never was," Zeus responded. "Punches and counterpunches go on to this day. The new physics, examining the realm of subatomic particles, trespassed into the realm of time/space. There physicists uncovered a new, unsettling paradoxical way of looking at things that usually raises more issues than it resolves. However, science has a powerful tool that lets it drill ten additional holes into the strainer. Using symbolic shorthand and the ten integers, 0 to 9, they have been able to develop mathematical expressions for the so-called world around the corner. It's been said that mathematics—along with its analog, music—is truly the language of the gods. Some of these equations are brilliantly constructed representations of the mysterious world beyond the Veil. However, interpreting their full meaning has turned out to be a sticky wicket indeed.

"So the battle rages on. Apparently, in the view of quantum physicists, Schrödinger's cat exists in two parallel, nonlocal universes simultaneously. In one, he is very much alive; in the other, quite dead. This curious indefinite system can be described mathematically as a superposition of all possibilities, and crazy as it seems, it can even be demonstrated experimentally. However, once such a system is observed or measured, it collapses into a definite state. The cat is either dead or alive.

"Some would go a step further and argue that matter doesn't actually exist unless it's observed. Following out this suggestion to its illogical conclusion can lead to some riotous sidebars. If matter requires an observer to exist, will God do? How about the conclusion that all matter must be conscious? Doesn't that suggest that Schrödinger's cat might have a say in determining its future?"

CHAPTER 15

The Voice

As they talked Larry and Zeus wended their way among the white tank monzogranite boulders shimmering in the dazzling morning sun. Their conversation was interrupted by a distinct voice emanating from the rocky cliff face to their immediate left.

> "There was once a man who said, 'God
> Must think it exceedingly odd
> If he finds that this tree
> Continues to be
> When there's no one about in the quad.'

"And the reply:

> 'Dear Sir, your astonishment's odd:
> I am always about in the quad.
> And that's why the tree
> Will continue to be,
> Since observed by yours faithfully, God.'"

The two burst out laughing. "Cool one," Zeus said. "Where did that come from?"

"Don't really know," came the reply. "We heard it some-where, perhaps from Monsignor Ronald Knox himself, and simply latched on to it. We recite it from time to time to remind ourselves that we do exist. After all, if we had to wait for people to wander by to let us know we're really here, we'd probably die of boredom—although that would be quite impossible for us to do."

"Who are you talking to?" Larry asked Zeus.

"Haven't a clue. It's just a voice in my head. Since you laughed at the limerick, I gather you heard it too."

"Yep."

"Hi, guys. My friend Larry and I are just trying to dope out some quantum stuff. You're more than welcome to join in, if you like. By the way, who are you?"

> "Look around
> and what do you see?
> Pieces of mountains,
> all parts of we!"

came the reply.

"You're the rocks?" Larry asked.

"Bingo! The two of you have been climbing, jumping, and sitting all over us for the past two days. It's about time you stopped and introduced yourselves."

"I'm Larry, as you already know, and my little four-legged friend here is Zeus. But don't let his size fool you; he's one smart doggie. This is only our third day in Joshua Tree and he's already taken me from being a wide-eyed wanderer to well past the no-fly zone of back and beyond."

"The pleasure's all ours," the Voice replied. "We got a pretty good idea of who Zeus is when you two first met Gathering

Cloud. It's been a while since we counted, but give or take a few hundred millennia, I'd say we've been hanging around this neck of the woods for about eighty-five million years. We're beginning to think that's long enough for one place, and we're about ready to go see another part of the Universe."

"Can rocks do that?" Larry asked.

"No, but *we* can."

"*What? What?*" The bird's high shrill jarred Larry and thoroughly amused the Voice.

"Aha, we did it. We made ourselves a bet that we could get ol' What-What to appear within the first fifteen minutes. We did it in under three. Now, that's got to be a record."

"What are you talking about?" Larry asked.

"It's a game we play. After you've named all the stars, counted the grains of sand, and played host to the antics of four-leggeds, two-leggeds, and innumerable creepy-crawlies, your imagination starts to find other ways to amuse itself. Our latest diversion is to tune into park visitors and see how long it takes us to trigger a predictable event. In your case, the challenge was to answer your questions honestly while trying to confuse you enough to evoke the bird.

"Now we'll expand upon our answer, if we may. We're not really the rocks, just as Zeus is not simply a dog and you are not totally contained within your human form. Your visible body is merely the local aspect of your presence, the one where the wave form happens to be the most dense. Visible matter is created by the interference patterns of wave forms frozen in the illusion of space/time to define what you bipeds like to call reality—the last grand illusion of the mechanistic Universe. Last night when you took a trip out into the Void, you left your body behind. When we're ready, we'll simply do the same. And judging by recent happenings, that'll be sooner than any of us have believed."

"What do you mean by that?" Larry asked.

"It's part of what you two have been discussing. There's been a gradual buildup of quantum nonlocal events that have already begun to collapse into a determinate state on this side of the Veil. Or, to put it in human terms, things have been cooking in the center of the galaxy and they've already begun to impact Earth in a big way. How humanity chooses to act over the next ten years will be critical to how God's dice fall."

"What events are you talking about?" Larry asked.

"Come see for yourself," the Voice answered. "You and Zeus are invited to join us, if you'd like."

"We'd be honored to," Zeus interjected. "How do you suggest we proceed?"

"Continue walking along the base of the cliff. Once you pass that spill of boulders ahead, you'll see a little cavelike hollow. Walk into it as far as you can so you are out of the sun, and find some place comfortable to sit."

Larry and Zeus followed the instructions and sat within the shallow cavity, their backs to the rocky wall.

"Now, close your eyes and simply follow your breath. . . ." The Voice led them into a deep state of meditation, then instructed them to drift upwards, out of their bodies, and find a tiny crack in the face of the cliff that would permit them to enter. They no longer had physical form; they were pure Consciousness drifting through solid rock as if it were as permeable as morning mist.

"What do you see?" the Voice asked.

"This is amazingly beautiful," Larry exclaimed. "I'm in a crystal cave, surrounded by millions of sparkling points of light reflecting off perfectly formed iridescent spires."

"And you, Zeus? What do you see?"

"I see you."

"And we see the two of you. Welcome to our world, gentlemen. Sorry we can not offer you tea. Perhaps what you are about to experience will partially compensate for this slight suspension of gentility?"

"*Au contraire,* kind sir," Zeus quipped, "it's not every day that we are invited into such an exquisite presence. I suspect that in the time we spend with you, we're going to suspend a great deal more than the outer trappings of cultural refinement."

"Quite so," the Voice agreed. "Perhaps we should have erected a portal into our realm of consciousness with a caveat that states: 'Abandon belief all ye who enter here.' As you quite rightly suggest, clinging to your previous concepts will effectively shield you from what you are about to experience. In your world, it would be much like donning a raincoat before showering.

"Let us begin by saying that we have been following Master Larry's progress over the past few days with great interest. We have been aware of the strong probability of your joining us for some time and cannot tell you how pleased we all are that it has come to pass. Zeus, you and your friends are to be commended. This is as fine a piece of work as we have ever witnessed."

"Thanks," Zeus responded, "I'd like to say it's all in a day's work, but I'm afraid we can't take too much of the credit. Larry did most of the work himself—although in his current condition, I doubt he'll admit to anything."

"Larry, what Zeus says is well taken. You must begin to acknowledge who you really are and the important role you are to play over the next, decisive decade. You are one of the few among us who has actually experienced incarnation in human form within the third-density dimension. Your insights into the emotional and psychological makeup of the human experience will be invaluable as we assess how to be of service during this time of transition.

"Zeus, why don't you take it from here and give Larry a little background briefing before we embark into esoterics?"

"A splendid idea," Zeus responded. He then directed his remarks to Larry: "As you are well aware, the outward state of this planet is not very encouraging. What you see now is merely the predictable outcome of a process set in motion quite early in human history. From our perspective, the entire Grand Experiment taking place over the past fifty thousand years on this planet appears to have ground to a halt. Although you have advanced technologically, outside of a few isolated exceptions there has been virtually no significant spiritual growth. It's like one of your old phonograph records spinning around with the needle stuck in the same groove, unable to play the rest of the song.

"As I told you earlier, this is only the second time that animals have been permitted to talk directly to humans." Larry smiled, recalling Zeus's reference to Noah's Ark. "Well, that's only part of the story. There have been several authorized interventions in the past when sixth-density entities were given permission to interact directly with humans, just as we're doing now. The only difference is that they were permitted to come to Earth in human form without going through the Veil of Forgetting. These earlier visitations were meant to help the evolution of Awareness on this planet move forward—interfering as little as possible while gently moving the needle to the next groove. Without getting into details, let me simply say the results were less than anticipated. Instead of advancing humans along the path of Awareness, these visits only produced misconstrued myths that unfortunately found their way into what many people revere as sacred texts.

"Recall your own words as you addressed the Council of Nine: 'You are well aware that this planet is at the very end of the current and final great cycle and that she is already shifting into the fourth density. You are also aware that human Consciousness has not evolved as expected.'"

"I recall saying that," Larry responded. "But if advanced beings from the sixth density couldn't set things right when they were here before, how do you expect me to make any difference now?"

"Easy there, big fella," Zeus cautioned, "don't get too far ahead of yourself. Remember, you are not the same person you were two days ago and you can't even imagine what you will become before leaving this magic place. Now's not the time to ask questions or jump to conclusions. You simply don't have enough information to do either intelligently."

Zeus took Larry's silence as tacit agreement and continued: "Earth's shift into the next dimensional octave is proving more difficult for humankind than originally intended. It's an inviolable law of Creation that an early fourth-density planet cannot support third-density life forms. In other words, as the planet's shift continues, the energetic conditions become progressively hostile to humans if they insist on holding onto their old patterns of belief. This is why there's such a marked increase in abusive relationships at every level of your societies, with unparalleled atrocities pervading your families, churches, schools, sports, nations, and environment.

"As we were just reminded, there is precious little time left. Visualize each person on Earth hanging onto two rungs on a jungle gym—one representing the Consciousness of the past, the other the direction forward along the path of Awareness. Part of each being wants to move ahead, part is afraid to let go of the

familiar rung behind. This is collective humanity's condition—
stuck in indecision. Now that time as you know it is running out,
a new twist has been added. As Earth undergoes her transition,
the space between the rungs is slowly expanding. This began
some seventy years ago, hardly noticed except by a few sensitives
who almost no one took seriously. However, the widening has
accelerated markedly since the new millennium, and it's beginning to cause real angst at the inner-knowing level of every
human on the planet.

"The special blue-indigo-star-crystal-AIDS children are being
born by the millions, and they are holding the energy of the next
density as an open invitation. These kids have entered the illusion with a double body in activation, so they can adjust to the
instreaming of higher-octave frequencies without disrupting their
third-density physical forms. This is not the case for the balance
of people now on Earth. They are subject to a lot of vibrational
stress, which is why so many bizarre events are taking place—the
death throes of the old guard, terrified of the prospect of change.
The Earth and the children will be fine. We have come to serve
those who are entangled in the illusion's web, unable to break
free. Our fondest wish, during our time on this side of the Veil,
is to assist anyone who chooses to ask—those who have the
courage to let go of the past and move joyously into the next
level of experience."

"An excellent summary, Zeus. Thank you very much," said
the Voice. "Now, as we recall, the two of you were deep in your
exploration of nonlocal quantum worlds when we interjected
our little ditty. We recognize where your discussion of
Schrödinger's cat was leading. Perhaps this would be a good time
to continue—especially as it has major relevance to the facts we
will then share."

"Thank you," Zeus said. "You're quite perceptive. We *were* about to explore the holographic nature of Creation." Zeus's voice took on an almost professorial tone. "It is said, 'When a sparrow falls to the ground, God knows.' How is this possible? How does a mother know instantly when her child at school breaks a leg during recess? What mysterious process allows telepathic connection between lovers or very close friends or twins living on opposite sides of the world?

"One answer lies in a curious observation first made by Schrödinger in 1935, which he termed 'entanglement.' In the nonlocal world of quantum mechanics, once two subatomic particles—including some of the bigger guys like neutrons and protons—come together and interact, they become intertwined and remain so, regardless of how far apart they later separate. For example, if the first particle is determined to have a spin *left,* the second invariably has a complementary spin *right.* The two form a single coherent system that can be mathematically described as a single wave function. Curiously, according to a whole contingent of your quantum physicists, neither particle has a definite spin characteristic until it is observed. Until then, both particles float blissfully in quantum superposition heaven, experiencing all possible spin states.

"As Niels Bohr inscribed on the coat of arms he personally designed when the Danish government awarded him the Order of the Elephant, *contraria sunt complementa*—opposites are complements."

"If we may interject," the Voice said, "and borrow once again from this great Dane—no offense meant, Zeus—'The opposite of a true statement is a false statement, but the opposite of a profound truth is usually another profound truth.'"

"No offense taken, I assure you," said Zeus, retaining his

polished tone. "Besides, despite my diminutive stature, I wouldn't be surprised if there wasn't at least a little Great Dane blood in me somewhere."

"Quite," the Voice said. "But let us not wander too far afield. Entanglement has considerable philosophical implications. If two particles can become inextricably linked, is it any surprise that the same occurs with human beings? What do particles and humans have in common?"

Larry volunteered an answer. "Consciousness . . . and, I would presume, God."

"Bull's-eye!" The Voice sounded for a moment as though it was grinning. "Zeus, my man—or should we say, my dog?—this kid will do just fine! Yes, Larry, you're quite right. Even at our level of Awareness, we are little better than the six blind men groping about the elephant, trying to express our understanding of All That Is. Concepts like God and Consciousness, Love and Light, Free Will and Awareness are but dim shadows cast by the Mystery we seek. Yet they are all we have, so we carry on as best we can.

"Creation teems with processes and happenings. The semblance of inert objects fixed in definite locations within the space/time continuum is just that—a mere semblance. You have already been given substantive proof that all of us are far more than we appear. Strip away your physical, emotional, mental, and spiritual outer garments and you won't have reduced your essence by a whit.

"We three are far more than a dog, a man, and a rock engaged in the exhilaration of philosophic discourse. We walk the Consciousness path in the true spirit of the paramecium!"

"What? . . . What? What? . . . What?"

"Bingo! We did it again! Sorry, gentlemen, this conversation was getting a bit heavy so we couldn't resist throwing in a little curve ball. We do love the sound of that little bird!

"Paramecium are those fuzzy little one-cell creatures you studied under the microscope in high school biology class. They have a most extraordinary way of creating entanglement. Every so often, they find a suitable partner and conjugate—that is, they cozy up to each other and exchange a bit of their DNA. They don't reproduce this way, but if they fail to make it to the swap meet in time they run out of the chemical that allows them to reproduce asexually, and so they expire.

"Do you think these little fellows ever forget each other? They can't! They *are* each other! By the same token, when the three of us eventually part, a portion of us will go with each of you, just as a piece of each of you has already been integrated into our collective being. We are forever entangled. The magic of it is that you, in turn, will convey part of us to every single person you interact with from here on. In this way, during the course of a lifetime each person actually makes a meaningful contribution to several million others on the planet.

"This is why the concept of separation would be so laughable, except that the vast majority of people have chosen to believe it. Larry, you think of Marianne a lot more than you care to admit. It's not because the two of you have parted; it's because you haven't. In fact, you never can, just as you can never part from any person you have every met, any book you have ever read, any piece of music, any ball game or crossword puzzle—anything you have ever experienced, including each of your dreams.

"We'll illustrate the process with a simple mind problem. Let's suppose two people, a bully and a timid fellow, are represented by two identical bottles containing different colored fluids. The bully is dark blue and the weakling is pastel pink. The two entangle, and the bully gives the other fellow a black eye. Using our metaphor, the blue infuses twenty drops of itself into the pink bottle. The pink, on the other hand, manages to shift only one drop of its liquid into the blue bottle. Each bottle is thoroughly shaken.

"The two combatants withdraw, and each returns to equilibrium. In the example, this means the fluids in both bottles are returned to their original levels; that is, the bully reclaims nineteen drops of liquid from the pink bottle—the twenty he forced into the pink bottle minus the pink one he received.

"Which has been more transformed by the interaction? Is there more blue in the pink bottle or more pink in the blue bottle? We'll give you a hint: This is true entanglement!"

"Thanks for the hint," Larry said, half in jest. He assumed the question was directed at him, since Zeus was humming his "Get Along Little Dogies" theme song to himself with just enough amusement to warn Larry that the answer was not going to be obvious. Clearly, more blue was poured into the pink than pink into the blue. But once the fluids were fully mixed, the liquid in the victim's bottle was still pink, the few drops of blue having almost no visible affect. So when the nineteen drops were returned to the blue bottle, they too were almost pure pink, with just a trace of blue.

"How about another hint?" Larry pleaded.

"With pleasure," the Voice responded. "Direct your thinking into the nature of the system itself. Change your perspective from the microcosm of the mathematics involved in measuring dilutions to the macroscopic view that sees the entire interaction at once. If both bottles are returned to their precise original liquid volume, would you not agree that a small amount of the blue still remains in the pink?"

"Absolutely," Larry said. "Since the original nineteen drops were thoroughly mixed into the entire volume, it's impossible to isolate them when the liquid goes back into the blue bottle. In fact, most of those original nineteen drops of blue would still be in the pink bottle"

"Quite," the Voice agreed. "Ergo?"

I think I've got the answer," Larry said, though his tone sounded more like a question than a statement.

"And what would that be?" the Voice chided.

"The two bottles make a closed system. So when both are returned to their original fluid levels, any blue remaining in the pink bottle must displace an equal amount of pink in the blue bottle?"

"That is quite correct," the Voice said, "yet I can see the penny has yet to drop. You present the solution, but the meaning still escapes you. Zeus, perhaps you can find another way to explain entanglement to Larry."

"Be happy to," Zeus said. "His mouth makes the right sounds, now let's see if meaning can follow suit! Larry, how many atoms are in your body?"

"How many what?" Larry sputtered. "Who knows. Billions, I suppose. What's that got to do with entanglement?"

"You're selling yourself short again. It's not just a few billion atoms. Your body contains more like seven billion atoms times a billion times a billion, or 7×10^{27} atoms. That's a seven followed by 27 zeros! Now, how many of those atoms are actually yours?"

"All of them are mine," Larry replied. "Who else could they belong to?"

"Oh what tangled webs we weave when first we practice to believe," Zeus chimed. "Do you recall what you said just a few moments ago—that all particles contain Consciousness?"

"Yes, what's your point?"

"Patience, my good man. This is tricky business. If the role entanglement plays in Creation isn't perfectly clear, nothing that follows will makes sense. So stop being defensive and listen carefully. Your mind can eavesdrop if it wants, but it's your heart I'm addressing here."

"Okay," Larry said with an amused chuckle. "I'll keep my personalities out of it."

"Consider your breath. What happens every time you inhale and exhale?" Zeus asked.

"I breathe oxygen into my lungs and release carbon dioxide back into the atmosphere."

"Would you agree that every time you breath in, you take millions of atoms into your body?"

"Yes, of course."

"And would you also agree that every time you breath out, you release millions of atoms back into the air?"

"If I didn't, I'd blow up like a balloon," Larry retorted.

"So much for keeping the personalities at bay!" Zeus said. "Okay, wise guy, think about this: Each time you exhale, you eject millions of atoms loaded with your Consciousness into the air. They intermingle with the countless atoms exhaled day and night since humans first populated the planet. They mix with the breath of animals and the oxygen released by plants. They merge with the pollution of smoke stacks, the pollen of flowers, the salt air scooped from the surface of the sea by passing winds.

"Every breath you take infuses you with the Consciousness of every man, woman, child, plant, animal, and element that has ever existed on planet Earth. Christ is within you as surely as Rasputin. You drink from a cup that still bears the lip marks of every saint and sinner that ever lived. Now ask yourself, how many of your many billions of atoms are really yours?"

"Wow," Larry said. "I never thought of it that way."

"Hardly anyone ever does," Zeus replied, "which is precisely why the world is in its present condition. Now can you appreciate how all Creation is entangled? Everything connects to everything else. Nothing exists in a vacuum. Nothing resides outside of the All That Is."

"I think I get it now," Larry said. "Going back to the two bottles, I can now see how the fluids are connected, even though they appear to be in separate bottles. No matter how many drops of blue are mixed into the pink, when the amounts in both bottles are returned to their original levels, the number of drops of each color remaining in the other is equal."

"Bull's-eye!" the Voice said. "That is precisely the quantum nature of entanglement."

"Except for one thing," Larry said. "If the bully was so forceful, shouldn't he be represented by a larger bottle?"

"The size of the bottle doesn't matter. As long as the fluid levels are returned to their original positions, there will always be the same number of drops of pink in the blue as there are drops of blue in the pink. However, as you are about to say, the percentage of dilution depends completely on the original size of the bottle. Here's where entanglement becomes very, very interesting.

"You have already discovered that *all* things are God. Since God is infinite, can you understand that, by extension, any one thing must be infinite as well? So you see, the size of the container *is* completely irrelevant. In this holographic Universe, a little piece of Creation is no less infinite than the totality of Creation."

"Theoretically . . . I suppose," Larry mused. "But in real life this certainly doesn't seem to apply."

"If by 'real life' you mean this illusion, we would have to agree with you. But now we have come full circle—since this false appearance is promoted by the delusion of separation—one of the main characteristics of your earthly experience.

"From our perspective in the quantum nonlocal universe of

time/space, the energetic nature of the experience was the same for the bully and the timid chap; once they returned to their original volumetric states, each had given and received equal amounts of fluid, or Consciousness. Why isn't it the same on your side of the Veil? In your world, the bully walks away from the entanglement with a smile on his face, ready to prove his machismo again, while the poor victim may be so traumatized that a shadow is cast over the rest of his life."

"Why not ask, 'How long is a piece of string?'" Larry replied with a glimmer of irritation. "How does one even begin unraveling a question like that?"

"This is very important," the Voice persisted. "Please answer as best you can. This is precisely why you entered the illusion through the Veil—to provide insights from points of view that we cannot fully access."

Larry dropped into thought. Why was the bully apparently not affected as much as the victim? Why did the theoretically equal interchange leave the two in such different states of mind? He deliberated for quite a while over ethnic wars, religious zeal, soured relationships, even the World Series—anything that boils down to winning and losing. Then he thought about rape, and the penny dropped. "I think I'm beginning to understand. It has something to do with violation of Free Will. If the two protagonists were enlightened, neither one would be affected emotionally. Both would know they are pure conduits siphoning the fruits of experience into the cosmic data bank Zeus talked about yesterday."

"Like the Buddhist monk?" Zeus asked.

"Don't tell me." Larry glanced in Zeus's direction. "You have another story?"

"So happens I do," said Zeus, "and it should serve well in this discussion. May I continue?"

"Please do," said the Voice.

Larry knew by now that when it came to Zeus, it was best to bow to the inevitable. Besides he actually enjoyed the stories. They were one of the few aspects of the teaching his mind didn't fight. So he gladly echoed permission to proceed.

"It seems," Zeus began, his voice tinged with a spicy, pleasing subcontinental flavor, "there was a little farming village tucked into an obscure valley in the Himalayas. An unmarried teenage girl of the village fell pregnant by consequence of a forbidden relationship with a young man from a neighboring town. Caught between the proverbial rock—no offense meant—and a hard place, she opted to keep her little indiscretion under wraps. When she could no longer do so, she blamed her now very visible condition on a monk who lived at the top of a nearby mountain.

"The village folk were aghast that a supposed man of God could commit such a deed. So once the baby was off the breast, they wrapped it in sheepskins and proceeded single file up to the monastery to confront the 'father.' Knocking on the wooden door of the hermitage, they were greeted by the monk himself. 'You disgraced your order; you fathered this child. Now you take care of him.'

"'Ah, so,' replied the monk, taking the baby into his arms. The people, in disgust, returned down the mountain path to resume village life. Fourteen years later, a terrible accident befell the child's mother. As she lay on her deathbed she confessed that she had wrongly accused a man of God in an attempt to shield her lover. The people of the village were deeply ashamed. How could they possibly remedy the unwarranted accusations leveled at the monk?

"After careful deliberation, they decided that all those still alive who had partaken in the original journey must return to the monastery. Once more, in single file, they ascended the steep path. Again, knocking on the door, they were greeted by the monk.

"'We have done you a great injustice,' they confessed. 'It turns out our accusations that you broke your vows and fathered an illegitimate child were baseless. We have come to apologize and to take back the child so it may grow up with its grandparents.'

"'Ah, so,' said the monk."

"Ah, so," the Voice repeated. "Entanglement. It is said that the Great Tao, the Way, is easy—provided one has no preferences."

"I think I understand what you're trying to say," Larry mused. "Both the girl and the villagers had distinct preferences. The monk, on the other hand, saw all the events as equal. He was falsely accused. He was given a baby to rear. The child, who he had probably bonded with over the fourteen years, was taken away. To him it was all the same. There was no guilt, no need to defend, no pain on encountering the unforeseen bumps on the path. There was only 'Ah, so.'"

"True," the Voice said. "We would like you to consider something else. You said violation of Free Will was the deciding factor between our two friends. Both of them also had distinct preferences. How would you differentiate preference from Free Will?"

"Well, it's obvious," Larry responded. "The bully expressed his preference to be belligerent. He used his Free Will to override the preference and Free Will of the victim."

"I don't think so," Zeus chided.

"What do you mean, 'you don't think so'? It's as clear as day, isn't it?" Larry said.

"Thank you, Larry." It was the Voice speaking now. "You have just explained something that has puzzled us a very long time. If the distinction between preference and Free Will isn't clear to you, we suspect it isn't appreciated by most third-density beings. How would you define Free Will?"

"It's what I decide to do solely by my own determination, without any influence or coercion from an outside agency," Larry said, quite pleased with his quasi-legalistic phrasing.

"Do you really feel that any choice you have ever made—with the possible exception of your decision last night to return from the Void—was made freely?"

"Of course," Larry answered. "I almost always exercise Free Will. After all," he said, feeling a sudden need to defend his position, "I live in America—the land of the free, with the freest democratic government on the planet. If I don't freely decide what I want to do, then who does?"

"Bull's-eye!" the Voice responded. "*That* is the sixty-four-thousand-dollar question. We wonder what Rocky would have to say about this. Why don't we take his advice and 'look into the I's of Infinity?'"

"What do you mean?" Larry asked.

"A few moments ago you confirmed that all matter, from particles to humans, is conscious in nature."

"Yes."

"Would it be fair to say, by extension, that *every* part of Creation contains Consciousness?"

"Sure. What's so surprising about that?"

"It's not at all surprising. However, you've just opened up an interesting avenue of exploration. Consciousness is not only resident within all energy and matter, interpenetrating every aspect of Creation; it is also the subtle matrix on which manifestation stages its infinite dance. At the higher levels of the I-continuum, Consciousness is both self-aware and aware of its interrelationship with every part of the Universe. All existence is holographic, each part containing the imprint of the whole and each affecting the Universe in intimate and extraordinary ways.

"Recall your earlier insight regarding 'crevolution,' when Zeus pointed out the ongoing exchange between organism and environment. Now, take that one giant step further and explore this interplay on a cosmic level."

Larry focused on this exercise for quite a while, straining his imagination to visualize a boundless process of perceiving, transmitting, integrating, and creating as it exchanges information throughout limitless dimensions. "My God, it *is* God!" Larry exclaimed. "Taken universally, it's the sum total of All That Is experiencing itself infinitely."

"Exactly so! That's the big picture. Now hold it in your mind's eye as you narrow your focus to the current conditions on this planet. There is no difference except in terms of scale. You know the cliché: 'As above, so below.' What does it mean that all Creation is connected by zero degrees of separation? How does this affect the workings of the human mind as it makes choices?"

"I've often wondered about decision points," Larry said. "When I wake up in the morning I lie in bed for a while. Eventually I get up. Why precisely at that moment and not a few seconds earlier or later? Is it random, or is something actually happening on a deeper level? Or, why does someone decide to give up smoking a hundred times only to fail; then something inside them goes 'click' and suddenly they succeed?

"Now—assuming I've got a handle on this stuff—in the context of a quantum universe this takes on a different meaning altogether. When I lie there in the morning, I am getting up and staying in bed simultaneously each moment. Every possible choice, conscious or not, creates another fork in the road, and I follow both paths. A series of simultaneous parallel universes unfold, in which the consequences of each choice are played out.

"When I finally act, it's like the observer opening the box to find out what happened to Schrödinger's cat. The alternate realities collapse into what is happening in the now. I, the observer, create the reality of my own experience. I choose one path and the others simply dissolve—unless a portion of my Awareness particles decides to hold some of them in place."

"Interesting that you put it that way," the Voice said. "So is your final decision made randomly?"

"No, I don't think so. Even with something as simple as getting out of bed, I'm aware of a flood of information bombarding my mind—the joy of lying there a few more minutes, the need to start my day, the clock ticking, the thought of a shower or exercise. . . . It just goes on and on until I finally make the move."

"Then what determines how and when you ultimately decide?"

Larry wrestled with this question for a long time, eventually revisiting his experiences with Junie, when he met his subpersonalities. Somehow, he knew intuitively the answer was there, buried in the cauldron of psychoemotional soup he had explored with her.

Zeus, following the erratic stream swirling through in Larry's mind, broke the extended silence. "You're on the right track, kiddo. Where do these individual thoughts come from?"

"They're voices in my head."

"Go on," Zeus urged.

"Holy shit!" Larry exclaimed. "Each one comes from one of my subpersonalities. Eventually, one is loud enough, or powerful enough, to win out and cause an action."

"Does that sound like your definition of Free Will?" the Voice asked.

Larry laughed. "I see what you mean. As long as one of my subpersonalities drives the car, I remain bound and gagged in the trunk. I can't make a choice except through one of the voices. They mean well, but they're only limited viewpoints, and they're frozen. Each one believes that what it sees is *all* there is to see.

"So let me ask you this: If I and all the other humans on this side of the Veil don't exercise Free Will, then why does the *Interdimensional Survival Manual* call it the ultimate gift of the gods? And why is everyone in the higher densities so careful not to violate it?"

"Just because you haven't exercised Free Will doesn't mean you aren't able to," the Voice said. "It is available to you—and to every man, woman, and child on this planet—in an instant, to use whenever you choose. In fact, nothing would please us more than to see this happening worldwide.

"However, Free Will is not exercised in the mind; it doesn't function at the egoic level. Free Will belongs to the realm of the soul. It is a function of the wordless intelligence of the soul which resides in the heart and finds expression there through the heart's mind. The analytical mind, on the other hand, resides in the brain. It is the stage on which the personalities play out their human dramas. That is where lower-level choices are made, based on a potpourri of cultural influences, impressed dogma, and a multitude of belief modules. Free Will, I'm afraid, hardly enters the picture."

"Is the mind of the heart similar to intuition?" Larry asked.

"Good question," the Voice said. "There is an important difference between the intelligence of the heart/mind and the gut-feel of intuition. We'll begin by pointing out that the human brain processes cognitive information in the two lobes of its cerebral cortex, left and right. The popular conception that women are right-brained and therefore creative and intuitive, while men are left-brained and therefore logical and practical, is not entirely correct. Although they are independent structures, the left and right lobes are connected by a rather thick cable of nerves that facilitates the sharing of information. So biologically there is no reason for any being not to have full access to the input from both spheres. In practice, however, this is rarely the case. Your societies selectively favor certain responses and breed these into your children. As a consequence, brain-sequencing patterns form early and generally remain throughout an entity's life."

"I'm confused," Larry said. "There's no question that my experiences here in Joshua Tree are right-brain. If I couldn't access the part of me that's willing to suspend reality and jump into this weird fantasy world, I'd either have bolted or gone mad. On the other hand, when I'm working on a client's case, it's all left-brain stuff. Hard core facts and logic. Doesn't that mean that I use both spheres?"

"Ah, the imprecision of language raises it's ugly head yet again," Zeus interjected. "Larry, exactly which *I* are you referring to?"

"Huh?"

"It's not much of a mystery," Zeus continued. "In fact, you'd have figured it out yourself had you paid more attention to your own words. You say you're experiencing through your parts and have mentioned two: the feeling, intuitive persona spearheading your recent adventures and the practical realist who leads the way in legal battles. They just happen to be sharply polarized examples. They've set up their preferred brain-sequencing patterns, just like every other subpersonality."

"Are you saying that every single part sets up its own sequencing pattern—adjusting the levels by which it chooses to receive information from the practical side or the creative side—depending on its makeup?"

"Why is that so surprising?" Zeus responded. "A subperson-ality is simply a fixed point from which to view. It naturally chooses to receive information that expresses and reinforces its energetic signature. If it didn't, it couldn't hold its position."

"Then every time I make a decision, it's with input from only fragments of my brain?"

Larry's last question amused Zeus. "Do you think the world would be in such a mess if people accessed input from their *total* brain? When it comes to data-processing on the lower levels of the I-continuum, you guys don't score too high. In fact, its pretty comical. On one side you have your hardcore scientists who abhor anomalies and would insist on double-blind, fully replicat-ing toilets before they'd relieve themselves of a single obsolete concept. The other side is championed by new age butterflies who fancy they can fly through the cosmos and communicate with the ascended masters but have difficulty meeting their rent payments or making their relationships work."

"Then what are we supposed to do? How do I link up both sides of my brain so they work together?" Larry asked.

"It seems we have come full circle," the Voice said. "This is where one relies on the intelligence of the heart rather than the output of the brain. The heart/mind is able to synthesize the data streams from both the rational, intellectual brain and the emo-tional, feeling brain into a higher, more balanced state of know-ing. Because the heart/mind operates at the soul level, it has a more pervasive perspective. It transcends the personal to process incoming information in terms of archetypes. The heart/mind is capable of levels of understanding far beyond sensory percep-tion, allowing it to continually add its observations to the collec-tive Consciousness of the All That Is.

"Intuitive input, on the other hand, comes as a sudden flash of inspiration. Unless it is fully integrated by both spheres of the brain—which seldom happens—it doesn't add much in the way of understanding. In fact, it often merely confuses and immobilizes. People would do well to flavor their intuitive 'hits' with a grain of analysis. At the same time, they would be well advised to access their creative side, to think outside the box, while tackling any practical matter.

"Zeus, perhaps you can shed some light on this matter for our young friend here."

"Be glad to," Zeus said. "As you reminded us a moment ago, Larry, Free Will is the ultimate gift of the gods. From your experience on Inspiration Peak, you've learned that letting go requires nothing less than complete surrender. Although you tried to resolve your Higher Self's proposition with your intellect, you ultimately discovered that the analytical mind was not up to the task. Even after you thought you'd accepted the proposition fully with your heart, it was still not enough. It was only after you braved your own death by exhibiting enough faith to leap into the Void that you actually surrendered. With that act, your heart/mind opened up and you penetrated the realm of Absolute Knowing."

"Bull's-eye!" said the Voice. "Thank you for that insight, Zeus. Illuminating indeed. In fact, it leads to another point that might serve you well in your tasks ahead. It has to do with the temporal nature of the lower will, as articulated by the lower, egoic I, and the expression of the higher will, emanating from the realm of the soul.

"The lower will manifests intention in the realm of prayer or desire to create something that does not already exist, eliminate something that does exist, or alter something from what it presently is. The lower self sees only linear time, so it envisions a process through which betterment of either conditions or the self is achieved by dint of prayer or personal diligence. It asks for a happening to take place some time in the future.

"On the other hand, higher will flows from the soul, which resides in the time/space continuum and thereby perceives time as nonlocal. It is here, in the Infinite Present, that all possible realities have already been manifested in superposition. They merely await the pleasure of the cocreator. Free Will is the act of selecting what already is.

"Larry, what do you seek except what you already are? For unless you are conscious of being that for which you thirst, you can never find it. The Father dwells within, and you will surely miss Him completely until you awaken to the realization that He is *you*."

"My God," was all Larry could say.

"Yes," the Voice replied, "isn't it miraculous that the Great Unknowable Mystery can be expressed so completely in two words?"

CHAPTER 16

Wherever You Go, There You Are

The Voice's last, rhetorical question hung suspended in time. "Tell, me Larry, what were you experiencing in your body as you spoke just now?"

"I'm still tingling all over. It's as if a large tuning fork inside of me was vibrating. I feel alive . . . activated . . . as if a new part of me has been opened."

"What part of you feels the vibration?" the Voice asked.

"No specific part," Larry responded. "It seems to be coming from deep inside, extending through every part of my body out into a large circle around me."

"Ah, very interesting," the Voice said. "You are experiencing Love."

"I'm not sure I understand what you mean," Larry said. "This feeling is certainly not like anything I associate with pretty girls or puppy dogs. There doesn't seem to be an object involved. It just seems to be there. Does that make any sense?"

"It makes a great deal of sense," the Voice replied. "Consider that Love is expressed along an infinite continuum, similar to Rocky's I's of infinity. An attraction to tangible objects or people is simply a lower harmonic of the universal form of Love—it's love as perceived by the egoic I. We expect what you have just experienced is quite different?"

"I should say so!" Larry said. "It's far more encompassing—if that's the right word for it. There was definitely no object involved. In fact, I don't even think there was a 'me' involved."

"Ah," the Voice declared, "then you do understand. Well done, indeed!"

"Understand what?"

"Why, the difference between I and me, of course."

"But I am me," Larry protested.

Zeus coughed, obviously intentionally, and the merry-go-round in Larry's mind came to a screeching halt. "Larry, m' boy, don't sell yourself so short. Let me help clear this up for you. Where are you now?"

"Somewhere between the moon and the Pleiades," Larry offered, only half in jest. "I remember leaving my body in a small cavelike hollow outside a large rocky outcrop. Next thing I know, I'm in a crystal cave with you and some extraordinary intelligence having these amazing experiences."

"Good. Are you aware of having thoughts as all these experiences occur?"

"Of course!"

"Well then," Zeus exclaimed triumphantly, "there you have it. You have separated the *things*—all the objects and experiences—from the *thoughts* that allow you to examine and learn from the things. Now, there's only one more part remaining—the *thinker*. That part is the I that observes the me."

"Like the Aware Ego observing the various parts?" Larry asked.

"Exactly so," the Voice said. "Now, apply that same distinction to the realms of Love. Each of your parts seeks to experience Love according to its particular energetic distortion. It relates to preferences, desires, and urges in terms of its unique concept of 'me.' And it wants to give and receive Love in a way that enhances its own sense of survival. The Love that the Aware Ego seeks, on the other hand, is far more universal. This is the Love you just experienced—the Universal Energy from which everything springs. One could rightfully say Love is God and the Creation itself. Just as God is all things, so is Love."

"Like the words from the Beatles' song 'All You Need Is Love'?"

The Voice seemed to enjoy the idea of equating the All That Is with a pop song. "People still haven't realized just how profound an impact the lads from Liverpool have had on the planet's Consciousness. The literal answer to your question is yes, Love is all you need. But if you really want to get to the heart of the matter, immerse yourself in the lyrics of one of John Lennon's later songs, 'Imagine.'"

"I remember being devastated when I learned he'd been killed. That was sometime in the early eighties. Was he really shot by a crazed fan or was something else involved?"

"Larry, you have put a toe into treacherous territory better left unvisited at this point. When it is finally appropriate for you to read the Akashic records' hidden files, you will learn much about the purposeful engineering of events throughout human history. For now, it's sufficient to acknowledge that on the night of December 8, 1980, when Mark David Chapman took John Lennon's life, a beautiful light on your side of the Veil was extinguished.

"Let's direct our attention more productively. We spoke earlier of Consciousness being the matrix supporting manifestation. Well, Love is the underlying matrix on which Consciousness rests. It is the universal constant that finds expression in myriad forms throughout Creation. It is the attraction of gravity, the force compelling flowers to turn toward the sun, the invisible cord interconnecting every aspect of Creation with every other.

Love is the very clay with which Free Will shapes the many universes."

The Voice paused for a few moments, allowing the fullness of these statements to percolate. "You see, Larry, saying 'Love is all you need' is like saying all that's required is All That Is. It is a perfectly accurate statement but essentially meaningless until one arrives at a much higher level of Awareness, where it becomes so self-evident that it never needs to be expressed.

"The energetic essence of Love—regardless of how it may be expressed—is crystalline in nature. This is what makes the holographic universe possible."

"Are you saying that all Creation is made of crystal?" Larry asked.

"What clever devices, these words," the Voice mused. "Why is it they convey only to ensnare?

"Let us define our terms more carefully, then, since much of what you are about to learn hinges on your precise understanding of this fascinating concept. The term 'crystalline' refers to the purposeful, structured nature of Creation, meaning it is not amorphous or random. Our entire universe—as you saw when you encountered the Council of Nine—is based on sacred geometries expressed through the twelve dodecahedral principles of Creation. All energy, whether thought or matter, is expressed through a geometrical form.

"At the level of Universal Love, the vibrations of crystalline intelligence are superluminal, that is to say, they are infinitely faster than the speed of light and can transmit information across unspeakable distances instantaneously. This point sheds light on some of the galactic physical events unfolding around us. Every organism in Creation is quantum coherent."

"What do you mean by that?" Larry asked.

"Allow me," Zeus offered.

"Be our guest," the Voice replied. "Perhaps you can explain quantum coherence to our young student in a way that allows him to dig even deeper into the nature of Creation."

"Larry, humans typically see objects and systems as separate from each other. Consider a still-life painting. There might be a bowl containing fruit, some flowers, a table, a candlestick, and so on. But there's also the canvas and the frame, the wall on which the picture hangs, the building surrounding the wall. . . . You could extend this exercise to include the entire planet, solar system, galaxy, and, ultimately, the entire universe."

"Yes, but all you've described is just a clever way of expanding the context." Larry said. "You can't seriously be saying that the apple in the picture has any connection to Alpha Centauri?"

"Oh, but I am," Zeus rejoined. "Indeed, I'm saying precisely that and more. You'll soon discover that the connection goes deeper than a piece of fruit and a local star system. We've only considered the relationship of the various factors in a given instant of time. Let's also consider the artist and everything that went into the process of painting: years of study and practice, planning the composition, the painter's mental and emotional states—in fact, every single interaction the artist ever experienced is incorporated into that painting."

"That sounds like entanglement to me," Larry said.

"Exactly so!" How can it ever be otherwise? Look at your own body. To the scientific world it's a compendium of separate systems somehow operating together to create a mysterious whole called life. But it's more than that. Although the mechanisms of circulation, metabolism, muscles, and nerves go on simultaneously and independently, it takes more than physical connectivity to resolve them into a coherent whole. Just because observers are unable to find a measurable link between mind and body, or the phases of the moon and emotions for that matter, doesn't mean they don't exist."

"Is nothing as it seems?" Larry asked.

"Bull's-eye!" the Voice interjected. "Nothing is precisely the *only* thing that is as it seems. Thank you, Zeus, for that explanation. It appears our lad is now ready to receive the next lesson in our little discourse.

"Larry, when we stated that every organism in Creation is quantum coherent, we were really saying that every organism—past, present, and future—is connected in instant, nonlocal time/space. Each one emits its own coherent wave field, which intersects with similar wave patterns emanating from every other, resulting in a vast quantum hologram containing the sum total of all experience. This universal field of Consciousness allows any object to be in instantaneous and constant two-way communication with every other object, as well as every event and every thought, in the Universe. It is exactly as you said earlier: 'Taken universally, it's the sum total of All That Is experiencing itself infinitely.'

"Each human is actually a microcosm of the universe. This fact is mirrored in every human brain. The brain does not, as most people believe, emulate a classical digital computer. Rather, it stores and manages data more like an analog device, processing the constant inflow of nonlocal information from the quantum hologram and comparing it with recalled data stored in its memory banks—a significant portion of which resides in nonlocal holographic reservoirs. Consequently, the human brain never records precisely repeatable patterns. Why? Because, no matter how similar to a previous perception it may seem, each successive perception is unique, being influenced by everything preceding it on both individual and cosmic scales.

"You questioned how a piece of fruit might be informed by a distant star system. When you appreciate the cascade of fractal harmonics—contemplated by Plato in his analysis of the various forms flowing from universal archetypes—you begin to grasp the implicit and pervasive order of Creation. There is a hierarchal flow of information through the Universe that traces the course of 'crevolution,' as you called it, especially its macroscopic changes. Modern, mechanistic human thinking would find this a radical notion, but your so-called primitives have appreciated it since the beginning of recorded time. You still find traces of this wisdom in their songs, dances, and rituals.

"The individual human organism is informed by the intelligence of its heart/mind, which receives ongoing signals from the heart/mind of the Earth. The Earth, in turn, receives direct input from the sun. Where do you suppose the sun looks to for its informational cues?"

"I guess it would simply move up the scale and look to the galaxy?" Larry answered.

"Indeed it does," the Voice responded. "And it seeks a very specific point in the galaxy, the one that gave it birth. This, too, is a matter of quantum coherence. Most people would agree that your solar system is made up of ten planets—if you include Chiron—plus their moons, the comets, the asteroids, the meteoroids, and the interplanetary medium. Instead of perceiving these as separate bodies, consider the entire structure as a single coherent, sentient, and intelligent being."

"Do you mean the sun is the head and the planets make up the body?" Larry asked.

"Not exactly. Let go of your anthropomorphic view of intelligence. It's too limited. Believe me," the Voice chuckled, "the Universe is not created in man's image. It is far too exciting and diverse a place to be contained in such a miniscule test tube.

"Your solar system is an intricate and diverse set of dynamics—many parts together performing a divinely choreographed ballet, hurtling through space for the sheer joy of it!

"Consider this: The Earth rotates on its axis at 1,100 miles an hour. As it spins, it orbits the sun at 67,000 miles an hour, taking approximately one year to complete the circuit. The sun, with all its retinue in tow, plunges through space at an incredible 486,000 miles per hour in a giant orbit around the Milky Way's central sun that requires some 226 million years to complete. All the while, your galaxy—consisting of 100 billion suns or stars—is moving in its own vast orbit. So you will never return to the same place in space/time again."

"But," Larry asked, "if our solar system is just passing through, doesn't that mean it had to come from someplace and is on its way to somewhere else? Doesn't that imply a beginning and an end to Creation?"

"Perhaps—if the Creation existed solely in terms of space/time. But such is not the case. The Universe is infinite; it extends beyond the limitations of space and time into dimensions that continually recede beyond our grasp. However, there is much we have learned during our own journey about the nature of All That Is—some of which might be beneficial in guiding your future inquiries."

CHAPTER 17

The Myth of Creation

"Do you mean you can actually explain God?" Larry asked.

"That, my boy, we would never presume to do," the Voice responded. "However, why let a little impediment like our inability to fathom the fullness of infinity get in the way of a good story? If you're ready, we'll give you the latest rewrite of the Ramayana and the Upanishads from India, dreamtime legends from aboriginal Australia, Kojiki from Japan, and countless other traditional sagas that have attempted to make sense of the unknown. We'll call it simply the Universal Myth of Creation—the timeless tale of how the Oneness became the All That Is. You will soon discover that it is a never-ending story—like the circle of Uroboros, the ancient Greek name for the symbol of eternity represented by the snake swallowing its own tail."

With this brief preamble, the Voice began a narrative destined to so utterly invert Larry's sense of reality that nothing would ever be quite the same again.

"Once, long before anyone conceived of Time, the Oneness, wishing to know itself more completely, devised a plan so it could experience diversity. It birthed, from its own totality, the fundamental impetus of expression: Free Will. But Free Will in and of itself could accomplish nothing in the Void of nonexistence. Becoming Aware, Free Will focused Infinity into Infinite

Energy, giving birth to Love—the indivisible quanta of Infinite Energy—and thereby providing itself with the substance with which to form All That Is.

"Having separated Free Will and Love from itself, the Oneness allowed the potential for cocreation. Free Will infused itself into Love, and Love then came to know its own existence. Following the Oneness's example, it separated out parts of itself so it could explore its own possibilities. And so, the first point of Consciousness was cast out from the totality of Love. But attracted to the Oneness, that Consciousness immediately sought to rejoin its source and once again feel whole. Thus Love knew the first glimmer of duality: the whole, knowing all its parts, felt complete; but the parts, separated from the whole, longed to merge back into the One.

"Secure in the knowledge that it could emit and shift these points of Consciousness at will without sacrificing its wholeness, Love began to arrange them in pleasing patterns, causing energy to flow among them in great swirling spirals. Love invested vast quantities of itself into each of these points so each could hold its position and resist the overwhelming desire to return home. This allowed Love to view the Great Dance from multiple perspectives. And so were born viewpoints—the ultimate archetypes of your subpersonalities—from which Creation could experiment and explore its limitless diversity.

"Positioning billions of these points of Consciousness throughout the Void, Love infused each with a full measure of Free Will so they, in turn, could advance the Great Experiment. These became what your scientists call black holes—seminal cores of pure Consciousness so dense that nothing entering their sphere of influence can resist the desire to merge into them. Some of these great beings, feeling complete in their connection to the Oneness and all the other points of emanation, were content to remain observers of Creation. Others, emulating their parent, used their Free Will to send portions of themselves out into the Void to continue refining the Dance.

"These became the logoi—the primary instruments of Creation as we know it. These supremely intelligent beings, discovering their own infinite natures, were able to explode vast cascades of Light into the Void without diminishing themselves in the slightest. With absolute delight they organized measureless quantities of Light into billions of suns. These suns became their galactic bodies, while each logos became an axis, a central sun, around which a vast spiral of its own beingness revolved. The logoi invested each sun with large portions of Free Will and Love—cores of pure Consciousness—so that it too could experience itself any way it chose. These became the sublogoi of Creation. Your sun is one of them. And some of these, in turn, explored their own inventive natures by begetting planets and the myriad visible and invisible aspects of their own, local Creations.

"The Oneness, observing this process unfolding, delighted in the diversity, knowing that the perception of separation from itself was nothing more than a quantum concept in the heart/mind of the All That Is. The intriguing game of Creation was allowed to continue, each part expressing itself according to its own imagination. And so billions of galaxies, and solar systems within galaxies, were fashioned.

"So you see, there is only the Oneness. Nothing can possibly exist apart from it. The separation that dims the fullness of Infinite Awareness is only an illusion."

"Does that mean that the entire Universe is the equivalent of God—or the Oneness, as you put it?" Larry asked.

"Would that it were that simple," the Voice replied with a touch of humor. "What we experience as the Universe is only one of the infinite universes through which the Oneness seeks expression. Take your own remarkable realm of cosmic experiences, for instance—your local universe. The galactic logos facilitates it through a series of seven energetic veils, each successive veil causing the beings living behind it to believe they are one step farther removed from the Oneness.

"The seven veils partition Consciousness into eight densities, each of which has seven major energetic subdivisions, which in turn are partitioned into an endless series of ever-smaller heptagonal subsets. The upper boundary of each density is defined by a marked energetic ridge that requires a strong act of faith and will to cross. The transition from one density to the next is what is commonly called a 'quantum shift' or a 'leap into the next paradigm.' You have heard references to these varied states of Consciousness in the past few days.

"Although this is a circular story with no identifiable beginning or end, for the sake of convenience let's start with the snake's tail—just before it gets devoured by its head. We'll call that portion the beginning, or the first density. First-density beings—those perceiving Creation with all seven veils in place—are composed of your four classical elements: earth, water, air, and fire."

"If you don't mind my asking," Larry interjected, "since the minerals are first-density beings, then how come *you* have such depth of knowledge?" With a smile he added, "You don't sound like the average rock to me."

"Kind of you to notice," the Voice said. "Outward appearances can often be deceiving. In our case, our level of Awareness provides access to sixth-density knowledge, the same as Zeus and his friends who have come to entertain and instruct you."

"What do you mean by sixth density?" Larry asked. "If a rock is first density and you're at the sixth, where does that leave me? And what about Buddha or Christ or the Ascended Masters?"

Again, the Voice was clearly amused. "Easy there, Larry. You ask important questions, but to answer them now would only add to your confusion. We will explore this fully as our little story unfolds. The term 'density' simply refers to a range of Awareness, analogous to the color bands in the visible spectrum. However, even at the higher densities we are influenced by the distortions built into the points from which we view. If you find what we say helpful, you are welcome to make it yours. Any part with which you do not resonate you are free to discard."

"I know," Larry said, "Zeus gave me the same disclaimer yesterday. But if you are from the sixth density—whatever that really means—why did you have us enter this large piece of rock to meet with you?"

"We chose to invest ourselves into the crystalline formations in the white tank granite of Joshua Tree National Park because of the exceptional strength of its vibrational fields. As you have no doubt noticed, the energy amplification available here aids our exploration of Consciousness considerably.

"To answer your question more directly, we are not of the rock, we are merely in it . . . just as you are no longer of the world."

"I think I understand," Larry said.

"Good," the Voice responded. "Now, where were we? Ah, yes, the first density, composed of the four classical elements, earth, water, air, and fire. These seemingly inanimate rudiments are the most removed from the Oneness. Nevertheless, they serve the All That Is as they experience Awareness filtered through all seven veils. In their earliest stages of development they cannot even conceive of their own existence. As the first glimmer of Consciousness emerges, it encounters only chaos. Gradually the mineral and water life receive instruction by perceiving the heat of fire, the formative movement of the winds, the sounds of the silence, and other energetic impulses streaming through their crystalline structures. Eventually they become cognizant enough of their own being that one of the Veils falls away."

"What causes them to wake up?" Larry asked.

"All of Creation is subject to the spiraling Light energy that inexorably draws everything back to Oneness."

"But if the Oneness calls everything back to itself, how does anything stay in existence?" Larry sounded completely confused.

"It doesn't," Zeus interjected, "except when it does. Larry, stop trying to make a mental diagram of everything. We're dealing with nonlocal reality here. Everything from manifestation to destruction occurs simultaneously—hence the image of the Uroboros. Light spirals out from the logoi to form the cosmos even as it is called back to the Source so it can begin endless new cycles. Visualize great breaths simultaneously inhaling and exhaling Creation."

The Voice resumed its discourse. "Humans might call this force gravity, but it is much more than the physical attraction between objects based on mass and distance. Spiraling Light is too powerful, too pervasive, too exquisitely subtle to fit comfortably in a predefined container. It does not yield to mathematical analysis, nor can it be tagged by the mind's blindman's-bluff gropings. This is the unspeakable force of the black hole, the magnetic quality experienced by lovers, the call to delve deeper into the Unknowable Mystery. It shapes the land and urges water into seas, lakes, and rivers. It calls even the most elemental aspects of the All That Is to become Aware.

"Once elemental life forms have fully integrated the extraordinary realization that they exist, they are ready to emerge as rudimentary organisms in the second density. This is the density of growth into self-awareness. It is expressed through the dual kingdoms of animals and plants and, in rare instances, through certain mineral deposits located in a major power vortex, such as where we are now."

"Aren't animals more evolved than plants?" Larry asked.

"What do you think Junie would have to say about that?" the Voice responded. "No, Larry, plant life and animal life are equal branches of the second-density experience. Here the path of Consciousness forked, no doubt to offer the Oneness greater diversity of experience. You are voicing your society's bias, which holds that an increase in purposeful animation and concrete manifestation equals higher intelligence and Awareness. Using this absurd yardstick, you would attach greater value to a corrupt politician or an egocentric entertainer than to a monk praying for the well being of the entire planet in total anonymity.

"Animals may seem superior because they consume plants—although in a few instances the reverse is true. And they may appear intelligent, more social—more like humans. Plants, on the other hand, seem to just sit there, doing nothing but looking pretty, providing shade, and converting carbon dioxide into oxygen. This view is merely human narcissism. By and large, people simply cannot imagine a kind of information transference outside of their own five senses. Yet experiments have conclusively proved that plants—especially trees—not only have extraordinary means to communicate among themselves but show astonishing evidence of being able to read the thoughts of humans.

"We assure you, plant Consciousness is every bit evolved as animal Consciousness. Notice, for instance, the distributional similarity among species in both forks. In this density's early stages, the Consciousness of each species is profoundly vested in the group. Animals live in herds, plants of the same species grow close together, sharing a common, nearly undifferentiated

Consciousness. However, the spiraling Light energy calls them on. Eventually individual flora and fauna realize they possess a personal, discrete essence. This process is greatly speeded when a second-density being, such as a pet or a houseplant, receives a third-density being's attention—much as your own awakening is enhanced through your interaction with us. Once a second-density entity fully realizes it has an individuated Consciousness, it is ready to move on.

"This brings us to the third density, arguably the most challenging—the density of self-awareness and choice. Humanity on your planet has been experiencing this vibrational frequency for the past seventy-five thousand years, and it is due to end shortly. This is why we are all here—and why it is essential that you make the information you receive during your brief visit to Joshua Tree available to the planet's collective Consciousness."

"When the third density ends," Larry asked, "will all of humankind evolve into the fourth density? And what will happen to the beings in the second and first densities?"

"Very perceptive questions, Larry. The Earth is but one of many third-density planets. If a human is not sufficiently advanced to make the leap into the next density, he or she can continue experiencing third-density challenges within another illusion. The first and second densities simply remain as they are as the Earth emerges into the fourth density. Those humans who choose to evolve with her will remain, as fourth-density beings. But as we indicated earlier, early fourth-density planets cannot support third-density life. Entering a new density requires significant adjustment and balancing—much like a baby first learning to walk. The refined energy of the fourth density is too dissonant for third-density entities who have not mastered that density's two lessons.

"This is a good moment to explore the third density's unique opportunities for growth in some detail, so you can better understand the challenges now confronting humankind.

"In the third density, several new ingredients are added to the experiential soup. As the second of the seven veils dissolves, each entity gains, for the first time, a rudimentary overview of Creation. It sees the unity of the Oneness expressed as All That Is, and it learns that it possesses Free Will and can assume its first, fledgling role as a cocreator.

"The logos crafted the third veil in an extraordinary manner. Like an energetic barrier, it impedes direct flow of information between the conscious mind and unconscious mind, so the third-density entity forgets what or who it really is. It also constructs the phantasm of space/time, which in turn facilitates the illusion of separation and duality even while allowing the use of Free Will. Why? Simply so the Oneness can explore more varied and previously unknown aspects of itself. It takes many lifetimes for an entity to complete the cycle of this density's lessons."

"So, there really *is* reincarnation?" Larry asked. "I mean, people actually were other people in previous lives?"

"Why do you ask?" the Voice inquired.

"I've never quite known what to make of reincarnation," Larry said. "Everyone talks about being an Egyptian priest or priestess, or walking with Christ, or being some great historical figure. There are more than six billion people on the planet—how can all of them have been someone famous?"

Zeus broke into laughter. "Let me try to tackle this one," he said. "We're back to the problem of trying to stuff concepts through the strainer's twenty-six holes. The reason reincarnation isn't making sense is because you are trying to understand it from a human point of view. Let me share something of value from the *Interdimensional Survival Manual*—page 217, I believe:

*When caught in a fog bank, you can always see more
clearly by moving above it.*

"In other words, when you find yourself caught in a problem, keep shifting to a higher perspective until the problem is reduced to a single tile in a mosaic.

"Here's an example. Imagine you are a kindergarten teacher who suddenly notices a commotion in the sandbox: Johnny and Bobby are fighting. The issue is simple. Johnny is pushing a toy car along the roads and ramps he just built, and Bobby wants the car so he can play too. Left to their own devices, there would be two bloody noses and a major disruption involving the entire class."

"Sounds familiar," Larry interjected. "Just like the world we live in!"

"Yes," Zeus said. "The dynamics of both the problem and the solution fit. So what happens next? What would you do?"

"I would realize, "Larry said, visualizing the entire scene in his mind's eye, "that all problems are defined by the boundaries of the illusion that contains them. Johnny and Bobby are so focused on their little world of sand and the car that they cannot see a greater universe. So my job is simple. All I have to do is think outside the sandbox."

"Bull's-eye!" said the Voice. "You've hit the nail right on the head. How can you solve this problem in an instant?"

As the Voice spoke, Larry viewed himself as a character in a mini play. He was acutely aware of his own presence along with Johnny and Bobby, and was able to trace the perceptions and emotional references that each one consulted to create his individual response. "Amazing!" he said. "I can see it all so clearly. . . . It isn't about the cars at all. That's just surface stuff. My

God, I can feel the pain and the fear deep within these kids. They *really* don't know who they are."

"Whoops," said the Voice. "We didn't mean to take you in that deep. Let's stay with the 'surface stuff' for now." The deeper projection became fuzzy as Larry's Consciousness refocused on the events unfolding in the foreground. "What would you, as the teacher, do?"

"Oh, that's better . . . a lot easier on the heartstrings. Thanks," Larry said. "I would notice the small size of the arena containing the problem, then shift my point of view—like you just did with the projection—so I could see the larger picture. This lets me access possibilities unavailable to the two children. Looking around the room, I notice several other toy cars on a shelf. I add a few of them to the sandbox, and the two children begin to play together."

"Exactly," the Voice continued. "In the process, you give the youngsters insight into the Creation's unlimited potential, and you also provide a small crack through which they might later travel to explore their inner worlds. You have nudged each child gently towards the realization that nothing limits Consciousness except the illusion of limitation. Now, let's apply the same expansion of perspective to your question regarding reincarnation.

"Picture the life cycles of each entity in the form of a sine wave—a series of curves tracing successive arcs above and below a horizontal midline. The curves above the line represent the periods between incarnations and the ones below the line are individual incarnations in space/time. The line symbolizes the Veil of Forgetting, which affords the experiences of the third density. During its sojourn above the line, each entity has access to Infinite Intelligence through its unconscious. It is aware of the role it plays in expressing creative Free Will and thus assisting the

Oneness in experiencing itself. With this awareness it constructs a blueprint for its next journey into the illusion. But once it embarks on its journey—or lifetime, as you would call it—the Veil of Forgetting blocks easy access to higher knowledge, and the entity is plunged into a sea of confusion.

"One comment," the Voice added. "We use a sine wave only because it is easy to visualize. Please don't think the process is as smooth and regular as the symmetrical tracings on an oscilloscope. The time lapses on both sides of the Veil vary greatly, depending on circumstance. For example, if an entity had a particularly unsettling life—like Adolph Hitler's—that deviated significantly from the original plan, there is much delicate work to be done, with the assistance of many helpers, before it is ready to undertake the next lifetime experience.

"On the other hand, sometimes the dip below the line is extremely short—lasting a few years, or even just a few weeks of gestation. Perhaps the entity wishes to refine a particular point of understanding, or elects to serve as a catalyst so another being can reap the fruits of experiencing certain heightened emotional situations."

"What's the purpose of all this?" Larry asked.

"The macroscopic answer is exactly what I just said," the Voice responded. "All Creation is simply the Creator experiencing itself as part of itself. The microscopic answer deals with the third density's very purpose. In the first density the entity learns it is Conscious. In the second, it realizes its Consciousness is individuated. In the third, it learns to intentionally engage in cocreation with Love/Light energy and it achieves balance. These last two are the lessons you and all the other third-density beings on your planet are here to master."

"Zeus talked earlier about the distinction between Love/Light and Light/Love," Larry stated, "but I'm still missing an important piece of information. Exactly how are Love and Light related?"

"Again, you ask excellent questions," the Voice offered.

"Thanks," Larry acknowledged. "Zeus told me I should ask for clarification whenever a term isn't crystal clear. You may think your discourse is a 'little story,' but the concepts you present are anything but little!"

"Actually, Larry, the concepts we submit are relatively simple. They are challenging only when they don't build on what you already believe. Your conscious mind would probably rather put up a blockade and sink into torpor than relinquish its ingrained preconceptions.

"Your present query is a prime example. You recall that the Oneness triggered the unfoldment of Creation by permitting Free Will to come into being and that Free Will, in turn, begat the energetic force of Love. In a sense, each of these is a lower vibrational analog of its predecessor. In the same way, if the frequency of Love is slowed, it manifests as Light. And when the frequency of Light diminishes, it manifests as matter. We use the term 'Love/Light energy' to refer to the basic building block of the cocreative process as it moves from the Oneness through the All That Is and ultimately to you.

"The cocreative process is precisely what an entity engages in for the first time as part of its third-density lessons. Through successive dips into the illusion an entity gradually discovers the value of balance, and between incarnations it carefully and consciously chooses the prime objectives for acquiring greater balance in the next lifetime. We will discuss these concepts in detail as our little story progresses. For now, let's focus on the illusion of incarnation.

"In the realm of space/time—the part of the sine wave below the line—events appear to occur within a linear, past-present-future time frame. In the nonlocal universe of time/space—above the line—the entity's unconscious mind connects to Infinite Intelligence. From this elevated point of viewing, Creation is perceived as simultaneous. Multiple universes, containing all conceivable possibilities, happen concurrently. The future informs the past, and the present expands in infinite directions. If it could be seen from within the illusion, it would look like the imaginings of Lewis Carroll on LSD. Trying to decipher its meaning would be as futile as a frog trapped in a well contemplating the ocean.

"However, when, like the kindergarten teacher, you shift to a higher, more encompassing point from which to view, something entirely different is revealed. You perceive yourself as having two distinct aspects—the unconscious and conscious, the Aware and unaware, the Higher Self and lower self, the universal and limited, the knowing and not knowing. . . . The list could go on and on, but we think you get the idea."

"Yes," Larry said. "It's as if part of me is here, within the illusion, while another part watches from above, trying to guide me through occasional insights, chance meetings, books falling off shelves, tuning in to a radio station just as it broadcasts a vital piece of missing information."

"Quite so," the Voice said. "That's exactly how it works. Throughout the third-density experience, but especially during its earlier phases, the Higher Self has a devil of a time making a conscious connection with its lower-self counterpart. So it throws out subtle hints such as those you just mentioned. As you can imagine, this is not a very efficient way to communicate. That's why the bulk of mapping the course for each incarnational dip below the line is done during the interval between what you perceive as death and rebirth. The Higher Self does this very carefully, working with as much assistance as required—especially during the early stages of the third-density experience."

"Why does the Higher Self need help if it's connected to Infinite Intelligence?" Larry asked.

"While the Higher Self has access to vast stores of experiences and information, it is not omniscient. It cannot handle the full measure of Light/Love energy required to access the entire cosmic hologram. There are many unknown possibilities arising out of the use of Free Will in third-density interactions. If left to its own devices, before it has gleaned the wisdom from observing many third-density lifetimes, the Higher Self would tend to be overambitious and create a learning experience too challenging to be productive. That's why each Higher Self seeks input from its own social memory complex counterparts to guide its early decisions. Maximizing the chance for success calls for great care in balancing the entity's historical memory, physical form, and emotional patterning with the environment into which it is to be cast."

"Like a fly fisherman?" Larry asked.

"Not a bad analogy," the Voice responded with obvious appreciation. "The Higher Self selects the fly to tempt a certain fish—the lesson to be learned by its third-density self in a certain lifetime. That fly, assiduously imprinted with the memories of previous incarnational experiences, will be cast into the illusion.

"Since the fisherman can choose among the entire panoply of exotic flies, does it make sense to settle on a drab one that won't interest the fish? If you were free to select energetic vignettes from the Akashic record's vast archive to attract certain lessons you want to learn, wouldn't you pick from the richest, most pregnant lifetimes on file? If you are drawn to Egypt, why not be a priest or a pharaoh? Certainly their lives contained more spice and catalyst than that of the slave who swept the temple. If you could board any train in the Universe, why choose one that arrives on the wrong continent twenty minutes after Christ has left the planet?

"The fly, replete with all its appropriate memories, is tied onto the hook and cast onto a carefully chosen spot in the stream where the fish are known to be. That is, each entity chooses its parents, the time and place of its birth, the race, culture, and religion—or lack of it—into which it is born, and every other formative aspect of its incarnation. Once Consciousness descends into the illusion by crossing the Veil of Forgetting, it is subject to the perception that it is on its own, abandoned, left to fend for itself. Then the fun begins in earnest!"

"How does an entity know what it needs to learn next? What stops it from simply declaring itself 'evolved' and skipping on to the next density?" Larry asked.

"Moving through the densities is not like your game of Snakes and Ladders. There are no serendipitous short cuts. Each entity must take the full curriculum. The logos constructs levels of Awareness within its Creation by interweaving Light/Love energy through it. For beings at the lower densities, the Light/Love energy appears subdued, since the Light is filtered through many Veils. As an entity advances and these screens gradually dissolve, more Light can penetrate.

"After each incarnation, the entity moves along the beckoning spiral of Light back toward the Oneness to the point where the intensity becomes too blinding and it can advance no further. It cannot enter a realm for which it is ill-prepared. If the entity's ego causes its reach to exceed its grasp, it will be instantly rebuffed—an experience comparable to awakening from sleep in a dark room to find a bright flashlight shining into your eyes.

Even the light from such a tiny bulb may distress when the entity is unprepared. However, when you are fully awake, you can go outside and acclimate even to the sun's brightness; the flashlight beam is hardly noticeable. In the lower three densities, entities are still very much asleep, so even a modest measure of Light can be painful.

"The spiraling Light/Love stream is like an energetic umbilical cord connecting every individuated aspect of the All That Is to the Oneness. This is the two-way track along which Consciousness flows, acting much like the leader and streamer strokes of lightning, entangling every aspect of Creation, illuminating the way home. As a cocreator, each entity is free to gather experiences and advance as far along the path of Infinite Awareness as it wishes. Nothing impedes or limits its choices other than itself. As it progresses, mastering the lessons of experience, each entity is able to accept increasingly brighter Light in growing comfort. The greater the measure of Light/Love at its disposal, the greater its ability to cocreate."

"That makes sense," Larry said. "I can see now why every incarnation has to be purposefully planned and how the Higher Self decides what fly to use and where to cast the line. But I'm not clear on whether my past lives are mine or not."

"Permit me," Zeus offered, assessing the considerable gap between the Voice's instruction and Larry's comprehension. "Apparently our prize student has painted himself into a rational corner and his little mind needs rescuing before it'll allow him to continue on his journey."

"Larry, you're confusing the 'I' and 'me' again. Let me give you a visual image that might put it in a larger perspective."

"Thanks," Larry replied. "Sometimes I think I've got it; but when I try to retrieve it, it seems to disappear and I'm left with nothing but the confusion you're talking about."

"Score one for the glorious limitation of the mind and its unyielding need to understand everything in terms it already accepts," Zeus cracked. "Let's see if we can throw it a bone or two. Imagine, if you will, a single drop of water (you) and a river (your lifetime) emptying into the sea (at the time of your death) as you depart from the illusion of space/time and enter into the nonlocal universe of time/space. When the single drop enters the sea, it not only merges with all the other drops, it also loses its integrity as a drop. It separates into its component molecules. Got any idea how many?"

"Nope," Larry answered, "but judging from the tone of your voice, I'd say it was more than I can count."

"You got that right. It's a whopper of a number: 1.7×10^{21}. That's 1.7 followed by 21 zeroes . . . far more than all the stars in the Milky Way galaxy! Now, imagine each of these molecules as data units, carrying back the fruits of your incarnation to the mother sea.

"When you're about to take another incarnation, it's time to reassemble a new drop of water. It's up to you and your Higher Self to gather data units from the vast archive available to you. What you ultimately select determines the 'history' of your past lives as well as the gifts and challenges you bring with you when you reenter the illusion."

"Thanks. It's beginning to make sense. When people get caught up in the details of their past lives, they're missing the point completely, aren't they?" Larry asked.

"Why so?"

"Because they get caught up with the glamour of the surface and fail to go deeper. Instead of feeling special about who they were, wouldn't they be better served by pondering why a particular previous lifetime was chosen and how it impacts their current life?"

CHAPTER 18

Why Nothing Is As It Seems

The Voice took a long pause before continuing. "Let us reiterate that this illusion as you know it—the Earth and all its human inhabitants—is fast drawing to a close. Visualize the path of the solar system circling the galaxy as the sweep of the outer portion of a minute hand on a clock. It is now well past the fifty-nine-minute mark, almost touching the twelve. As it enters this final segment of the arc, the solar system is subject to the first influx of the fourth-density's vibrational spectrum, which operates by a markedly different geometry than the third density.

"Your planet is in the process of realigning its electromagnetic reception centers—akin to the chakra system of the human body—so it can hold the matrix of fourth-density experience. Unfortunately, most beings on your planet are not prepared for this shift. For them, it is like being confronted by a light too painfully bright to bear.

"The logos never intended the transition to be painful. The original plan called for the planet and all its inhabitants to change over smoothly, as an interconnected unit. However, humanity's collective thought forms—concretized in belief systems—have made such a unified passage to the fourth density quite unlikely. The growing energetic disparity between humanity and the planetary sphere is causing a marked increase in entropy and unusable heat. Some predict that this will cause a dramatic intensification in volcanic and tectonic plate activity over the next few years.

"To understand the process that is underway in more detail, you need to expand your knowledge of how the Universe communicates with all its parts. What do you know about chakras and how they function?"

"Not much," Larry replied. "I remember reading that they are energy centers in the human body. I think they're usually described as spirals, or something."

"Yes," the Voice replied. "That's pretty much how they have been viewed in your traditional literature: seven main chakras, each a separate energetic portal tuned to a certain vibratory range. In your libraries you can find illustrations depicting seven energy vortices along the vertical axis of the body."

"I think I've seen something like that," Larry replied. "but I always assumed they were the product of someone's overactive imagination."

"Larry, m' boy," Zeus interrupted in an absurd imitation of a hillbilly drawl, "there ain't nothing in the entire Universe which ain't the product of *someone's* overactive imagination. Fact is, that's exactly what Creation's all about. Take away what you call overactive imagination and you can kiss bye-bye to the Hoover Dam and the Great Wall of China—not to mention the Andromeda Galaxy and fantastic sex . . . which, of course, I just did . . . mention it, I mean. Just 'cause you can't see, smell, or touch it, don't you go assumin' others can't. Why, there's a host of folks who can make chakras dance and sing—even cause 'em to spit cider in your left ear, if they'd a mind to."

"Stop the funny stuff, Zeus," Larry protested. "I'm trying to understand how I connect to the All That Is and you're making jokes."

"Now, there you go assuming again. Every time you do, you just prove the old adage: 'When you ass-u-me, you make an ass out of you and me.' I, for one, would rather remain a dog, thank you. You, on the other hand, are free to bray at any altar of your liking."

Larry could only shake his head in response to Zeus's blindside assault. He felt like a yo-yo. Every time he gained momentum in one direction, his beloved dog yanked his chain and abruptly changed course.

"To continue," said Zeus, "unless there are other barnyard entities you'd like to emulate? I'll take your muffled giggles as a no and elucidate, as I was about to do before I was so egregiously maligned. The energy vortex arising from each chakra is quite real. Almost anyone with a little training can easily feel it. If you hold a small weight on a thread over a chakra while a person is lying down, your little pendulum will actually begin to move in a circle driven by the energy field coming out of the body."

"Quite so," the Voice agreed. "Typically, the seven main chakras are correlated with the colors of the visible spectrum, from red, the lowest vibration, for the chakra at the base of the spine, to violet, the fastest vibration, at the crown chakra just above the head.

"The chakras can be compared to a set of CB radios whose crystals are tuned to specific frequencies, establishing two-way communication channels with the quantum hologram that is the matrix of Creation—otherwise known as the Infinite Intelligence. Each energy center simultaneously receives and transmits information through its bandwidth of interest or perception.

"The need to achieve balance in the third density pertains specifically to the chakras. Unless all the chakras are cleared and properly modulated, reception is distorted and the entity feels alienated from itself, other beings, and all of Creation. Moreover, blocked chakras tend to attract more blockages, so the disharmony increases, leading to a wide range of physical, emotional, and spiritual malaises.

"Your societies have entirely missed the importance of seeking balance. The hedonist tends to glorify the pleasures of the lower three chakras while neglecting the centers at the heart, the throat, and the third eye. Conversely, most devotees of your consciousness-seeking philosophies overemphasize activation of their higher chakras while denying the lower ones."

"Like celibacy?" Larry asked.

"Yes," the Voice replied. "But the three lower chakras deal with more than sexual expression. The root chakra, the one linked with the color red, deals primarily with survival issues. All the information an entity receives during its lifetime is filtered through this portal first, before it moves to the higher centers. The first chakra, which by the way is linked to the first density, holds the energy of tribal memory—concepts involving family, religious convictions, superstitions, and similar group beliefs. Attitudes toward basic issues such as food, shelter, and financial security are stored here as well.

"The second chakra, associated with orange on the color spectrum, is tuned, as you might expect, to the harmonic of the second density. Here the entity stores all of its decisions regarding its personal and emotional identity. This chakra holds imprints concerning sexual activity, creativity, and manifestation as well as patterns of blame, guilt, power, and morality. And it is the major center through which the entity processes its perception of duality and the panoply of emotional feelings triggered by its interactions with other third-density beings.

"It is only after the first two chakras have consumed their fill of the meat of each experience that the remainder passes along to the yellow energy center, associated with the third density.

Here the entity processes the significance of each event in terms of its social relations. The data stored here deal with self-confidence and access to personal power. This is the seat of the ego, the home of the lower self, the egoic I. Restriction of this center leads to low self-esteem, fear of rejection, oversensitivity to criticism, and deep-seated fears of one's secrets being exposed."

"Can the blockages ever completely shut down a chakra?" Larry asked.

"A rather unlikely development indeed," the Voice replied. "That would most likely cause the entity's death. However, as we said, any chakra restriction causes a corresponding malfunction in the entity's mind/body/emotion/spirit complex."

"How do the blockages get into the chakras in the first place?" Larry asked.

"Bull's-eye!" came the reply. "You've just ventured into a critical area of exploration for any entity attempting to advance beyond the third density. How would you answer your own question?"

"I wouldn't know where to begin," Larry said.

"Okay, I'll give you a hint. Almost every infant is born with its chakras already partially restricted. From then onward, the distortions and blockages generally worsen, unless the entity works to reverse the process. Start there."

"Thanks heaps," Larry said, wondering if Zeus would come to his aid. But Zeus was silent. Larry continued, feeling his way. "You said earlier that before it's born, a third-density being chooses both a collection of past-life memories and the circumstances of its birth. These two choices color its entire incarnation. It inherits a certain gene pool, which includes the cellular memory of that particular family, as well as the karma of the previous lives it's adopted."

"Continue," the Voice encouraged. "How do you suppose

those two choices affect the chakras?"

"They load the deck, don't they?" Larry mused. "The genes and the karma must act like filters in each chakra, coloring whatever information is flowing through, like the color gels used in theaters to create different lighting effects on stage."

"Excellent," the Voice said. "Moreover, they have the same effect on input from everyday experiences as they do on the more subtle information constantly flowing in from the Universe. What else warps the frequencies within these seven receptor sites in a major way?"

"I haven't got a clue," Larry responded.

"Is that your final answer?" Zeus quipped. "How terribly sad. Allow me to be your lifeline. What happens each time you project into a new incarnation?"

Larry reviewed the process of entering from the nonlocal world of time/space into space/time, following the sine wave down into the illusion. "Of course!" he exclaimed. "The Veil."

"Correct," the Voice exclaimed. "And where does each entity moving through the Veil store the blocking programs it downloads?"

"In the chakras?"

"Precisely. A special code is deliberately imprinted into each energy center, inhibiting the entity's ability to remember who it really is. Once again, the logos does this to add richness and diversity to the time spent within the illusion, thereby enhancing the experience with which to gift the All That Is."

Larry slowly absorbed the information that was pouring into him. "My God. From what you say, we come in blindfolded with our hands tied behind our backs. We've sure gone to a lot of trouble to give ourselves a real challenge. And to think that's only the start! From there, as you said, it's one distortion after another, isn't it?"

"In fact," the Voice said, "some life-altering distortions are imprinted into the chakras during gestation, as the fetus is completely aware of everything taking place around it. Consider the distortive effect in the third chakra, the locus of self-esteem, if the child perceives, for instance, that it is unwanted. But, as you already know, the Higher Self would have programmed this too as highly probable when it chose the circumstances for that lifetime. What happens once the child is born?"

"It's subject to a grand conspiracy perpetrated by its parents and society." Larry offered. Both the Voice and Zeus actually laughed. Apparently they found Larry's answer amusing. "I don't get it. What's so funny this time?"

"Sorry," Zeus interjected. "Couldn't help ourselves. What you just said couldn't be farther from the truth. To say it's a conspiracy assumes—there's that word again—the schemers have a method to their madness. In fact, they're just following the dictates of their own imprints, passed on to them from the previous generation—like a fraternity hazing, inflicting the same sophomoric silliness on newcomers simply because that's the way it's always been done. You might say it's the totally blind leading the partially blind. Only here, the kid's mentors actually believe that sharing their distortions is going to help the little guy. Please continue. How do the misguided actions of these well-meaning adults affect the child's chakras?"

"I think I understand what you're driving at," Larry said. "The collective input a child receives from birth onward conditions its entire life. That sounds like an obvious statement, but it isn't. The real damage takes place below the waterline, where nobody's looking."

Larry's tone suddenly became more animated. "Parents can't

help but screw up their kids. By passing on their beliefs, however noble, they actually build an identity for the child that imprisons it in a cultural cell. Each piece of skewed information absorbed by the child as *fact* adds another restriction to one, or maybe several, of the chakras."

"Well done," Zeus said. "You're catching on. Now, how do you suppose these blockages manifest in the personality?"

"As all the crap that keeps us from getting along. If I had to narrow it down to a short list, it would include preferences, judgments, desires, obsessions, asocial behavior, unhappiness, confusion, anger, bitterness, victim consciousness, aggressor consciousness, low self-worth, sexual dysfunction, emotional and physical disease, intolerance. . . ."

"Okay, enough!" Zeus laughed. "You've got it. Moreover, you've just explained how human societies have boxed themselves into such a corner. The world is a mess because its people are a mess. Do you see now why there's no grand-scale solution to the world's problems? The only way out is for the Consciousness of each person to be raised—assuming he or she is willing—one person at a time.

"By the way, you said something important when you called the information 'skewed.' What did you mean by that?

"I'm not sure," Larry said "Part of me just blurted it out. 'Skewed' means slanted, like something that is more developed on one side or in one direction than another; it's asymmetrical—out of whack."

"And what do you suppose that has to do with the two most important lessons to be learned in the third density?"

"Well, one of the lessons is achieving balance. If a third-density kid's been loaded with skewed information from the moment it's conceived, it's going to be way out of balance long before it can walk or talk," Larry said.

"Quite so." said the Voice. "And what must that entity do to repair the distortions caused by imbalanced perceptions?"

"Balance them?" Larry asked.

"Yowzer," Zeus exclaimed, "the kid's a veritable rocket scientist. He got the answer on the first try!"

"C'mon guys, give me a break," Larry pleaded. "I'm just cracking my way out of the shell and you're giving me advanced calculus problems. How am I supposed to know about balancing my chakras when the other six billion people on this planet don't seem to have a clue?"

There was a considerable pause before the Voice said, "A most interesting emotional display, Larry. What chakra, do you suppose, holds the programming that triggered your response—using a self-deprecating piece of humor to evoke sympathy?"

"Ouch," Larry winced, feigning pain. "You two never give me anywhere to hide. Since there's no easy way out, I guess I'm going to have to train myself out of the old tricks of my ordinary mortal trade.

"As to my response, it felt like a voice telling me I needed to live up to your expectations to earn your approval. It was afraid of being overwhelmed and looking bad. So I'd guess it came from the third chakra."

"If you were to verbalize that thought form, what might it say?" the Voice asked.

"It would say, 'Pleasing people to get their approval is necessary for Larry's survival and well-being.'"

"How would you counterbalance that thought form?" the Voice continued.

"I would use an affirmation like 'I am good enough just as I am,' or 'I am a child of the Universe and don't need anyone's approval for me to be perfect in every way.'"

"Larry, if it were that easy to balance skewed imprints," Zeus interjected, "the world wouldn't be where it is today. Affirmations make great refrigerator art, but they're about as useful with a deeply imprinted energy pattern as a Band-Aid on an infected wound. They're generally the ego's attempt to take charge. By and large, other forms of focused thought—like laying on of hands, prayer, ritual—are much the same."

"Then how come energetic healers have so much success?" Larry asked.

"Allow us to respond," the Voice said, "for this is a particularly interesting question. If you mean that healers can eliminate symptoms and diseased manifestations in the body, then perhaps you are correct. However, do not equate the eradication of unwanted physical and emotional states with true healing. The condition of even the healthy beings on your planet shifts constantly—wonderful one day, middling the next, certainly not a balanced state of affairs. The term 'healer' is also unfortunate, as the healing is in fact done by the entity itself. The facilitator—the name we prefer—offers two important services. First, he or she acts as a conduit of Infinite Intelligence, intensifying Light/Love energy in the entity's field. Second, he or she helps the entity create a sanctified space where the entity can focus its own attention and intention into the healing process.

"Disease of any kind results from blockages within the chakras and is subject to the Law of Purpose, that is, the underlying intention behind an entity's incarnational experiences. An unwanted condition cannot be eliminated without unanimous consent along the entire continuum of the entity's I's that the diseased state is no longer a catalyst for growth. For example, a great deal of information is presented within your illusion on how to attract wealth or obtain better relationships or succeed at some form of competition. Keep in mind, however, that the circumstances of each entity's life were purposefully and carefully woven to maximize the opportunity to increase Awareness. How can it possibly help to remove these carefully placed impediments before the entity has gained what they were designed to facilitate?"

"Then how does a person get better?"

"Ah, a more complex question than you suspect. From our perspective, 'getting better' means coming into phase with the purpose of one's incarnation. To truly know what this is requires contact with one's Higher Self. Illness can serve to shift an entity out of the inertia of its day-to-day existence and away from the distractions of life. If used properly, such periods of distress become prime opportunities for advancement."

"What's the best way to use an opportunity like that?" Larry asked.

"To answer that we need to return to the concept of blockages in the chakras. These are caused by energy biases imprinted in each chakra's core matrix. They have four distinct sources and purposes, and four corresponding levels of penetration. The first, and most deeply ingrained, set of implants is put in place by the Veil of Forgetting as the entity passes through on its way to a third-density life. This primary program creates the experience of duality, eclipsing the entity's identity as an eternal part of the Oneness. A third-density being cannot completely erase this particular imprint and remain intact in physical form on this planet.

"The second category of blockage is also embedded deep in each chakra's core—although not quite as permanently as the first. These are the incarnational memories the Higher Self selects to assist the entity in learning the lessons needed for its advancement.

"The third set of imprints accompanies the physical vehicle the Higher Self chooses for a given incarnation. The genetic markers in the parents' bloodlines can predispose family members to particular physical or psychological conditions (sometimes called miasms) for up to seven generations. In most cases—unless specifically selected by the Higher Self for learning purposes—genetically caused diseases respond favorably to energy healing.

"The fourth, and to us the most perplexing, type of distortion is contributed by the entity itself through precipitous emotional decisions made throughout its life. Fortunately, these are not as deeply rooted as the other three forms of blockages and can be easily dislodged through various energetic and psychological therapies."

"With all that gunk jam-packed into each chakra, how am I supposed to know how to start untangling the distortions so I can begin my journey into the fourth density?" Larry asked plaintively.

"Stop whining, kiddo," Zeus responded. "Your mind's pushing so hard you're scraping your nose against the bark. If you loosen up a bit, you can step back and see the forest. Ask not what the illusion can do for you, but what you can do for the illusion."

Larry's groan only encouraged Zeus to play more mind games with his master's head.

"The trouble with humanoids is they're so vain—they think every song is about them. Larry, if you waste all your energy trying to solve the puzzle by looking out through your 'what about me' personality, you're gonna get nowhere."

"Why do I forget you can read my mind?" Larry mused. "Perhaps I should rephrase my question. If the distortions are so indelibly imprinted on *one's* chakras, how is *one* expected to advance to the fourth density?"

"Quite so," the Voice agreed. "In probing universal mysteries, it is always more fruitful to seek answers that pertain to the collective. Consider that you did not volunteer to enter the illusion at this particular time simply to escape it. We suspect you had a far nobler purpose in mind.

"As to your concerns about overcoming the blockages held in the chakras, you will need to think outside the box. Remember Einstein's famous words about problems not being solvable at the same level of Consciousness where they were created. You will hardly succeed in defusing the imprints lodged in your chakras by merely introducing opposing thought patterns.

"It is the nature of Creation to maintain equilibrium. This is reflected in the tensions held between opposing subpersonalities, in the complementary nature of white and black holes, and in what you call manifestation and destruction. Every expression in thought, word, or deed has its antithesis, whether evident or hidden. Moreover, we are part of a quantum hologram in which every possible permutation ultimately finds expression. For example, in some parallel universe, or O-world, your emotional imbalances are a mirror image of how you are imbalanced here. Instead of trying to get attention by evoking sympathy, the you in that O-world attempts to survive by making others see you as the Universe's intellectual gift to the planet."

"But how can that be?" Larry asked. "If everything was perfectly balanced, wouldn't one side always cancel out the other, leaving an absolute sea of nothing?"

"Bull's-eye!" the Voice exclaimed. "Larry, shall you never cease to amaze us? You are like a diver who has mastered an inward triple somersault with a double twist yet is still unable to climb the ladder to the diving board. It would seem you have inadvertently happened upon the ultimate paradox: 'Nothing' happens to be the most powerful force in the Universe. Let us quote you a riddle we once overheard:

What is greater than God,
More evil than Satan,
Poor people have it,
Rich people need it,
If you eat it you will die?

"The answer, of course, is 'nothing.' Unfortunately, most people view this riddle as merely a clever confirmation of their beliefs. It would never occur to them to take it literally. For to move to the point from which you see that all Creation is merely illusion, and the entire algebraic equation—despite its complexities—can only equal zero, is to approach the brink of madness. However, there's a key hidden in the folds of this enigma that, if used properly, can unlock door after door along your journey home."

"Thanks for 'nothing'!" Larry said, quite bewildered by it all.

"Oh, don't thank me," the Voice responded, seemingly oblivious to Larry's sarcasm. "However, your memory appears short, indeed. Have you already forgotten the Ultimate Proposition? 'Nothing' is the ultimate gift, for in truth it is everything; just as infinity is the consummate expression of the One. The most curious belief in your dualistic world is the idea that one can own 'things,' and that the more 'things' one has, the happier one will be. From our perspective, we are already rich beyond measure. The compulsion to own, acquire, or control simply clouds our perception of the grandeur of existence. I refer you to the last words of Rocky's famous rap song: 'If you wish to transcend mere Platitude, move past your ideas of Gratitude, master the art of Desuetude, and embrace the world of Omnitude!'"

"Oh, I remember," Larry said. "Zeus told me I'd eventually understand, and I think I'm beginning to. The difference has everything to do with the I's of infinity, doesn't it?"

"Correct." came the instant reply. "Gratitude is the lower self's appreciation of what it perceives as material, emotional, or spiritual abundance. Omnitude moves way beyond the mind's limited realm of objects and concepts and expresses the joy of gravity—the inexorable pull of Consciousness gradually revealing itself to itself. Omnitude is the realization that every entity is an aspect of All That Is, blessed with the ultimate gift of bearing witness to Creation's infinite unfoldment. Anything else the entity might value only diminishes what it already has. In other words, nothing equals everything!"

"Amazing," Larry replied. "It all ties together. Rocky's words, the Ultimate Proposition, the chakras, the densities . . . everything in Creation relates. I think I'm really beginning to see that now. Still, I know there's a me, somehow separate from the whole. And I still can't help wondering why I'm here. What did you mean when you said there was a noble purpose for my coming to Earth at this time?"

"From the perspective of the higher densities," the voice said, "it is clear that humanity on this planet needs considerable assistance in the current transition to the fourth density. Consequently, tens of millions of advanced entities, primarily from the sixth density, volunteered to take human form at this time. You might recall both Zeus and your Higher Self speaking of Wanderers. The reason we are having this conversation now is that you are one of them. However, your passage through the Veil was not without consequence. You are subject to all the limitations imposed on third-density entities. Your task is no different from theirs, except for one rather important mandate: to serve."

"What do you mean by that?" Larry asked.

"What would be the use of descending into this illusion from a higher density only to depart as quickly as you can?" the Voice asked.

"Not much."

"Then, why are you here?"

"To serve," Larry said. "Isn't that what you just told me?"

"Quite so," the Voice responded. "And if you truly wish to commit to service, you must take the entire curriculum. No shortcuts. No getting out of here before you have fulfilled the purpose for which you have come. This is a cleverly designed density. The players, using their concept of Free Will, have created a very sticky wicket that has kept them immobilized for seventy-five thousand years. If your service is going to make a difference, it would behoove you to fully appreciate each step of the process experienced by those trapped within the illusion. Your knowledge of the chakras is vital in understanding both how the glorious mirage of this illusion is maintained and what must be done to move beyond it."

"Ouch," Larry said. "Sorry for the sarcasm. I guess my ego was asserting itself again."

"As it must," the Voice replied. "It is the expression of your lower will. Without it, you would have great difficulty operating on this planet. With too much of it, you would have great difficulty moving beyond it. As we said earlier, you are only seeking the balance that already exists."

Chapter 19

Lessons in Mastering the Illusion

"But with things on our planet so far out of kilter, how can you say that a state of balance already exists?" Larry asked.

"Ah, it seems you are failing to see the invisible," the Voice mused. "We will illustrate with a simple example. Imagine a tube of glass bent into the shape of the letter U. What happens when water is poured into one of the two openings?"

"The water moves down one arm of the tube, around the bottom, and up the second arm," Larry said.

"Precisely so. Is one column of water higher than the other?"

"No, they're equal because the air pressure pushing down on both of them is the same."

"Good," the Voice said. "Now imagine that the U-tube represents all of Creation. At the macrocosmic level, if you will, all matter is in one side of the tube, offset by an equal amount of antimatter on the other. The same model works at many different levels. Take personalities, for example. Every overt expression has an opposing counterpart held in tension somewhere in the psyche—that is, on the other side of the emotional U-tube."

"That's like saying each action has an equal and opposite reaction," Larry said. "So is the U-tube another illustration of entanglement—that whatever takes place locally must have an unexpressed counterpart somewhere else?"

"Quite correct," the Voice agreed. "Sometimes, as you have already learned, these unexpressed, or disowned, personalities are heavily suppressed. Sometimes they are simply dormant. But they always exist. You will find that the deeper you delve, the more you will find the subtle hand of entanglement at the helm.

"We referred to O-worlds a few moments ago—an excellent example of this principle. Imagine that the U-tube goes through a piece of cardboard so large that you can only see one half of the tube at a time, never all of it at once. Can you still accurately predict the level of the water—or in this case something less tangible, like emotion or Light/Love energy—in the other column?"

"Yes, for sure. The cardboard just obstructs my view, it doesn't affect the levels in the tube, which remain equal."

"Now, envision the cardboard as an infinitely large screen separating two parallel universes. Whichever tube you, the observer, are looking at is the one that finds full expression, or is explicate, if you will, while the other tube is suppressed, or implicate. Which one is real?"

"They both are," Larry responded. "It all depends which sea you decide to swim in."

"Excellent," the Voice said. "Is one more valid or desirable than the other?"

"No. Both simply *are*. Validity wouldn't have anything to do with it."

"Bull's-eye!" the Voice exclaimed. "By the way, the same point applies concerning the myriad doctrines and teachings that sprout up on your planet like mushrooms after a rain. Each one portrays itself as the golden path to the Promised Land. In the end, each is little more than a coalesced point of view offering adherents tenets of belief.

"You see, when it comes to balance, it doesn't matter which side of the seesaw you sit on. Being too high up in the air is just as unbalanced as scrunching down on the ground. Positively oriented beings—those seeking to serve others—who have not embraced their dark side are as out of balance as their negative counterparts, who delight in dominating others while disdaining the Oneness of all Creation.

"We would like to offer a method for balancing any system and keeping it in conscious equilibrium by defusing the distortive impact of implanted beliefs. This can be accomplished by taking advantage of the wormholes that interpenetrate the sheet of cardboard, as it were."

"I don't follow you," Larry said. "What do you mean by 'wormholes'?"

"Ah, the vagaries of language," the Voice sighed. "Zeus, can you help us with this one?"

"I'll certainly give it a try," Zeus chuckled. "Larry, in theoretical physics, wormholes are a geometry of four-dimensional space/time connecting two separate regions of the Universe. This is your science fiction writers' favorite explanation for time travel or hyper-lightspeed jumps through the galaxies.

"Unfortunately, wormholes open and close so rapidly that even light can't make it through. However, thought and Consciousness can! That's why our host here chose this particular term. Whenever you simultaneously view two distinct realities—even if only in your mind's eye—they are connected by a wormhole."

"Ah, I get it," Larry said. "It's like what Junie showed me. When my Aware Ego chooses a perspective that can hold the tension between opposing subpersonalities, it becomes like a wormhole. Then I can see both sides of the U-tube at once."

"Quite so," the Voice interjected. "Thank you, Zeus. Larry, it's through a wormhole that your Higher Self allows you direct access to the time/space continuum. There your Consciousness can connect to all possible alternate realities, so all events appear simultaneous. In theory, then, you can return to the exact moment a belief was implanted and create an equal and opposite viewpoint to neutralize it.

"However, in practice this process has proved time-consuming and not very dependable. Moreover, it is only useful in addressing the fourth kind of energetic implant, the ones the entity itself puts in place during its current incarnation. It can do little to dislodge the deeper energetic blockages put in place by the Higher Self and by the Veil.

"Fortunately, there is a much better way to achieve balance. It requires only that you become keenly observant, so you can produce alternate points from which to view.

"Let us take your earlier outburst as an example. You felt ridiculed for your response, and you reacted immediately. In fact, your words, 'balance them,' were the appropriate response. Zeus's comment was not meant to judge; it was merely an attempt at humor and a commentary on how rarely beings within the illusion are able to appreciate the obvious. However, because of patterning within your third chakra—where imprints dealing with self-image and fear of rejection reside—you took his words personally and felt the need to defend yourself.

"This, like all involuntary emotional reactions, provides a perfect opportunity to clear your chakras. We would like to offer a set of lessons on how to accomplish this and attain the balance required to move on to the fourth density. Are you interested?"

"You bet I am, " Larry responded.

"Very well," the Voice continued, "the first set of lessons deals with the mind. And lesson one teaches you how to balance your emotions. As you feel an emotional reaction rising, imagine a seesaw, and visualize that emotion sitting on one side of it. For the sake of this exercise, no emotion is better or worse than any other; just observe the amount of energy it carries. In a sense, emotions are simply energetic thought forms having amplitude and vector. They can thus be balanced by an opposite thought form of the same amplitude and opposite vector. For example, whenever you experience a moment of joy, pause briefly and visualize that joy causing one side of the seesaw to drop to the ground. Then imagine altering the current circumstances to create an equal amount of grief to add a corresponding weight to the other side. Then watch as the teeter-totter returns to equilibrium—into balance—again.

"Obviously, you are encouraged to run this process in the other direction as well, adding a positive emotion to counterbalance a negative emotion. Eventually you will realize how much you, and most other humans, depend on outside circumstances to trigger your feelings of self-worth and happiness. Does it really make sense that another's words or actions can so directly affect your emotional state?"

The Voice's last sentence triggered a torrent of memory vignettes in Larry's mind: the highs and lows in his relationship with Marianne . . . the way he felt when the pretty barista at Starbucks remembered his name and that he liked his wet decaf cappuccino extra hot . . . how he made himself feel whenever he looked in the mirror after a particularly groggy sleep. "My God," he gasped involuntarily, "there's no escaping those thoughts, is there?"

"Why ever would you want to do that?" the Voice inquired. "They are your most valued teachers. You must meet each of them head on, with as much Awareness as possible. In time, through this practice you will find balance and completeness within yourself, and so transcend the grasp of the Veil. Keep in mind that in the context of this exercise, even positive emotional thoughts, which tend to prop up your self-esteem, are as skewed as negative ones.

"So, Larry, when you felt we were mocking you, what counteracting thought could you have evoked?"

Larry was silent for several minutes, fighting off his unwillingness to see happiness, joy, and other emotional highs as undesirable. The Voice fully understood his dilemma but said nothing. In time, the internal dialogue settled into the amorphous repository housing Larry's growing collection of paradoxes, and he could turn his mind to the Voice's question. At last he spoke: "I guess I could have seen the three of us as a team, aligning our intentions to help the planet. If I'd shifted my point of view to match yours, I would have seen that my answer—simple as it was—was exactly what was required."

"That's excellent in theory," the Voice said, "but of course, that's not what took place. Before you had a chance to shift viewpoints, the horse bolted from the barn, so to speak—your emotional reflexes took charge. How might you use the lesson we just gave you to balance your reaction?"

"I like the idea of the seesaw," Larry answered. "If I place my feeling belittled on one side, I can see how heavy it was by how fast the seesaw tips. I know it originated from a subpersonality, or a thought form embedded in my third chakra, that doubts my self-worth. All I need to do is create a positive thought that tells that part of me, 'I understand what you said and the programming that makes you feel that way. But *I* am far more than you realize, and whether I goof or am brilliant has no bearing on who I really am.'"

"Precisely." said the Voice. "*All* thoughts—especially those with high emotional content—have an opposite. Your job is to identify each one that throws your seesaw out of equilibrium, whether it's positive or negative, and balance it with one of equal intensity. There's a subtle but vital difference between the processes we offer and affirmations, which imply a desire for change mixed with an element of judgment."

"Yes," Larry replied. "I think I'm getting it. Rather than trying to change things, I need to learn to embrace each interaction as a gift—regardless of whether it makes me feel good or bad. Although I have to admit, this is the first time I've heard anyone put a negative thought to good use. But it makes sense."

"May we say, we are gratified that you grasp the essence of this teaching," the Voice said. "It's actually a three-step process. First, recognize an emotional reaction as the reflex of a preprogrammed thought, imprinted in a chakra, that's been triggered by some external circumstance. Second, embrace that emotion as a valued teacher. Third, create an equal and opposite emotional thought-picture. Take the time to experience the opposite emotion fully, using the full panoply of your senses, so it matches the power of the original emotion.

"If this is clear to you, we'll continue with lesson two of the mind: accepting oneself as complete. Please listen carefully, as this point is easily misunderstood. The third density is not the place for you to overrule your dominant personality attributes. For the most part, these were carefully selected for you— and by you—prior to your incarnation. When you use your egoic self to judge your personality and then try to make changes so you are better liked or more successful or more effective, you simply load your chakras with more distortions. As you so correctly said, the object is balance, not change. You will come to realize that you are already complete, irrespective of how your personalities manifest within your illusion. All this transpires of its own accord—a natural by-product of your efforts."

"Wow," Larry said, "this sounds like the opposite of what everyone else is trying to do. All those self-help books and seminars are chock full of advice on how to improve yourself and your life. And you're telling me that all they're doing is rearranging the deck chairs on the Titanic? No wonder people can't make sense out of their lives."

"It's another paradox," the Voice said. "If you really want to affect major change in yourself, simply become more in tune with what you already are. All that's required is balancing the skewed polarity within your chakras. I promise, you will be amazed at the results!

"This brings us to lesson three of the mind—seeing the completeness of others. The gift of this exercise is that every entity you encounter becomes, for that moment, your personal guru.

"When you note an emotion or thought arising in another, follow the same three steps outlined earlier regarding yourself: First, recognize the energy as coming from an energy blockage within a chakra. Then, view that emotion as a valued teacher for both yourself and the other entity. Finally, in your own mind, create an equal and opposite thought or emotion and silently project, into the situation on the other's behalf.

"The key to this exercise is remembering that each entity you meet has its own continuum of I's. That is, when you meet another, do not merely acknowledge the beauty of physical form, the pleasantness of personality, or such outer trappings as financial condition, intellect, and social status. These are merely the outer shell. Consider that each of that entity's traits—both positive and negative—were put in place to help teach it lessons, just as you are learning from us now.

"The next aspect of this lesson requires you to visualize the other entity as your other self, complete with its own Higher Self, its own circumstances, and its own challenges. Appreciate that each of your fellow humans is making a unique experiential contribution to the All That Is, just as you are."

"Do you mean I should view everyone as my brother and sister?" Larry asked.

"No, this looking is deeper. You view the other not as separate but as an aspect of yourself. Acknowledge the Oneness in everyone you encounter. Realize that when any third-density entity—whether an individual, a group, or a nation—takes action, it is generally the egoic self interacting with the distortions in its own chakras. The other entity, like you, is being challenged to awaken and is trying, as best it can, to navigate through its own blockages.

"The exercise's purpose is twofold: first, it allows you to emotionally detach from any emotionally charged situation, and second, it teaches Compassion as you realize that all entities share the same path with you."

"I suppose that makes it easy to forgive some pretty dumb actions," Larry said.

"Like that statement?" Zeus interjected.

There was a brief pause, providing Larry a chance to recover from Zeus's latest thunderbolt.

"From now on, you might choose your words more carefully," the Voice suggested. "As you progress toward a higher quotient of Light/Love energy, your words take on increasing power. Be advised that from now on, what you think, what you say, and what you do will send greater and greater ripples throughout the All That Is. With Awareness comes responsibility. I strongly suggest you take a moment and balance your last words."

After several moments of silence Larry spoke only one word, "Sorry."

"Not at all," the Voice said. "Your apology is accepted, though hardly necessary. You simply spoke through the distortion of a restricted chakra, which, at this stage of your development, is to be expected. Your course of growth will continue to provide opportunities for learning until you no longer need them. Rather than sensing remorse, perhaps you can see the value of feeling joy in this moment?"

"When you put it that way, I guess I do," Larry replied. "Thanks for your forgiveness. I really appreciate it."

"Whatever gave you the idea that you've been forgiven?" the Voice responded. "Your new age movement so venerates this overused concept, yet few realize what it actually means."

"Doesn't forgiveness come from the Bible—when you are wronged you must turn the other cheek?"

"Not unless you want two matching cheeks," Zeus interjected. "Larry, you've uncovered yet another paradox of this illusion. Forgiveness does not really exist. It's an impossible act to perform."

"What do you mean?" Larry asked. Surprisingly, the What-What bird was nowhere to be heard.

"When you felt we were poking fun at you—didn't part of you feel hurt, victimized?"

"Yes."

"Didn't that part feel you were wronged and judge us as rather callous?"

"As I remember it, yes."

"And yet you were willing to continue listening to the Voice's discourse. Does that mean you forgave us?"

"Yes, I suppose it does. I don't seem to be harboring any ill feelings about it."

"No, Larry, that's not it at all," the Voice said. "Something else took place. Had you not addressed the distortions in your chakras, you would not have been able to balance the energies causing the feeling of hurt. Once you used the first lesson to create alternative points of view, and realized the intent of our remarks and the source of your reaction, the entire emotional content was drained from the incident. What was left to forgive?"

"Nothing."

"Correct," the Voice said. "Now you've got it. Forgiveness is not an act, it's a state. Forgiveness is simply the suspension of judgment. When you go back to an incident and balance its polarities, all emotional content is removed. You are no longer invested in defending or being stuck in a single point of view, so you are free to appreciate multiple perceptions simultaneously. In the process, all judgment is suspended. Where there is no judgment, there is nothing to forgive.

"This principle lies at the very heart of the third lesson of the mind. When you have fully balanced the emotional and conceptual content of any interaction, there is no longer the impetus to judge. When people offer therapies allowing you to look back at past incidents and forgive yourself and others, they are on the right track. But, unfortunately, they have not gone deep enough. What is the value of simply saying, 'I have been profoundly wronged by my parents—or my wife or the IRS—but I forgive them?'"

"Another Band-Aid on a festering wound?" Larry offered.

"Precisely so," the Voice said. "There are other exercises one can perform in the realm of the mind, but these will do for now. If you're still interested, we can proceed with the lessons of the body."

"Yes, please, go on."

"Very well, then. Lesson one of the body is the balancing of love and wisdom. The current intensification of the instreaming Light/Love energy provides an excellent opportunity for refining one's attitudes toward sexual interactions. This area of contact between humans has become so heavily distorted precisely because it offers such a rich potential for experiencing the I's of infinity.

"Craving another's company to combat the feeling of loneliness, wanting to connect, to touch, caress, make love, wanting to join as one—these are products of natural bodily functions, yet they carry so much emotional overlay that they are a prime source of chakra blockages. Be aware of the thoughts concerning sexuality and balance them as they arise, using the process you have just learned. Try to distinguish between their physical aspect and their deeper, more sacramental meaning. If one is willing to make the effort, great wisdom can be gleaned from exploring the allure of sexuality.

"This lesson asks that you express physical love with Awareness. Be mindful of the exquisite entanglement that enfolds both entities into a powerful moment. Be aware of the suspension of time and local reality. Go beyond the perception of the senses, beyond the flow of hormones, and use the sacredness of love to catch a fleeting glimpse of the reflection of the All That Is. Do you not see a similar magnetic attraction between two entities in love, the tide's response to the call of the moon, and the return of all Creation to Oneness?"

"I think I do," Larry mused. "The one thing I miss most about my relationship with Marianne is intimacy. We actually did merge when we made love; all our local distortions were overridden and the two of us rocketed off the planet. I always got the feeling that at the moment of absolute connection, we became gods honoring each other's divinity. It was so perfectly complete, I always wondered why I couldn't sustain the feeling more than three minutes after orgasm. Now that I'm learning more about how the mind works, I can see why sex is so addictive—and so easily misunderstood."

"Sexual expression is one of the greatest opportunities for gaining Awareness," the Voice continued. "Much of human-kind's confusion in this realm is due to religious and societal taboos that denigrate the physical form.

"This brings us to lesson two of the body—understanding the connection between the body and the mind. The state of the body is very much a product of the mind. This is true of all thought, and especially of those decisive conclusions that embed themselves as energetic distortions in the chakras.

"It is productive to tune your attention to how emotions affect different parts of your body. With practice, you will be able to observe which thought patterns cause the stomach to tighten, which cause the back to hurt or the head to ache. You can then neutralize these sensations by balancing the causative emotions with their opposites.

"The third-density body is subject to the immutable ener-getic geometry of the illusion. That means it has a dual nature. In this incarnation, you are a male. However, every biological male is also part female, just as every female is also part male. You need not physically express the opposite sexual bias, but you must become aware of its innate presence in yourself and balance it within your energy centers. Explore first one and then the other gender within you so you can understand the jewels each presents."

"So tell me, sport, how do you feel about having both 'him' and 'her' alive and well within you?" Zeus teased.

Larry smiled. He was intrigued by the thought of people carrying the opposite gender within them—being complete in themselves—yet still finding such richness in union with that opposite outside themselves. Zeus's question opened up endless limerick possibilities. After a few moments to collect his thoughts, Larry said:

You tell me that, strictly between us,
Although I'm endowed with a penis,
I come from the stars
Being programmed by Mars
With a little assistance from Venus.

The three of them, for the first time, laughed together, and Larry felt, despite his awkward attempts at balancing, as if he'd indeed scored another point or two.

"Ahem," the Voice asked, "shall we resume?"

"This brings us to the last lesson, the one regarding spirit. Larry, may I inquire whether any part of you is still interested?"

"Oh yes, Great One. Please, do go on," said Larry, obviously still under the influence of the moment of humor. "I eagerly await your venerable and most glorious wisdom." He'd never known he could speak with a Punjabi accent until now. This was getting very, very interesting.

"And so I shall, Little One," the Voice responded gently. "This lesson concerns contacting Infinite Intelligence. Unlike the others, it is not a process that the mind can consciously direct. Rather, it will flow organically once you have mastered the earlier exercises. Spirit's function is to integrate the upward yearning of an entity's mind/body energy with the powerful down-pouring of Infinite Intelligence—much as the streamer stroke reaches up to meet the leader stroke descending from above to form lightning.

"The spirit portion of your being is relatively free of the chakras' distortions, so it can be a pathway to the Infinite Intelligence and the higher aspects of your I's. When your body and mind have become receptive by clearing chakras through the practice of the earlier exercises, your spirit operates as a direct shuttle between your third-density self and your Higher Self and beyond.

"The purpose of this subtle lesson is to help you remember who you really are. The awakening occurs gradually, as you practice holding the viewpoint of a detached observer. In time, you succeed in piercing the illusion's glitter and deception and become aware of the core essence of your being.

"In the process of balancing your chakras, you will garner three important benefits: one, you consciously participate in the flow of Creation; two, you become aware of the awesome power of the Love/Light energy permeating All That Is; and three, you fully recognize yourself as the Creator. These major break-throughs are requisites for you to make the decision that will shape your existence for the next several million years."

I don't know what your destiny will be,
But one thing I do know:
The only ones among you who will be really happy
Are those who have sought
And found how to serve.

— Albert Schweitzer

CHAPTER 20

The Way Out

"You make it sound so permanent," Larry said, obviously concerned about the grave implications of choosing incorrectly.

"Only in terms of time," the Voice laughed. "As you will soon learn, it all comes together in the end. However, you are now at the crossroads. You must choose one of two paths prior to leaving the third density. Both paths use the same creative force of Love/Light energy; only the vectors differ. One allows you to serve Creation by dedicating your Consciousness to the service of other beings. The other also serves the All That Is, but the energy stream is reversed so it focuses your Consciousness on serving yourself and controlling other beings. In dualistic terms, the first is the positive path and the second is the negative. One is not better than the other. Despite what all your moral and ethical codes have to say, "right" and "wrong" have significance only in the polarized world of the third density. Once you have transcended the illusion, you begin to perceive that both positive and negative experiences allow the Oneness to know itself more completely."

"If that's all it takes, why hasn't everyone made a choice?"

"Oh, they have," the Voice said, "though unconsciously. In fact, an entity is usually well along on its chosen path by the time it becomes aware of its choice. However, certain conditions need to be met before the choice has meaning. To move on to the fourth density via the path of service to others, over 50 percent of every thought, word, and deed must be for the benefit of another entity, rather than your personal self. I'm afraid the overwhelming majority of humanity still has a long way to go before achieving that goal."

"Does that mean they've chosen the negative path?" Larry asked.

"Hardly. The negative path is extremely demanding, and few in human history have walked it successfully. It requires at least 95 percent of every thought, word, and deed to be for the benefit of oneself rather than another. As you might imagine, this demands a level of focus and discipline almost unknown on your planet."

"Wow. Can you name some people I might have heard of who accomplished this feat?" Larry asked.

"We do so reluctantly, as it is not our purpose to influence your view of history. However, some examples may shed light on the choice each third-density being is required to make. Taras Bulba, Genghis Khan, and Rasputin were all masters of the negative path. They had sufficient recall of some ancient Atlantean techniques for manipulating chakra distortions to directly access the gateway to Infinite Intelligence. This afforded them a concentrated source of Light/Love energy, which they used to manifest apparently paranormal abilities to influence others and control them. Given their intense focus on service to themselves, they spared no effort in personal discipline to maximize their access to this gateway."

"What happened to them?"

"They are currently enhancing and refining their abilities on a fourth-density negative planet."

"Does anyone on our planet today have that kind of negative focus?" Larry asked.

"That is not a question we will answer," the Voice said. "If we did, it would likely cause you to take action or make decisions you might not otherwise. That would be a clear violation of your Free Will. This type of information, like the answers to some of your other questions, is stored in the so-called hidden files of the Akashic records. Do you see now why these archives are not readily available? To access them requires a Light/Love quotient somewhat higher than what you have presently attained. However, you have come a long way in the last few days, and we shouldn't be surprised if you arrive at the necessary level of Awareness before leaving Joshua Tree.

"Do you have any more questions on this subject before we move on to discuss the higher chakras?"

"Yes," Larry replied, "Just one. What makes one person pick the positive path while another picks the negative path?"

"It seems to be in the nature of duality—some entities instinctively gravitate toward the light, others favor the darkness. To cite a simple example: we've noticed that some third-density beings prefer daytime activities and greet each morning with anticipation, taking delight in the sun and the wonders of nature. Others prefer going to sleep in the small hours of the morning after partying and partaking of the gifts of the night. The logos has created your illusion such that all these possibilities are available. Choice, based on preference and predilection, naturally favors the path offering the experiences that interest the entity most. When an entity becomes aware enough to exercise Free Will, it may choose to explore more deeply along its present course, or, in rare instances, it may switch to the alternative."

"Got it," Larry said. "I can't imagine what it would take for me to choose the opposite path."

"How 'bout a simple majority?" Zeus quipped.

"No way, Doggie-San. In this election, there's only one vote and I don't plan on casting it into a cesspool."

Turning his attention back to their host, Larry said, "If I'm to set my course for the next few million years, I'd best arm myself with all the information I can. Please continue with your explanation of the chakras and the other densities. I believe you were about to discuss the fourth chakra, which, as I understand, is in the area of the heart and corresponds to the fourth density?"

"Exactly so," the Voice said. "The fourth chakra is indeed centered in the heart, and it vibrates with the green ray of compassionate, unconditional love, which is tuned to the calling of the All That Is. For those who have chosen the path of service to others, this chakra opens the gateway to the fifth and sixth chakras. It is the springboard to the Infinite.

"However, on this planet, blockages in the lower three chakras tend to distort the operation of the heart chakra. If physical survival—a first-chakra issue—is an entity's primary area of concern, it is nearly impossible to develop the heart chakra, as the first and fourth chakras' primary energetic vectors are diametrically opposed. This is why entities absorbed in their own physical needs have difficulty manifesting unconditional compassion for others.

"The second chakra houses the entity's computations regarding its identity. When it is blocked, one has difficulty expressing personal power. One is also inclined to treat other entities as slaves or chattel, not as an individuated expressions of All That Is.

"The third chakra is the repository of issues involving ego and how the entity relates to groups and the society in which it lives. Restrictions in this energy vortex lie at the root of most political and religious hostilities now manifesting on your planet. Distortions here delude the entity into thinking its own group can dominate others by divine right and force nonbelievers to adopt its way of thinking."

"I'm puzzled," Larry said. "If getting into the fourth density requires balancing the fourth chakra, and if that means relinquishing self-centeredness and egotism, how can anyone on the negative path ever move on to the fourth density?"

"Our compliments, Larry," the Voice responded, "a very insightful question indeed. One who is balancing the fourth chakra cannot possibly walk the negative path. Those on that path consciously bypass this chakra altogether. Instead, they use certain ancient and arcane arts—as we just mentioned regarding Rasputin and the others—to open the gateway to the sixth chakra directly."

"Thank you," Larry said. "For some reason, I'd like to learn more about what drives some people to so completely disregard the welfare of others."

"In due time, we expect you will," the Voice responded. "But first we'll explore the fifth and sixth chakras, which is where experiences encountered in the third density can be linked to universal energies and principles. The fifth chakra, which is located in the throat, vibrates with a blue ray. It is a harmonic of the fifth density—the density of light, or wisdom. Third-density beings on your planet do not need to do much work on this center. Once they have cleared and balanced the fourth chakra, they can enter the fifth chakra almost immediately. This center's gift is in the realm of communication. As it opens, one feels great freedom, for one is accessing the part of one's self that is free of the illusion's restrictions. This leads to profound acceptance, which, in turn, enables one to communicate freely and allow others to express themselves without judging them.

"The throat chakra is also the first in which the entity encounters a palpable outpouring of personal energy that greets the inpouring from Infinite Intelligence moving upward through the lower energy vortices. Correspondingly, those who are blocked in this chakra often cannot grasp the essence of their own spiritual nature and frequently display difficulty accepting input from others. They feel a vague sense of alienation and separation. Deep inside, they are aware that by surrendering to the illusion of space/time they have become strangers in their own lives. There is a sense of living in constant shadow, waiting to emerge into a new, as-yet-undefined reality. This undiagnosed malaise infects the vast majority of humanity and is the root cause of much of the angst you and your fellow humans have been feeling in recent years. It expresses itself daily in random acts of belligerence that affect individuals, nations, and the ecological system of your planet alike."

"How do we get people to realize they are part of a larger universe?" Larry asked. "How do we get them to see that there really is no separation—that we are all one?"

"How, indeed," the Voice answered. "Larry, as you are learning, there is no simple, universal answer to these questions. The change, when at last it arrives, comes to each entity instantaneously, like a lightning bolt from the blue, acknowledging that it has earned the rite of passage into a higher state of Awareness. And there are no shortcuts. As we said earlier, each seeker must take the full curriculum.

"If you purposefully engage in the exercises we set forth earlier, the rewards will surely follow. If you wish to help humanity, you must begin with yourself. If you wish to lead, do so only by example. Have no doctrine, no thought of outcome, no expectations, no purpose save to open doors so others may follow—if they choose."

Larry sat in silence, allowing the words to percolate, syllable by syllable. Here was yet another paradox to add to his ever-growing collection: the greatest way to affect others is by focusing action solely on oneself.

Zeus smiled quietly, witnessing the labored contortions of a human mind attempting to deal with affairs of the heart. A wondrous tool, the mind, but so completely unsuited to the task at hand!

"This brings us to the sixth chakra," the Voice said, disrupting the two passing trains of thought, "the indigo-ray vortex of energy often called the inner eye, or third eye. It is located low in the center of the forehead. This energy center, like the heart, is a gateway to the Infinite Intelligence. However, the energy streaming into this center is considerably less distorted than the energy entering the heart, and thus it offers direct access to the realm of conscious cocreativity. Mastery of this gateway is not to be undertaken lightly; it is only for committed adepts on the positive path who have traversed the fourth and fifth chakras, or seekers of the negative path making the leap from the third density directly. The secret teachings of the ancient mystery schools instructed initiates how to open up portals in this chakra otherwise sealed to third-density entities.

"For those on the positive path who do not aspire to mastery, but seek only to clear the blockages and balance the energies in their chakras, this vortex can be activated simply by unconditionally accepting oneself not only as a polarized yet balanced being but also as a true co-creator. This realization comes only in the absence of both ego and false modesty, once the work of clearing and balancing the lower five chakras is complete."

"How can one be certain that the work on the chakras *is* complete?" Larry asked.

"In your mental universe," Zeus interjected, "certainty exists only in the dictionary, somewhere between 'cerebrum' and 'cervix.' What you're seeking has little to do with the head. You need to go a lot deeper, Larry. Your greatest ally is not the false comfort of certainty but Awareness."

"What do you mean by that?" Larry asked.

"Unfortunately, *goomba*, Awareness is a slippery concept, eluding the mind's efforts to capture it completely. It refers to more than realization or knowledge or a state of informed alertness. Think of it as an energetic link connecting the myriad O-worlds in which various parts of you reside. It deals with that state of multidimensional perception in which you bypass the restrictions of the mind to absorb simultaneous streams of information from divergent and often dichotomous sources."

"Huh?"

"Just having a bit of fun," Zeus retorted. "Best you forget the words and try to grasp the meaning of Awareness with your heart. As you gradually unblock and clear each of the chakras, purer flows of information will enter your being, and the full implication of Awareness will come clear to you. No doubt you'll find this easier to experience than to understand.

"The three major impediments to Awareness are addressed in considerable detail in the *Interdimensional Survival Manual*. Allow me to offer a simple abstract:

> *Immediately upon entering a third-density illusion such as Earth, you will be confronted by three Great Temptations:*
>
> *1. The compulsion to compare*
> *2. The overwhelming urge to judge*
> *3. The need to understand*

"So unless you want to be dashed against the rocks . . . have a herd of wild elephants stampede across your coccyx . . . be stuck in the eye by a red-hot poker . . . pecked at by a descent of demented woodpeckers. . . ."

"Okay, already," Larry said, grateful for Zeus's wealth of knowledge and his impeccable sense of timing—always shifting energies when one threatened to overwhelm. "I get your drift!"

"Okay, already," Zeus repeated, mocking Larry's attempt at humor as he addressed their host. "Did you hear what he just said? Do my ears deceive me, or was that Mr. Smarty-Pants brushing me off just because I got a little lost in the kaleidoscopic implications of submitting to the three major no-no's?"

With an abrupt change of tone, Zeus turned his attention to Larry. "Just trying to make a point, kiddo. This is important stuff; that's why I make light of it. There's no end to the mischief the Great Temptations cause you guys. Of the three, I would submit that the last is the most relevant at the moment. When it comes to learning how to think with your heart, it's best to simply recognize that the data comes from disparate dimensions and let them download into your consciousness. Here's the key: Do *not* try to integrate this information with anything you think you already know. Above all, do *not* try to synthesize it into a common, cohesive thread. Other than that, enjoy! As the Italians say: *Chi più sa, meno crede.*"

"What, in God's name, are you talking about?" Larry asked.

"E-z. I 'splain you," Zeus said, adopting a thick Italian accent. "De Italians, dey know. Watt'a dey say is'a simple: 'De more one'a knows, de less'a one'a believes!' I no'a kid you. Even in Italy de know dat when'a infomazione, she comm'a in, you just'a file. More infomazione comm'a in, you just'a fil'a some more. Soon'a or lat'a you get'a to read what you fil'a. It no gott'a make sense. Solo importante you just'a fil'a good. *Capisci?* Si, I'm a'think now you got it. Is a piec'a cake. You lik'a de cake?"

"Zeus, you are certifiably nuts. I hardly understood a word of what you just said."

"Ah, now you've *really* got it! Just stay with it. Don't seek anything more. I promise, it—whatever *it* is—will all make sense long after you have left here and no longer care a whit about it.

"Now that you're up to speed on the absurdity of treasuring certainty, perhaps we can deal with your question, which, if I may say, was quite perceptive, once the malignancy of certainty was excised. *Voce grande,* you can take it from here."

"*Mille grazie,* Maestro Zeus!" the Voice answered. "Larry, you asked how one knows when the work of clearing and balancing the chakras is complete. This, as you once phrased it, is like asking 'How long is a piece of string?' Instead of using the mind to direct the process, allow the process to direct you. As you do the suggested set of exercises, you will move up the line of chakras to the green energetic domain of the heart, and from there through the blue center into the chambers of the indigo ray. There will come a time during your sojourn in these rarified realms when you will be unflinchingly aware of yourself as one with the Creator. You will know—well beyond the feeble need for temporal certainty—because you will consciously merge with the Infinite Intelligence and be swept up by an unspeakable limitless joy, not unlike your experience last night at Inspiration Peak. It is this that makes the sixth chakra the ultimate stepping stone into the next paradigm."

"What about the seventh chakra?" Larry asked. "Isn't that the most powerful of all?"

The Voice and Zeus roared with laughter.

"What's so funny now?" Larry asked, assuming he must have said something particularly stupid.

"Oh, give it a rest," Zeus said, sensing Larry's twinge of self-denigration. "Don't expect to describe the top of the mountain in perfect detail while you're sitting in a cave at its base. Actually, you're doing far better than either of us ever expected. Every so often you toss in some comic relief. It reminds us that despite your flashes of brilliance, you are still very much under the illusion's influence. Consider the implications of what you just asked, and try to rephrase it more precisely."

"I just remember reading somewhere that the crown chakra is a thousand-petaled lotus that opens up to Cosmic Consciousness and that this opening process is the object of meditation and yoga and so on. Why is that so funny?"

"It amuses us," the Voice said, "because of the manner in which you perceive it. The seventh chakra is not in the same energetic parameter as the others." Discerning Larry's mounting confusion, the Voice continued before What-What could speak. "Consider a harmonious chord made up of six perfectly pitched notes. If the notes represent the balanced vibrations of the six chakras, the seventh chakra is simply the sound of the chord as its six composite tones are played.

"Attempting to directly strengthen the crown chakra by meditation or other practices is like trying to alter the shape of a projected image by painting on the screen.

"When it comes to matters of balance, power can often be more detrimental than helpful. If you want a pleasant, harmonious chord—or in the case of the crown chakra, the most balanced shade of violet—would you increase the volume of one note while ignoring the others?"

"I see what you're driving at," Larry responded. "It *is* all about balance. Each chakra has to be cleared of its blockages, and all of them have to be opened to a comparable level. If one is too strong or too weak, it affects what happens at the crown chakra. So if I go sit in a cave and try to experience unconditional love, or if I try to train myself to act holy, it only overactivates my fourth chakra at the expense of the others. If I haven't finished working on my lower chakras first, my crown chakra's going to show up as an unruly swirl of colors, reflecting my unbalanced condition."

"From your present vantage point," the Voice said, "you can appreciate in more precise terms how expanding the Awareness proceeds. Your mystics describe it as awakening the kundalini serpent from its coiled slumber in the first chakra. However, we prefer, once again, the metaphor of lightning.

"The Infinite Intelligence always seeks to express its Oneness with each entity in the Creation. So also, each aspect of Creation seeks to receive the Oneness more fully in its Consciousness. Thus the plot of the Great Play is set and the curtain rises.

"Infinite Intelligence is the leader stroke, eternally reaching down to you, calling forth your essence, unabashedly revealing itself in the Sacred Dance. Its energies enter through the root chakra at the base of your spine, the 'negative,' or south pole of your energy body. Until it is cleared, this energy center will absorb most of the impulse and emit only a weak, pseudo-streamer stroke in response. However, once you have unblocked and balanced the first center, the universal energy begins to flow upwards, to be met by and react with the spiraling energy descending from the crown chakra. As the clearing work is completed in the lower chakras, the meeting point of these two energies moves up the spine. When energy from the base chakra finally rises through the entire spinal column, the leader stroke of the Infinite Intelligence reaches the sixth chakra, where it is joined by the fully charged streamer stroke descending from the crown. The two join in Oneness. The portal to the next density is flung open, awaiting the decision of the awakened being to enter."

Chapter 21

Back into the Void

"That completes our brief tour of the chakras," the Voice said. "We cannot overstate their importance as stepping stones for evolving beyond the duality of the third density. If you are up to it, we will continue with the Universal Myth of Creation."

"Please do," Larry responded. "I'm especially interested in the fourth density, since that's where the planet and its inhabitants are supposed to go."

"In theory you are quite right. You were all meant to evolve in unison. Unfortunately, given the current state of affairs and the inherent right of each entity to exercise its version of Free Will, a large harvest does not appear likely in the few years you have left. However, nothing can be assumed. You have already confounded the odds with your progress over the past twenty years. Given your peoples' resiliency, and the present unfettered access to information and extradimensional assistance, anything is possible. After all," the Voice added with a touch of humor, "each of you is a god, albeit somewhat handicapped by a self-prescribed planetary dose of Prozac.

"The time has come in this extraordinary relay race to pass the baton to those who have entered the illusion in human form and are well on their way to recovery from the Veil of Forgetting. As Zeus might say, 'You're the man!'"

"I'll bark to that," Zeus affirmed.

"Come on, guys," Larry said, "give me a break. You keep telling me that I've volunteered to take responsibility for the entire planet. What do you expect one person to do?"

"Nothing. Everything," Zeus replied. "It's all the same. In fact, what you do has nothing to do with it. Remember Rocky's words: 'Don't matter where you've run, gotta come back from afar. Who cares whatcha' done? What counts is whatcha' are.' What do you think these lines mean?"

Larry remained silent as he contemplated Zeus's question. "Damn! Who would've believed that little raccoon clown could be so wise, or that his silly rap song could contain such depth of meaning?"

Zeus, in an unusually grave tone, asked, "Do you have any idea who that raccoon clown *really* is?"

"No, I don't. Who *is* he?"

"You have made the all-too-common mistake of judging a book by its cover," Zeus responded. "Would you have listened more closely had Rocky come in his true form? Would you be more impressed if he had descended in a chariot of flame and towered over the boulders with a twenty-foot sword flashing bolts of purple lightning?"

"Do you mean . . . Rocky is the Archangel Michael?"

"No, Larry, I didn't say he is—or isn't. I only asked, if Rocky had taken on that persona, would you have listened more closely?"

"Of course I would've."

"Ah, the three temptations rear their ugly heads yet again! Why are you always so quick to judge?" Zeus let his question sink in before continuing. "It's time to clear the cobwebs, little one. Over the past few days you've received a considerable instreaming of wisdom, lovingly aided by people, animals, trees, rocks, even sunsets. What is the one thing you are still unable to see?"

"God?"

"Precisely," Zeus said. "Go on."

"I can say the words 'God is all things,' but when it comes to really knowing what they mean, I seem to fall a bit short."

"And?"

"And . . . unless I can get past my deeply ingrained belief that form outranks substance, I will be forever locked into this density?"

"And?"

"And . . . I will remain an intellectual and material snob, failing to acknowledge the true worth of every being . . . every plant . . . every animal . . . every blade of grass . . . grain of sand. . . . "

"Oh, can it," Zeus interjected. "You're making me sick. You still don't get it, do you?"

"*What? What?* . . . *What? What?*" The unmistakably cry came right on cue.

"Help!" Larry said. "I thought . . . Oh, never mind. I don't know what I think any more."

"Good. Let's take it one step at a time. Look back over the past few days. What do Junie, Rocky, your current mentor, and I all have in common?"

"You are all my teachers?"

"Yes, but where I'm asking you to go is even more basic. Let's expand the list a bit. Add: the sky, the motel we stayed in last night, the left front tire on your car, the classified section of the *Los Angeles Times* in which you saw the ad for my adoption, 9/11, the Council of Nine, starving kids in Rwanda, your silly collection of cookie fortunes from the Peking Noodle Company. What do these all have in common?"

"*What? What? . . . What? What?*" The bird's second appearance within a minute confirmed that Larry had fallen deep into the abyss of confusion. Yet even he knew this was a wonderful sign, an opportunity for total destruction of old beliefs, making way for the Phoenix to arise anew.

"I don't know," Larry said weakly.

"Of course you know!" Zeus responded. "Don't settle. Go deeper. Ask for help."

Zeus watched as Larry focused on his breath to quiet his mind, beginning his descent into the delicious realm of nothingness. Zeus silently invoked a sacred symbol of Kofutu, one of the twelve teachings in the Mantura system of arcane study practiced by initiates in Atlantis. Within seconds, a holograph of the ancient image appeared above Larry's head and began pulsing slowly, radiating a glowing orb that eventually enveloped Larry in a sheath of golden-white light. Larry found himself transported once again into the Void. In this place, where the mind could not follow, his confusion, and all else, melted away. There was only peace. Then eternity. And ultimately, nothing. This was the domain of the Phoenix's great cosmic fire into which the soul descends and dies, only to be reborn again.

In time, Larry returned, exuding a remarkable clarity, completely free of doubt and confusion. When at last he spoke, his words were strong and clear. "The common thread is *me*. All the things you listed are present in my personal universe."

"Good job, kiddo," Zeus said. "Welcome back. It seems your short ventures into never-never land agree with you. You might want to schedule them more often.

"You see, you shortchange yourself when you settle for the first scrap of information that floats along. Somewhere within you the answer always lies. The only obstacle is your unwillingness to search for it. Unlike the hapless, *Gerris remigis*, you are not a water bug doomed to spend its lifetime striding across the pond's surface, oblivious to the rich treasures lying just below its feet. For you—and others who so choose—there's always more.

"Give it another go. Dive in as deep as you dare," Zeus challenged Larry. "What do you and every thing in your universe have in common? This time I won't assist you. You are now able to enter into the higher realms on your own. Simply shift the point from which you are viewing into your sixth chakra and seek to commune with the Infinite Intelligence."

Larry once more used the breath to align his Consciousness —this time with the frequency of the Great Bank of Cosmic Awareness. What he encountered defied cognition. His sanity, teetering on the edge of coherence, reeled and balked like a horse refusing a jump. Regrouping, he released the need to grasp at the fragments of reality disintegrating before him like snowflakes sublimated by fire. Directed only by some eternal instinct, he pressed on, eventually emerging into a boundless roil of realities snaking through each other in endless motion.

A sea of possibilities, ceaselessly touching, changing, and breaking away. . . .

Every possible thought playing itself out on the screen of apparent reality, fading, and merging. . . .

The immeasurable bank of collective experience, repository of the Universe's gifts to Creation, yet occupying no space and independent of time, incomprehensible. . . .

Larry merged with the All That Is. Yet the ocean was but a single drop within him. Pure paradox, poised at the brink of annihilation. This time he did not blink, and the Infinite Intelligence opened to reveal the prize he sought.

Zeus and the Voice waited quietly. Both understood the magnitude and potential danger of Larry's inner journey. Any sudden noise or dissonant energy could snap Larry back prematurely, fracturing his essence. It was vital that he returned only when he was ready, when his Consciousness had fully cohered again.

Eventually, Larry reappeared in their midst. His voice seemed strained, as if speaking for the first time after decades of silence. "They *are* me," Larry said. He was stunned by the simplicity of these three one-syllable words juxtaposed against the immensity they implied.

"Bravo, my friend," Zeus said. "You've been allowed a peek behind the scenes of the Great Mystery. You've seen first hand how the smoke and mirrors are placed to create the illusions of experience. In the process, you've perceived that in the Oneness of the All That Is, everything in your personal universe is a reflected aspect of yourself—Rocky, Patchuliti, me, even the tires of your car."

"Interesting thought," Larry mused. "If anything happens to me, you all disappear—poof!"

"'Cept for one small thing, ol' buddy," Zeus responded. "You're also only a player on my stage. If my electricity gets shut down, the curtain descends on you just as fast. So we'd better take good care of each other. 'Cause if I don't make it, you're in big trouble. And if you don't make it, I can kiss my uncropped tail goodbye.

"Unfortunately, human types have yet to get the message. You guys have a knack of making a mountainous mess out of the tiniest molehill. Take a look at your own life: every difficulty was ultimately blamed on some external circumstance. Your parents weren't perfect, Marianne didn't give you what you needed, work is too restrictive, world leaders are too self-serving, and the weather isn't exactly as ordered. Now you know the common denominator is you. Despite the challenges of all your experiences, the only *real* relationship you will ever have is with yourself."

"Third-density Consciousness is enshrouded in a conundrum within an enigma within a paradox. The illusion masterfully keeps you from knowing who you really are. Virtually every personal relationship within the lower, egoic realm is driven by projections. How can anyone exercise Free Will when each decision is born of belief or preference? Once you grasp this, you begin to appreciate the source of human suffering, why even the great among you are so easily driven to their knees. Cultivate compassion, be more gentle on yourself and others. Remember, all beings with whom you interact are the center of their own personal universes, projecting their needs and distortions onto you even as you project yours onto them. Is there a movie, play, or piece of fiction that doesn't try to choreograph this curious dance?

"So, now that you have uncovered one of the secrets of the Great Magician, are you more or less impressed with the show?"

"Wow! You've got to be kidding," Larry responded. "This is the most amazing show in the world, and I get to star in it as well as write it, produce it, direct it, and sit in the audience. I am the play within the play within the play . . . an infinite series of Chinese boxes each holding a surprise. God is all things and I . . . I am God."

"So, then, who is Rocky?" Zeus asked.

Larry laughed and laughed and laughed.

"The rest, as the Talmudists are fond of saying, is merely commentary," Zeus said. "But as long as you're on a roll, and now that you have the Creation's Rosetta Stone in hand, tell me what you know about illusion."

"It doesn't really exist," Larry answered.

"Then what makes it appear to exist?" Zeus asked.

"The charisma of time," Larry said.

"If I didn't know better," Zeus mused, obviously caught up

in Larry's merriment, "I'd swear you've been peeking at my *I-S-M* manual."

"Not me," Larry protested in mock indignation. "Not only have I never seen it, I didn't know it existed until we got here and you started talking. Besides, I think I'm getting the drift of these lessons." After a short pause, he added, "What does the great manual say about all this anyway? I'll let the two of you know if I concur."

"Indeed, my exalted master," Zeus replied. "Your merest wish is my command. I shall be only too pleased to provide the quote. The gods, I am certain, eagerly await your pronouncement in judgment of their work. Praise from one so venerable as you would be prized beyond measure."

"As I recall, what you seek lies in one of the earlier portions. Ah yes, I can see it clearly now, projected onto the screen of my mind:

> *Time is the canvas on which Creation paints the illusions of reality.*

"Huh?"

"Too deep for you? Shall I ask them for the annotated version with little cartoon animal drawings?" Zeus quipped.

"Never mind," Larry responded, his previous bravado slipping quietly away, "I'll work it out for myself, thank you."

"And so you shall," the Voice said, enjoying the rollercoaster ride Zeus had just provided for their student. "Allow us to restate the manual's wisdom, which, we may add, perfectly echoes your earlier insights. Now you know that nothing exists that isn't you and you are that essence of which nothing is made, which simply means that everything isn't . . . though of course it could be.

"When we suggested that it's time for you to take the baton from our outstretched hand, we hardly were referring to the little you. The bigger You must come to the party now. If we may quote that delightful little raccoon once again: 'It doesn't matter where you've run, you have to come back from afar. Who cares what you have done? What counts is what you are.'

"So, what are *you*, Larry?"

"I'm not certain how to answer that question. What I am exceeds any words I could possibly use."

The Voice did not respond, and Larry's last words rippled out well past the horizon of thought and beyond.

It was the Voice who broke the silence. "May we offer a word of advice? It's one thing to operate within your illusion while you are fast asleep. It can be quite another now that you have begun to awaken."

"My God," Larry gasped, "I hadn't thought about that. Talk about being a stranger in a strange land! Any suggestions before you pat me on the behind and return me to the slumbering masses?"

"What a lovely image!" Zeus chimed. "I can see you now, staggering between rows of beds, a ringing alarm clock in one hand and shaking somnolent bodies with the other; Paul Revere with amnesia—a true picture for the ages! Mind if we suggest a better way?"

"Suggest away," Larry replied, by now used to Zeus's offbeat sense of humor. "Off hand, I'd say the job ahead of me is far more than I can handle—at least that's the way it looks from here. I'm going to need all the help I can get."

"Very well, then," the Voice offered. "We offer three simple but powerful tools for dealing with your fellow human beings. The first is: in all interactions that threaten conflict, simply ask yourself, 'What do we have here?' These few words will help contextualize the situation, separating you from the energetic emotional snares that previously would have triggered your personalities.

"The second suggestion is: whenever you feel the beginnings of an emotional reaction, silently say to yourself, 'I need to just remember who I really am and why I chose to be here.' The word 'here' refers to both the situation and the incarnation.

"The third tool is founded upon the realization that nothing in Creation is random. When you find yourself in a challenging circumstance, consider that great effort was expended to bring it about. Each person involved spent his or her entire lifetime gathering unique experiences to bring to the table. Consider each to be your personal teacher and ask, 'What lesson is contained here for me?'"

"Thank you," Larry said. "I'll treasure your advice, and I promise to use it. Of course, it's easy to be detached and aware in your presence. The test will come after I leave here and some joker presses one of my buttons."

"Indeed," the Voice responded. "We will watch with interest how you choose to react.

"Larry, given your new insights into the current state of affairs on your planet and the road ahead, what would you say needs to be changed to help humans transition into the next density?"

"Nothing but me," Larry replied.

"Do you understand what you just said?" the Voice asked.

"Yes, I think this time I *really* do."

"Easy to say. Let's see whether you have seen deeply enough to unlock the files," the Voice said.

"What do you mean?" Larry asked.

"Remember earlier, when you learned that the information surrounding John Lennon's death was hidden in the Akashic records?"

"Yes."

"Do you now understand why it was hidden?"

"I think so," Larry said. "Until I could totally suspend judgment and know that everything is perfect exactly as it is, I would find myself emotionally embroiled, fueled by righteous indignation, trying to fix and save a world that doesn't need fixing and saving. Like a boy scout forcing an elderly lady to cross a street she doesn't want to cross."

"Precisely correct, Larry. Now that you appreciate why these files were locked, can you tell me who hid them?"

"Wow! . . . I did!"

"Clever man. You hid them to save yourself from being permanently distracted—as so many of your fellow humans already are—by the swirls and eddies at the edges of the stream. You knew you had to stay centered. As you have come to understand, there is precious little time left. If you choose to take up a particular cause, it must be picked carefully, as if it were your last battle.

"So let's test how deeply rooted your newly discovered insight really is. What do you know about the death of the famous Beatle?"

"Only what was written in the newspapers and what you told me before. As I recall, you said he was killed on December 8, 1980 by a guy named Mark David Chapman. He was shot just outside his Central Park apartment building in New York City. I have heard that certain people believe the incoming White House team serving Ronald Reagan sanctioned the hit."

"Interesting," the Voice responded. "It is time to see if you can answer your previous question. You've already mastered the process well. Focus your attention through your breath and access the Akashic records. See if the hidden files are now open to you."

Larry stilled his mind and once again reached out to the great Akasha. This time he found no secreted areas of information. It didn't take him long to locate what he was looking for. He returned within a few minutes, a smile of satisfaction illuminating his face. "You're right, of course," he said. "No matter what it looks like to the outside world, no matter who is doing whatever to whom, it is absolutely perfect exactly as it is."

"And what did you find?" the Voice asked.

"Isn't it curious that the killer's names all begin with roman numerals?" was Larry's oblique reply.

CHAPTER 22

The Prime Mandate of Creation

"Enough said," the Voice responded. "Now that you have access to the entire Akasha, you may explore it at your own pace. However, while uncovering deeper levels of information that conflict with your popular histories, do not forego the insight that permitted you full access to this planetary data bank in the first place. Having stated this vital caveat, we suggest that we continue our little jaunt through the densities."

"Bingo," Larry replied playfully, mimicking one of the Voice's favorite expressions. "As I remember, before we so delightfully interrupted ourselves, you were about to divulge the great mysteries of life beyond the pale of the Veil. Please sally forth with your learned exposition of the fourth density. Or, in the immortal words of the fourth estate, 'Press on.'"

Zeus and the Voice groaned their appreciation in unison. Larry was truly coming of age. "And so I shall," the Voice said. "I can think of no more pressing issue that must be shared than the must of the first pressing—the vaunted *première cuvée*—from the great vineyards cultivated in the density of love."

"Truce!" Larry cried.

"Truth," Zeus agreed, speaking with a marked lisp. "Letht we too glibly thacrifithe meaning on the altar of levity."

Speaking of 'truth,'" the Voice said, "what great truth or operating principle must one discern before the decision to serve others can shift from mere concept to effective service? Without a firm grasp of the ramifications of this truth, the transition into the fourth density is nigh on impossible."

"I'm not sure I understand," Larry answered, noticing he was having difficulty transitioning from the ridiculous back to the sublime.

Zeus immediately came to his assistance. "When in doubt, whip it out!"

"What the hell are you talking about?" Larry asked, stunned by Zeus's crude remark.

"Why, the *Interdimensional Survival Manual,* of course. Get your mind out of the gutter, lad. The information you seek is so foundational, it's included in the prologue. Permit me to quote:

> *Each life-form's motivation to action always accords with its perception of the Prime Mandate of Creation.*

"Which is . . . ?" Larry asked.

"Think about it," the Voice interjected. "What is the underlying purpose of Creation?"

"To allow the All That Is to experience itself more completely?"

"Quite so!" the Voice replied. "And as one advances through the densities what is the only thing that really changes?"

"Awareness, the point from which one views?"

"Precisely! Now, relate that to the quote from the *I-S-M.*"

"If I act in accordance with my perception of the Prime Mandate . . . ," Larry mused, speaking more to himself than out loud, "and that perception is simply a function of the point from which I view . . . and I, being part of Creation, also want to experience myself more fully. . . ."

"You're on the right trail, kiddo," Zeus said. "Keep it simple. Focus on the words in Rocky's rap song and look into the I's of infinity."

Larry paused for a moment before speaking. "When I add the I's of infinity to the words from the *I-S-M*, it means that each lower I, operating at the egoic level of the continuum, is nothing more than a stuck viewpoint so in fear of its own annihilation that it clings to its beliefs in order to persist."

"That's partly true," Zeus said. "But, as you so rightly said, the reluctance to let go only manifests in the lower vantage points of the continuum. Something else happens as you move higher. It's called realization of the Law of One."

"Oh, I see," Larry responded. "When you finally perceive that *all* Creation is the expression of the One, you no longer have to preserve the illusion of existence by defending a point of view. It's the clinging that keeps people locked into the lower levels, isn't it?"

"Precisely," the Voice said. "Then what is the Prime Mandate underlying every single action in Creation, whether the doer is an amoeba or an Ascended Master?"

"My God!" Larry exclaimed. "It seems so crass. But damn if it don't explain it all!"

"That it do, good buddy," Zeus quipped. "That's why this piece of information is the only sentence in the entire *Interdimensional Survival Manual* written in capital letters:

> **The Prime Mandate of all Creation is:**
> **WHAT'S IN IT FOR ME?**

"The only change as one advances through the densities is the perception of the word 'me.' At the lowest level of your third density, the concept of *me* is totally wrapped up in the egoic realm. As you evolve along the infinite continuum of your I's, it gradually expands. Eventually your concept of 'me' expands to include other selves as well. Then you can project yourself into another's point of view, and applying the Prime Mandate as an overlay, you'll find every thought, word, and deed is clear as a bell."

"Of course!" Larry said. The point struck home with such force that the words began pouring out of him. "It's a matter of knowing that we are One—that every other being is actually an aspect of myself. Otherwise, service takes on the yoke of martyrdom, sacrificing oneself for the benefit of another. True service, on the other hand, is uplifting and rewarding. When I empower someone, I maximize the Creation's ability to explore itself. I don't need to compete with anyone. In fact, the more others win, the more I win, because they *are* me."

"Larry," the Voice said, "when you *truly* know this—not just as a clever concept but at the core of your being—you will have stepped onto the fourth density's threshold. This realization releases the stranglehold of the lower egoic I. In the process, the illusion of duality, which fuels your wish to wage war in all its myriad expressions, is totally dissolved."

"What do you mean by that? Isn't war simply . . . *war*—a gross expression of frustration, an attempt to assert by might what diplomacy or reason fails to gain?" Larry asked.

"Adequate theory, kiddo, if you're content with nibbling around the edges and mollifying historians and sociologists," Zeus interjected. "But, if you want to gnaw on the bone—which always sounds delicious to me—go deeper where the fare gets meatier. Also remember your experiences with Junie."

"You mean, the battle among my subpersonalities?"

"That's a good place to start," Zeus encouraged.

"From what I learned yesterday," Larry said, "I'd say I have countless voices, each expressing its own view of reality, believing it acts in my best interest. But their views are usually skewed. They're definitely not in harmony with each other."

"Like relationships, families, religions, and nations?" Zeus asked.

"Exactly like that, except that they're all contained within me," Larry answered.

"Just as all those group voices are contained within the larger 'me' comprising the collective illusion on Earth."

"I see what you mean."

"What's the best way to deal with your voices, Larry?"

"Listen to each one as it shows up, honoring its belief that it's expressing its views for my benefit. But because I know that their views are distorted, not let any of them grab control."

"What if you couldn't stop a voice from taking control? What would happen then?" Zeus asked.

"War?"

"Perhaps," Zeus continued. "More likely, a major break in the usual state of tension, in which your primary personalities keep the unwanted voices at bay. As you recall, the apparent equilibrium on the surface simply conceals a cauldron seething with conflict just below.

"You gotta remember, most of us animals can read minds, one way or another. Present company included, I can't recall a single person who doesn't have three or four conflicting thoughts come up surrounding everything they do or say. The careful ones tend to think first, the others usually wish they had. The funny part is to watch how often humans think one thing and say another!

"Everybody loses control at one time or another. Some external circumstance triggers some of the suppressed voices, and they get so agitated that one or more breaks through the lid of the pressure cooker. That causes a sudden shift in personality, an unexpected outburst breaking the dominant pattern."

"Touché," Larry acknowledged. "Sounds too familiar for comfort."

"Ah, I see we have a shiny mirror to gaze into," Zeus said. "Now look even deeper. What creates the illusion of conflict between the voices?"

"I'm afraid that's a bit too deep for me," Larry replied.

"Cut the crap, kiddo. You're way past that knee-jerk self-effacing routine you've been getting away with all your life. You've already shown us that you have access to every piece of information you require, so stop pretending to be a helpless half-wit! Remember how when we first got to Joshua Tree—before you discovered that the voice in your head giving you road directions really came from me—I explained humor as the intersection of two planes of thought meeting unexpectedly at a common point in the now?"

"Yes," Larry said, smarting from the sting of Zeus's words. "Now that I've taken the baton, I guess I'd best crawl out from under the platform and start leading the orchestra."

"You got that right!" Zeus chuckled. "So how would you characterize the moment when the two planes of thought meet?"

"A big collision?"

"Exactly. The bigger the bang, the funnier the joke. The same applies throughout Creation. Imagine throwing two pebbles into a still pond. What happens to the two sets of concentric ripples as they meet each other?"

"Easy," Larry replied, "that's Physics 101. If two same-sized waves meet at a common peak or a common trough, they reinforce each other, the peak or trough gets more prominent. If they meet at exact opposites—a peak coincides with a trough—they cancel each other out and there's a moment of stillness in the pond. No matter how they meet, each wave contributes to what shows up next."

"Precisely so," Zeus said. "Now let's apply this rudimentary view of classical wave interference patterns to thought."

"I don't get you."

"Well, thought is merely the product of electromagnetic wave forms, which behave just like the waves on a pond."

"I get the idea of physical waves reinforcing or canceling each other, but isn't it a bit of a stretch to say the same thing happens with thought patterns?" Larry asked.

"Ah, it turns out you've been well and truly Madonna-ized," Zeus retorted, "very much the material boy, steeped in the heady brew of physical reality. Let me bridge the gap for you. Suppose you trained a video camera on one of the counters in a department store and it recorded one of the employees stealing cash from the register. What thought or emotion would the camera have?"

"Well, none. Cameras simply record. They're machines, so they can't think or have emotions."

"No, Larry. Actually, machines are quite capable of 'thought' and of what some consider quasi-emotion, though on a different level. A particularly 'intelligent,' or sensitive, camera can react to sharpness of focus or intensity of lighting and adjust itself accordingly. But the point is: the camera would never miss a frame because someone stole money. It simply records data without evaluating its meaning. Can you envision a human doing the same?"

"Wow, that would be tough!"

"Not really," Zeus said. "However, one big difference

between a human being and a camera is that the human is Aware that he or she is watching. It is precisely that part of you, the one that's Aware of being aware, that defines your essential nature as Consciousness.

"Mastering the simple exercise of observing is far more important than you might think. It teaches you the one skill required if you expect to increase your level of Awareness and make a difference to others on this planet. But it requires you to engage in one act that most humans find impossible to perform."

"And what, pray tell, is that?"

"You have to show up!" Zeus exclaimed. "It does no good to ramble mindlessly through events, reacting with the same old imprinted patterning. Not only must you bring your body, mind, and spirit to the party, you have to be Aware that you are doing so."

"That sounds almost impossible," Larry protested. "How can I be aware that I am totally present observing an event and not trigger some sort of emotional reaction in one or more of my personalities?"

"Piece of cake," Zeus replied. "Simply disengage from the personalities. It's really a very easy thing to do once you've experienced it. The trick is to be willing to experience something that your mind screams is impossible. That's why it's best to start with a very simple exercise.

"Imagine yourself lying on a hillside in the shade of a tree watching the clouds drift by."

"You mean, notice their colors and try to find angels and spaceships and other shapes as they change?" Larry asked playfully.

"Stop yanking my chain! What I mean is: simply lie there and record without processing. No thoughts, no emotions—just watch the clouds drift through the sky. See the sky's color, but don't allow your mind to identify it as 'blue.' Observe the play of light and shadow. Be present with each cloud's uniqueness without letting your mind say 'cirrus' or 'stratus' or 'spaceship' or any other descriptive label. The only way to do this without your mind drifting is to bring yourself totally into the present moment: you are Aware of yourself lying on the ground looking up into the sky being aware of the clouds. You 'show up.' You see the sky and clouds as if for the very first time and with such completeness that any involuntary intrusion from the past is simply impossible."

"Isn't that like a meditation?" Larry asked.

"Not *like* a meditation—it *is* a meditation. This simple exercise allows you to slip briefly through the crack in linear time and experience the now. When you are well into a meditative state—or if you are an evolved being—an event becomes like a single pebble thrown into your imaginary pond. The ripples flow out from the center without interference. This is the experience of the camera in the department store. It's also the nature of the constantly recording camera that's part of every sentient being."

"What do you mean by that?"

"There's a part—the pure Awareness inherent in every being—that simply records events without comment. As proof, there are documented instances of people in deep hypnosis remembering every detail of a surgical procedure conducted while they were under general anesthesia. It's this constant flow of pure Awareness that informs the universal hologram. It obviously contains a wealth of data the individual could access if they needed it or wanted it.

"However, most humans never consciously link up with this part of themselves. Let's say it's an unenlightened you, instead of the camera, who sees the employee stealing money. This visual set of ripples moves, as always, from your base chakra up towards your crown, meeting each energy center along the route. Each of your personalities, with its filters and distortions, has the chance to react. If the scene is a trigger—however slight—for one of them, it expresses its interpretation of the picture by casting its own pebble into the pond, creating interference waves.

"The process is a lot like splitting a laser light into object and reference beams to produce a hologram. Awareness provides the object beam; the aroused subpersonality contributes a reference beam. The interference patterns produce thought and its inevitable by-product, emotion."

"But if every subpersonality contributes a pebble, wouldn't that make for countless concentric rings all intersecting wildly?" Larry asked.

"Welcome to Planet Earth," Zeus replied. "The third density has been preprogrammed with the illusion of multiplicity—what you call duality and polarity. Now you are beginning to understand why all relationships on this side of the Veil are so challenging. And the challenge begins with your relationship to yourself. Conflict and war are unavoidable. Peace simply cannot exist as a stable state. It occurs only in those rare instances when waves with just the right amounts of peak and trough meet and cancel each other out. Then, just like in the pond, the moment passes.

"So, you see, thoughts really are waves. When two or more people—or subpersonalities, for that matter—are in agreement, the consenting wave pattern is reinforced. If you get enough agreement, it becomes a reality. If there is enough dissension, reality crumbles into yesterday's truth."

"Amazing, how complicated we humans are," Larry said, "constantly pelted by emotional triggers that set off time bombs waiting in our chakras. Does this same process precipitate dreaming?" Larry asked.

"Ah!" Zeus responded. "'Perchance to dream. Ay, there's the rub, for in that sleep of death what dreams may come. . . .' Larry, you do have a knack for asking fascinating questions. The simple answer is: yes and no. Perhaps I will let our host tackle this one."

"Our pleasure," the Voice replied, "for this is an exceptionally fertile field, worthy of careful consideration. Actual dream time—called REM, or rapid eye movement sleep—occurs in short spurts relative to the other phases of the sleep cycle. The most active dream period arrives in the early morning, just prior to waking. Dreams are typically more concentrated and vivid and have richer emotional content than waking experiences. For one thing, in a dream the subject matter is insulated from outside interference—although information can occasionally bleed through from a parallel universe. Second, the subject matter usually represents the most pressing lesson to be learned at the time. It's typically extracted from the previous day's events. However, if the person is coping with a major fear or upset, it may also draw on older memories. This is the basis for recurring dreams and nightmares.

"The rest is indeed similar to the department store camera. However, the scenes in dreams are obviously lit up, not by ambient light but by the laserlike object beam of Awareness focused through the Higher Self. All the vignettes to be processed are downloaded simultaneously. This tangle of data is sifted through the chakras, starting at the root and moving up through the spine. Imagine each 'byte' to be made up of a complex of energetic overlays, akin to the notes in a piece of music. As this mélange passes through the chakras' filters and distortions, it triggers preexisting imprints. These resonate—like a tuning fork—to the subject matter's energetic signature, that is, they drop their own pebbles into the pond. Those waves interact with the scene's subject matter, causing palpable interference patterns, which manifest as thought and emotion. The greater the match between the material and the preexisting imprint, the higher the peaks and troughs, and the richer the emotional content.

"During the REM phase of each sleep cycle, the subconscious projects portions of this mix of material and emotional overlay as a rich flow of coded data. The mind, trying to make sense of it, determines a sequence of events, creatively adding semiplausible segues to link apparently unconnected vignettes. That's why dreams are so fragmented, often jumping between unrelated scenes.

"'Follow your dream' may be one of the best pieces of advice you'll ever hear, provided you take it literally. Dreams are a veritable map of the state of your chakras. If you record your dreams in detail and take the time to observe how the interference patterns created by your various imprints ripple up your energy centers, the insight gained will speed up the elevation of your Awareness.

"However, if we may reiterate an earlier caveat: Avoid shortcuts. Don't resort to the simple symbology offered in so-called dream dictionaries, such as: a house represents your body, the ocean signifies your emotions. Instead, be willing to work outside the analytical mind. Ask your Higher Self or your Body Elemental for assistance. Replay the interference patterns in your thoughts throughout the next day and patiently wait for 'hits.' In dreams—as in all things, actually—the waters run surprisingly deep. Don't settle for skipping stones across the surface when the treasure lies in the depths. As the dream begins to reveal its meaning, enter into dialogue with the main characters. Assume that each of them is actually an aspect of yourself. Ask why it chose a particular form or a certain action. Ask what it wishes you to see."

"This seems like a lot of effort to me," Larry said. "Is there some way to understand your dreams while you are dreaming, so you don't have to mess with all the introspective stuff?"

"Good ol' Larry!" Zeus interjected. "Not thirty seconds after being told to avoid a shortcut, you're asking for a free pass out. 'Messing with the introspective stuff,' as you put it, is what Creation is all about. Why bother being here if you don't want to take the curriculum?"

"Indeed," the Voice agreed, "the value of each being's contribution to the Creation lies in the richness of its journey, not in getting through as quickly as possible. Each opportunity to delve into the mysteries locked in your personalities' skewed world is a gift to be treasured, so you should feel blessed, not burdened. But to answer your question directly, yes, you can be Aware of your dreams while you dream them. This is known as 'lucid dreaming,' and it generally emerges once you are well into the dream.

"In high-level lucid dreaming, you know that every element of your experience is a projection onto the holographic plate of the mind. You know you are actually asleep in bed and can suffer no physical, emotional, or other real-time consequence of the dream. There is also a lower level of lucid dreaming, in which you know you are dreaming but do not realize that the events are not taking place in local time. In both, you may be able to control the dream's course of events to suit your curiosity or interest. This level of command may also happen when you are not fully aware that you are dreaming. Again, you can be completely cognizant that you are dreaming and have no control of the dream."

"You make lucid dreaming seem like taking part in a virtual reality game," Larry mused. "Is there any other value to it than deliberately engineering events I wouldn't have the courage or opportunity to confront in my waking state?" Larry asked.

"Oh my, yes." It was Zeus speaking now. "From one per-spective, one might say that your lifetime on this planet is a dream sequence orchestrated by a higher Awareness. Look into the I's of infinity. When you have all these self-directed escapades in a lucid dream, who's sitting in the director's chair and who's experiencing the adventures?"

"Why me, of course."

"And which one of those 'me's' might that be?"

"I see what you mean," Larry responded. "One of them is directing and another is having the fun. That means that only a few of my viewpoints buy into the fact that I'm really here. The rest know differently. Maybe that's what Teilhard de Chardin meant when he suggested that we are not human beings having a spiritual experience but spiritual beings having a human expe-rience.

"I imagine that when I finally get enlightened, I'll come to know it fully. All my belief systems, all my priorities and respon-sibilities—everything that motivates my day-to-day existence—fall away. When that happens, I'm just pure Awareness—viewing through a multiplicity of viewpoints spread across an infinite continuum of I's, contributing to the collective experience of the All That Is."

"Quite so," the Voice interjected. "And what do you suppose comprises the totality of all viewpoints on all I-continuums?"

"Absolute Awareness."

"Indeed," the Voice agreed. "And who has access to this Absolute Awareness?"

"All of Creation."

"Then, what separates you from any other aspect of Creation?"

"Nothing," Larry replied in a near whisper. "Absolutely nothing. How could it? We really are all aspects of the One."

"Precisely," the Voice replied. "As we said earlier, realizing absolutely that all beings are One is the final stepping stone leading you out of the third density. The power of that perception completely dissolves your illusion's inherent duality and, with it, the expression of conflict as a primary experience. Then war in all its forms is truly gone. You emerge from the chrysalis of the egoic self flying free of distorted personas."

"Wow!" That was all Larry could think of saying.

Sit down before fact as a little child,
Be prepared to give up every conceived notion,
Follow humbly wherever and whatever abysses nature leads,
Or you will learn nothing.

— THOMAS HUXLEY

CHAPTER 23

What Happens Next?

"Wow?" Zeus mimicked. "You're given the key to the door out of the illusion and all you can say is 'wow'? At least make it a coda of note. How about bow-wow? Or even better, bowser-wowser?"

"Huh?"

"You're doing just fine, Larry," the Voice offered. "We are certain that once you have absorbed the full implications of this material, you will find precisely the right words to express yourself. When you completely perceive that all other selves *are* you, you will have mastered the illusion's prime lesson. From this elevated point from which to view, you can appreciate in a new way the pain and sorrow inherent in the polarized experiences characterizing the third density. With this realization comes overwhelming Compassion manifested as an intense desire to serve your fellow beings.

"Then you are ready to move on, to enter a new level of reality where the conflicts of duality fall away. The next density, the fourth, which all humanity is now invited to enter, is based on a completely different geometric principle than the third. Negative and positive, the pairs of opposites, begin to fall away. That is why it is called the density of compassionate Love. It is the first of the higher densities, purposefully hidden until now so your experience of polarity could remain intact.

"As we indicated earlier, every density has its own particular geometry. As one advances, the mathematics become progressively subtle—increasingly refined analogs of the distortive filters contained within your chakras. For there must be some level of distortion, or there would be no experience and we would not advance."

"That makes sense," Larry responded. "I have one question: Do we keep our bodies when we get to the next density?"

"No, not in their present form," the Voice replied. "Although the shape is similar, the chemical elements are not the same. The fourth-density body is appreciably denser in Consciousness, substantially lighter in physical composition, and considerably richer in life force. If it ever falls ill, it is easily healed."

"Does it need to eat?"

"Yes, but fourth-density beings are not attached to the complexities of food preparation you seem to enjoy here. I'm afraid cookbook publishers would find no market in the next density. The selection and preparation of foodstuffs is extremely simple by your standards, due to the increased level of communication between each being and its food. Meals are unimportant except as a means for learning patience."

"What a strange thing to say," Larry said. "What's the connection between eating and patience?"

"Ah, each density's unique geometry figures in all aspects of an entity's experience there. Consider what decision opened the gateway between the third density to the fourth."

"You mean the desire to serve others?" Larry asked.

"Quite so," the Voice replied. "In the fourth density that desire is so overwhelming that time taken for meals is viewed as a hindrance—and therefore an opportunity to refine the gift of patience.

"However, the fourth density involves more than serving, patience, and food. The overriding objective is to strive toward Wisdom. The fourth density reels under the weight of Compassion. Even though Compassion is the ultimate lesson in the third density, when practiced and refined as the prime focus of the fourth density it invariably becomes imbalanced, often leading to well-meant acts of folly."

"I thought pure compassion was a good thing," Larry interjected.

"'Good' and 'bad' have little relevance outside of your illusion. There is only balance and imbalance. Consider a seesaw with ten tons of compassion on one side. What would bring it into balance?"

"I don't know," Larry responded, "an equal amount of enmity?"

"Dummkopf!" The word clearly came from Zeus's direction.

"Stop thinking in terms of black and white," the Voice continued, ignoring the critique from Zeus. "As we said, opposites cease to carry the same weight in the higher realms."

"Does Wisdom balance Compassion?" Larry asked, realizing that given the subject's importance, this probably wasn't the best time to wisecrack.

"Indeed," the Voice said. "They form two sides of the Great Cosmic Triangle, the third being Power. The fourth through sixth densities deal with mastering Love—of which Compassion is an aspect—then Wisdom, and finally Power.

"Have any beings ever come back to our planet from the fourth density?"

"Yes, Larry. There is a sprinkling of fourth-density beings on the planet at this time. But more of the Wanderers who are here to serve during the transition are from the fifth density, and the majority, as we commented earlier, are from the sixth."

"Would I know of any of them?"

"Yes, I'm sure you would. While some work powerfully behind the scenes in anonymity, others are prominent teachers who attract large followings. It is not for me to reveal their names, as that would compromise your Free Will, tempting you to surrender your own power to belief. However, as the Akasha is open to you, you can browse the files whenever you wish. We ask only that you respect the Free Will of others at all times, just as we honor yours."

"You have my word," Larry said. "Can you at least tell me the names of fourth-density beings who were here in the past?"

"You don't need us for that," the Voice responded. "Look into your own histories to find those who came with messages of love and compassion."

"Jesus? Buddha?"

"Ah, it appears you already know the answers, so we shall turn over some new ground.

"As we were saying," the Voice continued, "unlike in your present experience on Earth, polarity is no longer the major catalyst for experience in the fourth density. The dimension's geometry does not sustain disharmony of any kind, neither within oneself or in relations with others. Individual differences abound and are valued, but they are automatically harmonized by group consensus."

"How does that happen?" Larry asked.

"On your side of the Veil, the distortive lenses and filters designed to create experience are lodged in the lower three chakras. In the fourth, fifth, and sixth densities, however, the energetic matrix that directs experience is focused on refinement of the higher energy centers. Duality is no longer required as an agent for growth. What were judged as negative and positive paths in the third density become, in the fourth, simply paths of service to self and service to others. Travelers on one path are not subjected to the energetic interference of the other path as part of their immediate fourth-density experience. This allows for unobstructed communication among all participants in a fourth-density community. Selves are not kept hidden from other selves. All imbalances are immediately apparent, and any illness is easily healed once the mechanism of any destructive or counterproductive influence is grasped.

"As the individuals' Awareness evolves, the group grows increasingly harmonious, gradually coalescing under a common purpose of service. The group memory—akin to the Akashic record—becomes known to the entire collective, creating a social memory complex. Then all the experiences of any member are instantly available to the whole group. Words are no longer necessary, as all is known to all."

"Something like a mini All That Is?" Larry asked.

"Yes, something like that," the Voice replied. "The fourth density is a baby step toward merging back into the Oneness. Each entity retains its individuality even while it is consciously connected to an integration of active viewpoints, which could include billions of other selves. The complexity of this union, as one moves higher along the continuum of the I's, increases exponentially and confounds our ability to explain it in terms readily comprehensible to you."

"I can't imagine many people on this planet being comfortable with the idea of others knowing their secret thoughts," Larry mused.

"For anyone experiencing a polarized density, granting another entity free access would be most unusual," the Voice said. "Even in the fourth density, this is a gradual process sustained over millions of years."

"Over *what?*" Larry exclaimed.

"It is difficult to translate time from one density to the next. For example, we have resided in these rocks for some eighty-five million years, arcing our Awareness between the first and sixth densities. To us, the passage of time is hardly noticeable. By contrast, your entire third-density experience is programmed to last for only three grand cycles—approximately seventy-five thousand years—probably a very long period to you. To paraphrase one of the finer minds who lived on your side of the Veil: time is relative; it passes more slowly for a man when he is sitting on a park bench waiting for his lover than when locked in her embrace.

"The fourth density lies somewhere in between. The lessons to be learned there are absorbed over approximately thirty million years. However, the typical fourth-density incarnation lasts some ninety thousand years—which doesn't seem long to the participants, as the experience is even more captivating than being lost in the love of merely *one* other self."

"How does one finally graduate from the fourth density?" Larry asked.

"It depends on the ability of the entire social memory complex to welcome a sufficiently high quotient of Light/Love energy. This is achieved as the collective attains greater levels of loving Compassion for the sorrows of their brothers and sisters still experiencing third-density reality.

"As you might expect," the Voice said, "the next area of exploration on our grand cosmic journey is the fifth density. Here the overwhelming, unbridled Compassion of the fourth density is countervailed by Wisdom.

"Keep in mind that the objective of each density is to move the self further along its infinite continuum of I's. In the second density, an individual breaks from the herd and recognizes its individuality. In the third, it overcomes its obsession with personal survival. In the fourth, the entity merges once again in the group mind while retaining an evolved individual identity; from this elevated perspective, it easily grasps the nature of immortality.

"In the fifth density, individuals can choose how they wish to gain heightened Awareness—as part of a social memory complex or as a singular entity. Both are catalysts for increasing one's quotient of Wisdom. One realizes that one contributes to the planetary Consciousness more through one's quality of being than one's ability to manipulate outcomes on the physical plane. As balance between Compassion and Wisdom is achieved, the individual is able to welcome a significantly greater quotient of Light/Love energy."

"And this, I gather, opens the gateway to the sixth density?" Larry asked.

"Precisely so," the Voice responded. "The sixth density has its own gift: unity. It is here that those who have chosen the negative path of service, once they fully know the Law of One, join their positive counterparts in service to all.

"As you correctly said earlier, this law states that infinity is equal to One. All Creation is One. Everything is an aspect of the One. There is only One. As a concept, this law is not far removed from what you have been experiencing the past few days. However, when perceived from the higher I's of your I-continuum, it ceases to be a mere concept. Perhaps the best explanation, given the limitations of words, is to ask that you imagine the equivalent of a tuning fork attuned to the cosmos embedded in each entity's core. When the Law of One is fully realized, the subtle vibration of Oneness—often expressed as the sound symbol Om—moves through the entity's energy fields. It actuates the tuning fork within, which then emits a sympathetic vibration that amplifies that entity's Love/Light quotient.

"Completion of the realization that All is One allows the sixth-density being to refine the balance achieved between Compassion and Wisdom. It is then able to use focused thought to access the Infinite Intelligence present in each particle of Light. At this level of Awareness, an entity is fully capable of manipulating energy to create whatever form it wishes to project into physical realms. Thus this density completes the Great Cosmic Triangle of Love, Wisdom, and Power.

"It is virtually impossible for us to capture the nature of the sixth density in words, as it involves a geometry beyond what your mind can grasp. But there is an exercise that can give you a preview of what the sixth density has to offer. Does this interest you?"

"You've got to be kidding," Larry responded. "That's like asking a five-year-old if he'd like to steer his dad's car!"

"Very well then, all you need do is ask. The exercise we are about to reveal provides you with a window into infinity, and insight into the process through which intention and attention are focused through the Cosmic Triangle to bring about manifestation.

"Using the breathing techniques you have been taught, enter into deep meditation. Imagine yourself becoming formless, just pure Awareness seeking points from which to view."

Larry began focusing on his breath, allowing his mind to drift into the Void, awaiting the arrival of anchor points from which he could re-form thought.

"Visualize a vast triangle, each side a portal with its own viewpoint. These are the portals of Love, Wisdom, and Power." Even as the Voice spoke, Larry found himself in the presence of a vast geometric form growing out of nothingness.

"First, move your Consciousness to the portal of Love. Allow yourself to merge with the portal so completely that you are consumed by endless waves of Compassion and unconditional Love. Remain deep in its embrace until your sense of personal identity has dissolved completely and you *are* unconditional Love."

Larry experienced endless waves of joy and peace until, much as the incessant lapping of the sea ultimately claims even the most durable granite, his entire being surrendered to the primal force of Creation.

"Next, move your Consciousness to the portal of Wisdom. Here too, allow yourself to merge with the portal so completely that you are consumed by the depth and pervasiveness of absolute Wisdom. Remain deep within the quintessence of Wisdom until your sense of personal identity has dissolved completely and you *are* absolute Wisdom."

This portion of the exercise absolutely stunned Larry. Nothing in his deepest imagination could have prepared him for the enormity of merging into the utter refinement of Wisdom. It embraced the pure distillate of infinite knowledge, the place where understanding and purpose are birthed.

"Once this Awareness is complete, move your Consciousness to the portal of Power. Allow yourself to merge with this portal so completely that you are consumed by the absolute certainty and causal presence of consummate Power. Remain deep within the embodiment of power until your sense of personal identity has dissolved completely and you *are* that which commands the potential to manifest all Creation."

The unbridled magnitude of the power Larry felt left no doubt about the origin of Creation. As he allowed himself to be carried by the boundless exhilaration of omnipotence, he felt his being expand beyond the realms of comprehension to merge with the essence of infinity itself.

"We can see that you have already realized that each portal, though an extraordinary doorway into the infinite, is somehow incomplete—like an object beam without a reference beam with which to create interference patterns. In the stillness of the Void, you will begin to become Aware of Creation's gravitational pull, seeking to complete itself.

"So return to the portal of Love, and once more become consumed by the energetic fires of unconditional, compassionate Love. Once this has been achieved, begin to focus your attention on Wisdom. Appreciate as fully as possible the gifts of Wisdom when viewed through the portal of Love. Note how the energy of Wisdom takes on a different signature when seen from here. Observe the flow of energy between these two portals.

"Now, leave Wisdom and return to the original feeling of being immersed in the vibration of Love. From here, focus your attention on Power. Observe how the raw, unbridled potential of Power is tempered by Love, how its energetic signature shifts when it is viewed through this portal.

"Continue this exercise, viewing Love and then Power from the portal of Wisdom. Once you have gleaned the knowledge you seek there, move on to the portal of Power. From there, view first Love, then Wisdom."

The Voice allowed Larry all the time he needed to fully integrate each aspect of the exercise, bending the third-density laws of space and time for this purpose such that the experience of eons was distilled into a few minutes of objective, local time. As the exercised progressed, the Great Cosmic Triangle began to spin with such rapidity that it morphed into a circle that expanded to engulf the entire universe, impelled by an irresistible centrifugal force. Larry now knew what the Voice meant when it said that the gift of the sixth density was unity.

The Voice and Zeus waited silently for Larry's return.

When at last he emerged, Zeus quipped, "Boy, you sure take some neat trips. When you get a free moment, would you

CHAPTER 24

Help from Above

"Ah," the Voice exclaimed, "perhaps we assume too much. What do you know thus far about your Higher Self?"

"Well, I met my Higher Self when I was working with Junie," Larry said. "But everything was happening so fast—as if it isn't now—I don't really know much, other than to say it's one of my subpersonalities. On the other hand, it might be the other way round. Among other things, it's the one who chooses the lessons for a third-density lifetime."

"This is too important a subject for you not to grasp completely," the Voice responded. "Zeus, perhaps you might clarify this matter for the lad?"

"Why not?" Zeus replied. "It seems attempting the impossible is my routine assignment these days. Larry, my man, you want paradox, you got paradox! You're about to meet yourself coming around the next corner!"

"Huh?"

"What color was George Washington's white horse?" Zeus asked. "You know, the high-spirited one with the long mane?"

"What in hell are you talking about?" Larry said.

Zeus found Larry's confusion amusing. "Sorry, couldn't resist. Why is the obvious always the last thing we see? Do you recall that a little while ago you explored your unwillingness to take Rocky's message seriously because of his funny outfit?"

"Yes."

"And what did you discover?"

"That he was actually a part of me," Larry replied.

"If you can see that Rocky is a part of you, why is it so difficult to work out who the Higher Self is?"

"Duh . . . ," Larry said. "Washington's white horse was white, wasn't it? What you're trying to tell me is my Higher Self *is* me?"

"Bravo. Now that we've gotten past the easy part, let's explore how you can be split into two levels of Consciousness at the same moment in time. Imagine talking to yourself in the mirror. You have a thought, your mirror image reads your mind and responds. The only difference here is that the response comes from a much higher point of view."

"You mean the me in the mirror is speaking from the sixth density?" Larry asked, with more than a touch of disbelief in his voice.

"Close enough for government work," Zeus responded with a chuckle. "That ain't exactly it, but if you don't get too caught up in the mirror business, it'll help get the idea across. Let me explain: It's all about nonlocal time being simultaneous rather than linear. If you remember, that's another way of saying there is no past or future, only a whole bunch of nows going off in all possible directions. Since you've already arrived wherever you think you're going, doesn't it make sense to reach back and give yourself a helping hand from time to time?"

"You mean the Higher Self is actually a more evolved 'me' in the future coming back through time to assist me?" Larry wondered.

"You see," Zeus said, speaking more to the Voice than to Larry, "that wasn't too hard at all. I believe he's beginning to get it."

"But how is that possible?" Larry stammered. "If my Higher Self comes from the future, wouldn't he . . . or I . . . know everything that is going to happen to me?"

"Oops, looks like I spoke too soon," Zeus said. "No. As you have already observed, nothing is certain and all possibilities are played out in parallel universes. The Higher Self is like a road map that depicts your known destination—in this case, the state of Awareness to be achieved when you finally make it to the sixth density. The map offers many routes to get there. Although part of you has already reached the destination, the journey may have been tougher than it needs to be. So the Higher Self—if so requested—reaches back to guide your third-density Consciousness through an easier, more productive route. In a sense, your Higher Self gifts you with partial knowledge of what you've already experienced, so you don't have to repeat so many of the lessons."

"That makes twice in the last minute you've stressed that the Higher Self has to be invoked, it doesn't just appear. I gather that's an important point?" Larry asked.

"Indeed it is," the Voice interjected. "Recall that the overriding force animating Creation is Free Will. This mandates that each aspect along your infinite continuum of I's must be allowed the freest possible expression of experience at each level of Consciousness. Your Higher Self may create certain predisposing limitations to set up third-density incarnational lessons, but the rest is up to you and how you choose to exercise your Free Will. That is why your Higher Self cannot freely interact with your conscious mind unless specifically invited to do so in each instance."

"Isn't the Higher Self governed by the same laws as I am in my third-density state? Doesn't it evolve in Consciousness too?"

"Not exactly," Zeus replied. "Amazing how seemingly simple questions can't be answered by a simple yes or no. In some ways, your Higher Self is completely outside the evolutionary equation. It's a part of you that was bestowed on your sixth-density self by *its* own future self."

"You've got to be kidding," Larry said. "If my sixth-density self gets my Higher Self from its future self so it can help me when I'm my later self, how do I—whoever I am—ever get out of here?"

"Out of where?" Zeus asked with obvious amusement.

"Here. Creation. Infinity. Whatever," Larry said, annoyed with himself for not being able to see the humor of it all.

"How about inserting a few more pieces of the puzzle before trying to guess at the final picture?" Zeus offered. "Lighten up. What's the big deal? You're down on yourself just because you can't grasp how the future can fold itself so conveniently into the present to affect the pathway by which it has already reached its destination. It's no more than another shining example of pure paradox—piece of cake, once you stop trying to understand it. Let's step back for a moment and revisit the Myth of Creation, this time from the point of view of a particle of Awareness rather than the All That Is."

"Okay, show me what you mean," Larry answered.

"Cool," Zeus said. "Now hang onto your hat, 'cause this is going to be a mouthful. As an Awareness particle emerges from the earliest densities, it's drawn deitropically—if I may coin a word that, from this day forth, shall mean being drawn irresistibly toward the Oneness."

"Like heliotropic—the way a sunflower moves its face toward the sun?" Larry asked.

"A perfect analogy," Zeus replied. "As I was saying, an Awareness particle is drawn deitropically by the gravitational attraction of the spiraling Light energy back toward its source. This pull increases exponentially at each successive density until, in the final phases of the seventh density, the exquisite intensity causes Awareness to lose all sense of personal identity. Its final act before merging with the Oneness is to shed its Higher Self. That portion of Consciousness is then gifted to Awareness's sixth-density self, so it can assist those portions of its own Awareness yet to follow on the vast circular course of existence."

Larry's silence testified to his confusion. Zeus continued, "Ah, so. It appears I had better try another approach. Imagine that your entire continuum of I's is represented by an enormous, slowly spinning disk containing all the colors of the rainbow. Larry, other than the obvious difference of hue, what actually distinguishes one color from another?"

"Their frequencies," Larry replied, trying to anticipate where Zeus was headed. "As I recall, the vibrational rate of red is the lowest and violet is the highest."

"Go to the head of the class!" Zeus exclaimed with feigned enthusiasm. "You remember Physics 101. In our example, let's equate the color bands with levels of Awareness. As Consciousness emerges from the Void, it passes through the first veil to enter the red realm. It remains there as long as necessary to increase its Awareness. What happens to its hue?"

"It gradually shifts from red to orange."

"You're on a roll!" Zeus teased. "Absolutely correct. Even though the colors flow into each other through infinitely subtle gradients, let's agree for the sake of this illustration that there's some energetic point where red becomes orange and orange becomes yellow, and so on. Those points all lie on radials that define the beginning and end of each color, separating them into seven vibrational compartments."

"The seven colors of the visible spectrum?" Larry asked.

"Yep. Let's call these seven radials the veils defining the entry points into each of the eight densities."

"Now you're trying to confuse me," Larry said. "How can there be eight densities if there are only seven veils?"

"Lordie, ah do declare . . . why, you're actually listenin'. How sweet. Ah just love an attentive audience," Zeus offered, reverting to his hammy southern drawl. "Why, Larry, ah coulda sworn ah already told you 'bout how first-density babies were born."

"Can the Kentucky fried chatter," Larry retorted. "I'm seriously trying to get this, and I'm not sure your little asides are helping. The first density arises out of the All That Is."

"Now don't get heavy here," Zeus replied, dropping the deep-South affectation. "This stuff is far too important to be taken seriously. Just hang in and keep your thoughts out of it. You've reviewed how a being enters the Wheel of Consciousness; where does it go when it graduates from the seventh density and is ready to get off?"

"Why, it merges back into the All That Is," Larry answered.

"Now you see, you've been trying to make a mountain out of a molehill. You really understood all along, didn't you? The veils create the distortions marking the onset of each density. Since the eighth density is the Great Unknowable Mystery—the One Supreme Infinite Creator—there's no veil blocking it from those ready to enter. All Consciousness is directly and intimately connected to it at all times, limited only by each individual's tolerance for pure Light/Love energy. Consciousness arises out of the Oneness only to return to the Oneness, in a constant, simultaneous sweep. Except, of course, that it never leaves it."

"*What? . . . What? What? . . . What?*" The screeching was right on cue.

"Ain't ol' What-What the cat's meow?" Zeus said. "He's always ready to break the tension and pat professorial pups on the paw to remind them they've strayed a bit off the path."

"Get real, Zeus," Larry offered. "Even the bird thinks you're absurd. How can one get on the Great Wheel, go through an entire process of gaining Awareness, to finally get off and still never leave it?"

"Ah, a perfect catch for two JAPs!"

"Zeus, what the hell have you been drinking? I give up. What's a JAP?"

"My! You have led a sheltered life," Zeus goaded. "Remind me to do something about that as soon as we get home. A JAP, mon cher, is a special subspecies of the human experiment, the crystallized perfection of doting parents and a dedicated supporting social cast of hundreds—a Jewish American Princess, of course."

"I still don't get it. What's a perfect catch for two Jewish American Princesses?"

"Why, a paradox, of course!" Zeus and the Voice roared their delight. It took a fair while for Larry to join them.

"Stay cool, dude," Zeus continued, "you're doing just fine. Let me add a few more ingredients to the story before we give it a final stir. I promise, it'll all make sense soon.

"As the gigantic disk rotates, it draws cosmic plasma in its wake, creating countless interference patterns within each segment of Awareness. These wondrous, intricate weaves of peaks and troughs constantly inform each range of Awareness, adding more and more spiritual mass, thereby increasing the density levels of each segment. There comes a point when the segment with the greatest quotient of Awareness—the violet seventh density, in this example—becomes so dense that it merges once again into the black hole from which it sprang. In the same instant, its place on the clock is replaced by the faintest shadow of a newborn red segment just beginning its journey through the first density of Creation.

"You see, this is the snake swallowing its own tail. There is no beginning and no end, only the Oneness of infinity. The totality of who you are *is* the disk. Each wedge of the Great Circle, akin to the seven densities, simultaneously experiences every possible aspect of Conscious Awareness."

"I'm trying my best to follow you," Larry said, "but I still don't understand a couple of things."

"And what might they be?" Zeus asked.

"It seems that all portions of the disk spin together. Doesn't that mean that all of the densities last equally long and that all beings graduate from their respective densities at the same time?"

"If the disk existed in local, linear time, that would be true. But it doesn't. What you call time is quite relative and subjective, depending on the point from which the observer views. Rather than encasing it in months, years, and eons, think of it in terms of too little, too much, and just right. From that perspective the time spent in each density is just right: no more, no less. Regardless of how long it takes, it all happens simultaneously anyway.

"You might try gift-wrapping that and giving it to one of the JAPs as a wedding present. And your second question is?"

"I don't know why I even bother asking," Larry mused. "If the seventh-density entity finally merges back into the Void, how can it simultaneously reappear as a newborn first-density entity?

"Well done!" Zeus cried. "Now that's a really good question. It points to the very heart of the Unknowable Mystery. Consider the seventh-density self—just after it bestows the Higher Self to its sixth-density counterpart—as it passes through the final portion of its radial. What becomes of it?"

"It ceases to exist?" Larry asked.

"In one sense, since it's forsaken all individuality. But in another sense, just the opposite happens. It merges into the absolute Oneness of the eighth density. Yes, it becomes nothing, but that, in actuality, is everything. So it can't help but be in the portion of the One reintroduced onto the first section of the disk, just as it is a miniscule part of the portion of Consciousness spun out onto a different disk in a different universe, to experience a completely different aspect of All That Is.

"If this makes even rudimentary sense, how can you consider even the *possibility* of escaping the hologram? How can you ever again doubt that you and all Creation are One? You ask how you can get out of here; there is *only* here. Where in the infinite Oneness could you possibly go that isn't here?"

"I need a beer!" Larry groaned.

"I agree, this is heady stuff," Zeus said. "But if you wanna' stay true, eschew the brew. The minutes left are getting few, and as you can see, there's much to do. Pardon the rhyme, but—as I just said—it's all about time."

"What's about time?" Larry asked.

"Why, the paradox, of course," the Voice interjected. "If you take Zeus's suggestion and eliminate time and space from the equation, it all makes perfect sense. If you are going to shift your Higher Self from theoretical concept to practical reality, you must first deal with your restrictive concept of linear time. You'll need to give up the belief that you have a beginning and an end. What you perceive as space/time is simply part of the third-density illusion created by the Veil. Viewed from the sixth density, all events appear simultaneous—one experiences the entire disk at once. The Infinite Instant contains all that ever was and ever will be experienced, from the first glimpse of Consciousness to the final merging into the All That Is.

"Herein lies the dilemma: How does one hold onto third-density reality and at the same time invoke the Higher Self's assistance?"

CHAPTER 25

You Can't Get There from Here

"It sounds pretty impossible to me," Larry said, "like trying to get somewhere while having one foot in the boat and the other on the dock. Either I'm here, in linear space/time where I can't access my Higher Self, or I'm in nonlinear time/space, where I lose all sense of my egoic self and the illusion I think I'm living in. How can I evoke my Higher Self without going stark raving mad—unless of course I have the help of someone like Junie?"

"Do you consider yourself mad now?" Zeus asked.

"No."

"Well, you've spent a portion of almost every day of your life communing with your Higher Self. If you hadn't, you'd have flipped out many times over by now."

"Zeus, what in God's name are you talking about?" Larry asked.

"Ease up, buckaroo. I'm referring to the only time you human types actually give your ego a rest. We were talking earlier about sleep and the immense pool of information it offers. You guys are preprogrammed to spend a few moments while you sleep each night with the part of your Consciousness that's outside the illusion. I also alluded to a beam from a higher energy source that selects the scenes for your dreams and illuminates them."

"Yes, you said it's like a laser's object beam projecting images through the chakras," Larry answered.

"And where do you suppose this beam comes from?" Zeus asked.

"My Higher Self?"

"Excellent," Zeus said. "Now, why do you suppose this process is so vital?"

"I don't know much about dreaming," Larry responded, "but I do remember reading about a study in which the subjects were deprived of REM sleep. They were woken up whenever the eye movement associated with dreaming was detected. From what I recollect, they were not happy campers."

"To say the least," Zeus said. "Although they were allowed eight hours of sleep time—enough to recharge their physical batteries—they weren't allowed to dream. If the experiment had continued, they would have become nonfunctional zombies. What do you suppose is so vital about the dream state that third-density beings can't survive long without it?"

"I gather it involves the Higher Self, but I can't seem to put the pieces together," Larry responded.

"And which I was that speaking?" Zeus chided. "Congratulations, my man, you've once again delivered a masterful rendition of third-density dysfunctional alchemy, complete with the stirring 'I can't' chorale reprise. Suck it up, kiddo. You can do a helluva lot better than 'I can't.' There's always a part of you that can't, just as there's always a part of you that can. It's up to you to pick the appropriate part in any situation."

"Got the message," Larry said. "In fact, why don't I shift gears and slide up the continuum and invite my Higher Self to chime in?"

"Good theoretical solution. But how are you going to make that happen without drifting off to sleep?"

"Kichi," Larry answered, remembering his Body Elemental. One of her prime tasks was to help him invoke his higher Awareness.

"Clever boy," Zeus said. "You're on track. Now just continue."

Larry quieted his mind and focused on his breath. In short order he felt the energetic presence of his beloved internal friend. "Kichi," he said, "I need some help. Could you shuttle between my lower Consciousness and my Higher Self? I'm trying to get some insight into the interaction between my Higher Self and dreams." Within a few moments, Larry found himself shifted to a more pervasive point of view. No longer tethered to the lower rungs of his I-continuum, he could easily access the information he sought.

"Very interesting," Larry said after a brief time. "Dreams stabilize our daily experiences by replaying them in present time. I know those are just words. I wonder if I can convey the fullness of what I've just learned? Let me take a whack at pushing it through the strainer."

Zeus was delighted by the prospect. "Ah, the paradox is about to be illuminated by the paradoxical," he said. "Good luck and welcome to the club. We can't wait to see what comes out the other side!"

"Cute, Zeus! Now I know what you two struggle with. Still, I'm going to give it my best shot.

"It all relates to time—just like you were saying—and the way it gets distorted on this side of the Veil into linear reality. Because of this, we're never really in the present as events unfold around us. Instead, we filter what reaches our senses through the preprogramming in our chakras, which links us back to the first imprintings of past events. This, like you said, produces interference patterns, which give rise to thoughts.

"The thought waves interact with the three Great Temptations you talked about—the urges to compare, judge, and understand. This causes another set of interference patterns that gives rise to emotions. The emotional patterns interact with the molecular vibrations of our physical form, causing yet another set of interference patterns. These ultimately embed themselves as palpable ridges of cellular memory and can ultimately show up as pain and disease. The whole cascading spiral would consume us if it wasn't for the Higher Self."

"Quite correct," said the Voice, impressed by Larry's new level of Awareness.

"Go on," said Zeus, "you're getting close to the mother lode and you've got our undivided attention. Now explain what the Higher Self does each night and why you would slip off the edge if the process was interrupted for too long."

Larry laughed as he struggled to find the right combination of words. "Now I know why you're so fond of metaphors. It's as hard for me to explain this without word-pictures as it would be for a concert pianist to play Rachmaninoff's Third with one hand."

"Got the picture," Zeus said. "Paint away."

"Let's say there's a ship sailing on the ocean skippered by a captain who doesn't have a sea chart or even a destination in mind. In fact, he's clueless when it comes to steering his ship. Its course is left to the whims of the weather and the conditions of the sea. To find the meaning of the journey, he tries to interpret the patterns of passing seaweed tangles or seek consensus among other captains' musings. But most of the time he just keeps busy making it to the next day.

"By and large, that's what it's like for us third-density beings. Instead of charting a course with intention, everybody's little ship is at the mercy of the three temptations. Some days are calm, and some are stormy. Without some kind of regular help from outside, the ship would end up on a rocky shoal somewhere. So every night the Higher Self steps in to help. When people drop into sleep, they slip out of linear reality into the nonlocal realm of the unconscious. This is the common ground where the third and sixth densities can interact. The Higher Self identifies the most provocative external energy patterns and uses a beam of Light/Love energy to replay the previous day's events. These vignettes are projected through the entire chakra system, which allows them to be reintegrated without being muddled by the three great temptations."

Exactly so," Zeus said. "The magnificent by-product of the process you've just described is the dream—a richly symbolic display of interference patterns generated by that Light/Love laser beam as it is split into the object beam of unfolding events and the reference beams projected through the skewed lenses in the chakras. Please continue."

Larry paused a few moments, collecting his thoughts. "A dream is a jewel offered by the Higher Self to its third-density self as an opportunity for growth. This gifting continues night after night, even though the person's waking Consciousness pretty much ignores it. But the fact is, if this process is interrupted for a significant length of time, the buildup of destructive patterns outstrips the Higher Self's ability to defuse them. The result is always some degree of madness, accelerated aging, and ultimately, death."

"Well done!" Zeus exclaimed. "Larry, may you never cease to amaze! You've described the Higher Self's role in most people's lives. However, this is just a sampling of its power to help. If a person drew on the Higher Self's full potential, his or her Consciousness could change in the wink of an eye."

"So if the Higher Self wants to help, why doesn't it simply tell the third-density self how to access more of its gifts?" Larry asked.

"Once again you manage to amaze, Larry; I just never know how. It's either a flash of pure brilliance or a clunking thud. Think, man! Why isn't the Higher Self permitted to do more on its own?"

"It would be a violation of Free Will, wouldn't it?"

"Of course it would," Zeus said. "The overriding imperative of Creation is to allow exploration and experimentation in infinite directions. Even though Free Will is hardly evoked in the third density, Creation honors the potential of any being emerging into present time at any instant. Consequently, even the Higher Self must wait backstage until it's summoned by the main player.

"The abdication of Free Will pervades the human condition. The strictures of your social institutions have become so deeply ingrained that people assume they can improve their lot only by adopting the view of someone in power. Almost any self-styled guru can attract a following; it hardly matters whether they advocate mass suicide, corporate raiding, terrorism, fundamentalist religion, or world peace. As long as one sheep moves, the flock willingly trails along. From our perspective, however, this only deepens the rut out of which your collective Awareness must climb."

"You make us humans sound so incredibly stuck," Larry said.

"Indeed, " the Voice offered, "we might have put it in more precise and less judgmental terms, but the meaning is inescapable. This planet's thinking could do with a little shaking up. And maybe—just maybe—if you can stop the merry-go-round long enough for folks to realize they've been going nowhere, they'll begin exploring outside the confines of their hand-me-down beliefs. That is precisely what is meant by the events of 9/11, which can be viewed either as a momentous tragedy that needs to be mourned or an unparalleled opportunity that needs to be seized. We are curious to see which of these paths humankind selects.

"And that goes triple for me," Zeus added. "But it don't look good. Last I checked the morning line, the smart money was betting against you guys. Here's my take on it, for what it's worth. Humanity is pulling as hard as it can in one direction while it pushes just as hard in the other."

"What do you mean by that?" Larry asked.

"Look at it this way: on the one hand, you're trying to complete the lessons of the third density, which require you to advance upward along the I-continuum. On the other, the mere thought of breaking free causes the egoic self to have a panic attack. The lower portion of your continuum has a major stake in staying around. It would rather explore a million ways to redecorate its prison cell than consider leaving it."

"It's all about *espavo,* the word Junie taught me, isn't it?" Larry said.

"Indeed it is," Zeus replied. "If you recall, she said it meant 'thank you for taking your power.' But this is a simplistic definition. As you experienced firsthand, the true meaning of *espavo* requires no less than a death/life experience such as you underwent on Inspiration Peak. The lower self, however, would rather take you down with it than relinquish the point from which it views."

"What a curious thing to say," Larry said. "Would you mind going a little deeper?"

"Allow us to address this issue," the Voice interjected. "As it is another area of particular interest to us, one we have been observing since humans first evolved on this planet. We are continually astonished by the presence of a problem so pervasive that it passes virtually undetected. And in the isolated, extreme cases when your societies acknowledge its existence, they scarcely know how to deal with it. Do you have any idea what this problem might be, Larry?"

Larry was silent, unsure how to respond.

"Let me give you a helping hand," Zeus offered. "What our esteemed host is referring to is the common factor in the following situations: obesity . . . codependent relationships . . . fanaticism . . . depression. . . ." Sensing Larry's confusion, Zeus continued, "Okay, I'll throw in a few more examples to make it easier: chocolate . . . sex . . . drugs . . . alcohol . . . gambling . . . smoking. . . ."

"They're all addictions," Larry blurted out.

"Precisely," the Voice said. "Here's the part we cannot fathom. Your view of reality is so biomechanistic that you seem to recognize addiction only when you locate a psycho-bio-chemical box to put it in. What you fail to recognize is that all addictions emit common wave forms that identify them as internally conflicted, self-destructive actions compulsively generated by the distortions implanted in the lower chakras interacting with a state of catalytic overwhelm the Higher Self has not been able to successfully process."

"*What . . . What? What . . . What?*" The unmistakable screeching verified that this made absolutely no sense to Larry whatsoever.

"Sorry about that. It would seem we got ahead of ourselves. See if this version helps: Think back to when you and Junie were discussing the source of your shadow parts. She shared something quite profound when she said, 'Every problem arises as the solution to a previous problem.' At the time, you didn't have sufficient Awareness to take that teaching any further, but now you do.

"You now understand how seemingly random events in an entity's life trigger interference patterns as they pass by the energetic biases lodged in the chakras. You also appreciate how and why the Higher Self attempts to reintegrate these experiences in present time. Well, Larry, addictions are what occur when that reintegration is not completely successful. The interference patterns accumulate in the chakras' distortive lenses and ultimately take over and redefine the entity's life."

Following Larry's inner thoughts, Zeus knew he hadn't fully comprehended the Voice's message. "Larry, have you ever been in a situation so overwhelming that you didn't know how to cope?"

"Of course."

"What did you really feel like doing then?"

"If you want to know the truth," Larry answered, "I felt like crawling back into bed, pulling the covers over my head, and staying there forever."

"That's it!" Zeus exclaimed. "That's exactly what addiction is all about. Any skewed activity—even the ones society praises—is a way of avoiding the challenges the third density poses."

"Yeah," Larry said, "when it gets that overwhelming, what hope is there?"

"Allow us to quote some words we overheard recently," the Voice said. "'Hope is what my Playful Rebel would certainly call a "woosie-wish" made by a gelded castrato crooning to a tone-deaf God. Asking people to hope separates them from their power and their innate exquisite nature.' These very words, unless our inner ears deceive, came from your lips. You are right, Larry, there is no hope for addiction. There is only *espavo!* And therein lies the heart of the problem.

"Tell me, Larry, what is your society's best plan for dealing with addiction?"

"Twelve steps, one day at a time," Larry responded.

"And in the lexicon of this twelve-step program is there any such thing as a cure?"

"No, there's only remission. People are encouraged to admit openly that they are still addicted while they count the days they have been clean, or sober, or abstinent."

"And which one of the I's is addicted? Which one is in the program? And which one does the counting and admitting?" the Voice asked.

"They are all the same I, the lower, egoic I—the I that developed the addiction in the first place and, from what you're telling me, would rather die than release it."

"Bull's-eye!" the Voice replied. "Now you're right on target. Can you see how having the addiction comes to define the person's life, itself feeding off the original, underlying problem that created it in the first place?

"Let's take smoking as an example—certainly a worldwide problem, affecting over one billion people, 80 percent of them in developing countries, one-third in China alone. The health implications of smoking are well known and publicized, yet every day thousands of new young smokers—did you know 95 percent of all new smokers are under the age of twenty-four?—take their first puff. One study confirmed that Joe Camel is as familiar to three-year-olds as Mickey Mouse. Hundreds of millions of smokers claim they would like to quit. Many try to break the habit. But few succeed. Why is all this happening?"

"Smoking must have seemed like a viable solution to a previous problem," Larry responded. "Since the majority of first-time smokers are in their teens, I suspect it must be an image thing."

"In part," the Voice said. "Among the young, the motto is certainly 'Image, über alles!' But like most easy answers, 'image' is, as you humans are fond of saying, just the tip of the iceberg. Smoking provides a sense of identity in what is often an impersonal and overwhelming world.

"The belief that smoking is addictive is accurate. The belief that it is solely a biological dependence on nicotine is less true. Smoking is considerably more insidious than mere chemical dependency. One has only to listen to the excuses of those who fail at giving up smoking: 'I can't quit, I'm hooked.' They are absolutely right. Yet every so often, a habitual smoker decides to quit and simply walks away, never again feeling the urge to light up. Larry, what do you suppose precipitates this apparent anomaly?"

"I don't know,' Larry answered, "but it is curious. I can remember dieting countless times—mostly a half-hearted attempt to eat grapefruits or take some magic metabolic bullet pill. They all worked for a while; then I slipped back to my old patterns and the weight slipped back as well. Then for some reason, about two years ago, something inside seemed to shift. I can't explain what happened, but my attitude toward food changed. Without thinking about dieting, I found myself cutting out a lot of the processed foods and fried stuff and losing weight."

"I know," Zeus interjected, "I was there. It was an interesting process to observe. Death always is."

"Huh?" Larry said. "Who died?"

"Kiddo, slow down and take a few deep breaths. It's time to read you another quote from the *I-S-M* text. This portion is not normally shared—for obvious reasons—with third-density bipeds. But now, given the short amount of linear time remaining, we need to pull out all the stops:

Beings entering the third density through the Veil of Forgetting perceive themselves as largely separated from their true essence. While this allows for richness of experience in an apparent reality defined by belief, thought, and emotion, it has one overriding consequence that lies at the root of all human behavior: third-density beings are not certain they exist.

"This fact causes all manner of paradoxes. On the one hand, humans can perceive infinity and the mysterious nature of Creation. They can delve into subatomic physics and discover that nothing is solid and that the state of matter itself is a matter of uncertainty. On the other hand, they can bump their knee against a table and be convinced it is solid, or lose a loved one and be submerged in grief. Palpable experience has a way of demanding center stage. It leads humans by the nose to adopt society's accepted means and ends, at times moving with the herd, at other times simply trying to better their position.

"Yet they are nagged by a sense that there is more to it all. And one recurring question raps incessantly at their mind's door, like the steady beat of native drumming: 'Who am I? . . . Who am I? . . . Who am I?' The way people deal with this question defines their entire existence. Almost all the 'whys' concerning the human condition—personal, family, tribal, national, global—have their roots in this core question. It is the base cause of ambition, the foundation undergirding all subpersonalities, the reason people turn to religion and compulsion. Addiction is a particularly effective way to drown out the drumming.

"I think, therefore I am . . . I believe, therefore I am . . . I am a Blood or a Crypt, therefore I am . . . I am righteous, therefore I am . . . I am a good parent, therefore I am . . . I am noticed, therefore I am . . . I stand for something, therefore I am . . . I cause something to happen, therefore I am . . . I am fat—or thin, tall, fit, pretty, ugly, well-dressed, famous, talented, rich—therefore I am . . . I smoke, therefore I am. . . .

"The more they doubt their existence, the grosser the addiction needed to assuage the doubt.

"The same line of reasoning leads humans to their anthropomorphic gods—the quintessential third-density paradox, a product of the belief that one lives in linear time. 'Creation exists, therefore there must be a Creator; and since I am able to view this Creation, I must also be a product of the Creator, separate from the other products He—or She or It—has created.'

"If you define your existence by what you and others perceive you to be, how can you alter it without risking annihilation at some level? Simply put, you can't. To write new words on the blackboard of this schoolroom requires erasing the previous notations. Death makes way for birth. That's simply the way of it."

"Ouch! No matter how much I try to duck and dive, you've just described me to a T," Larry said.

"Don't think you're getting out of it that easily, my friend," Zeus responded. "There's more work to be done here, and it gets trickier. Think about your many voices that you met with Junie's help—what exactly are they?"

"Each one is a singular point of view expressing itself as a subpersonality, contributing to the whole psychological me. Some are primary, and some are suppressed or unexpressed."

"Go deeper," Zeus said.

"What do you mean?"

"Larry, you've just described the psychology of personalities. Go beyond that and tell me what you know about their physiology and etiology. I want the nitty-gritty, get-your-hands-dirty stuff way down at the core."

"I still don't get what you're driving at," Larry said.

"Okay, let's play some mind games correlating personalities with chakras and time. Tell me how personalities are formed, where they're stored, and why they persist."

After a few moments' thought, Larry said, "According to Junie, a personality arises when somebody makes a formative decision about his or her survival. To survive as babies, we need our parents' continual attention, so we experiment. Some discover smiling and gurgling works best, others cry, others simply lie there doing nothing or find that grown-ups respond to them more when they're sick. The behavior that works best to get the parents' attention becomes the person's primary persona. Gurglers and smilers generally evolve into consummate pleasers. Criers typically become chronic complainers. The quiet infant may play a background role in another person's life rather than emerge as the star in his own."

"Fair enough," Zeus said. "Why does this pattern remain the primary persona?"

Again Larry took the time to find the portion of the iceberg hidden from view. "Oh, I see what you're driving at! When a major decision is made, it becomes an energy pattern embedded in one or more of the chakras. From that point forward, all life experiences pass through that imprint, so it shapes the person's actions for the rest of his or her life."

"Excellent," Zeus commended, "Now, in light of what you just said, can you simplify your definition of subpersonality?"

"A subpersonality is the outward expression of an energy pattern imprinted in the chakras."

"Not quite good enough," Zeus responded. "You said earlier that those voices could be dormant, suppressed, or unexpressed. Simplify it further to include these as well."

Again Larry paused in thought. "A persona *is* the energy pattern imprinted in the chakras."

"Bull's-eye!" the Voice interjected. "Now you *have* grasped the simplicity of the situation. Let's revisit, then, the question under consideration: why some decisions to give up addictions have instantaneous results while others are fruitless. It is simply a function of Rocky's I's of infinity—a matter of discovering which of the myriad I's is making the decision. Recall once again the famous quote from Dr. Einstein: 'No problem can be solved from the same level of Consciousness that created it'—quite pertinent to the case at hand.

"Consider the person who has started smoking to escape some of life's challenges and find an avenue for self-identity. When he desires to quit, he has two options. One is to embrace the world of psychologists, twelve-step programs, nicotine patches, and deprivation, all of which invite him to remain at the lower, egoic level of his I's, where the decision to smoke was initially made. Unfortunately, as he struggles to redefine himself as one who is overcoming the addiction, the unwanted behavior moves to center stage in the his life. The second option is to move to a higher perspective, one where smoking becomes irrelevant as an escape from life's tests and proof of his existence. Here quitting is a fait accompli—no effort, no additional thought required. We imagine you're wondering how it works."

Larry said nothing, allowing the Voice to continue. "It's quite simple, really. Consider again your experience on Inspiration Peak. That night part of you died, clearing the way for a new part to enter. The you who climbed down from the mountain to the empty parking lot was not the same you who had ascended a few hours earlier. In essence, you became a walk-in on your own life."

Sensing a thread of confusion remaining in Larry, the Voice went on. "Let us present a more graphic illustration. Imagine an entity deeply involved in an abusive relationship that threatens its well-being yet feeling powerless to move itself out of the situation. If you were magically projected into that being's mind and body with the full power to take over its life, what would you do?"

A tinge of anger colored Larry's words. "I'd tell my abusive partner to take a hike and I'd get my butt out of that torture chamber in a New York minute."

"Why is it you could change that entity's life in a heartbeat while it cannot?" the Voice asked.

The edge remained in Larry's voice. "Because that person is however he chooses to be, and I'm me. He may like wallowing in misery, but I sure don't."

"Could you perchance make your answer more creative and thought-provoking? Try going a bit deeper before presenting us with the pearls of your deliberations," the Voice gently chided.

"Sorry. I guess there's a portion of me that doesn't fancy abusive relationships. Let me take another whack at it—no pun intended, of course.

"I think I've got it." Larry said after a few moments thought. "The *I* that walks in to take over that life is not at the same position on the I-continuum as the *I* that got into the abusive relationship in the first place, then accepted it and fed off it. Its point of view is not attached to the energy patterns embedded in that guy's chakras, so it would have no history in the relationship or investment in maintaining it."

"Correct," the Voice said. "So what would happen to the old energy pattern in the chakras when the new *you* arrives on the scene?"

"They'd be neutralized. Totally inactivated," Larry said, amazed at his own words.

"Now, relate this to addiction and tell me what you perceive."

"Of course," Larry said. "To change a habit, all I have to do is shift the point from which I view—out of the personality that created the old pattern and into one with a more pervasive perspective. In other words, I have to evoke a higher point of view."

"Ah," the Voice responded. "Interesting choice of words. And just exactly how would you go about evoking a higher point from which to view?"

"Through my Higher Self?"

"Yes and no," the Voice said enigmatically. "It is true that we have been speaking of your Higher Self as a sixth-density version of yourself, obviously having a larger perspective and greater level of Awareness. However, the Higher Self is not to be viewed as a benevolent parent one evokes to make problems disappear. Rather, consider it an ally, helping you learn to shift your own point of view. A great deal is already accomplished simply by requesting its assistance. Do you know why?"

"I guess it means the person already acknowledges that part of his being exists outside his local universe."

"Quite so," the Voice said, obviously pleased by Larry's answer. "Now why is that realization so exceptionally significant?"

Larry felt encouraged by the Voice's tone and did not wish to miss an obvious opportunity to continue to impress. Zeus found his master's typically human thought process amusing but remained stoically silent. After several minutes of intense concentration, Larry said, "I think I see where you're going. Once I accept that I already have multiple points of view—

some of them beyond anything I've yet experienced—I'm implicitly acknowledging that parts of me also exist outside the problem consuming me."

"Quite so," the Voice acknowledged. "Your answer brings up collateral areas of interest. For instance, the term 'Higher Self' also has a relative meaning. It defines any point along the infinite I-continuum more elevated than where you are now."

"Huh?" The word slipped out on its own accord, much to Larry's regret.

"Pity," Zeus remarked, "you were doing great there for a while—til you started getting highbrow on us. My guess is you're losing sight of the gradient nature of the I-continuum. Picture again the giant disk on which each density is a different section of the color spectrum."

"Okay."

"Well, the same concept can be used to represent the I's of infinity. Imagine the lower, egoic portion of the continuum starting at pure red. With each small gain of Awareness, a drop of yellow is introduced until, over time, the color changes to orange and eventually becomes pure yellow. Then, blue drops are introduced and the color starts shifting toward green, continuing through the color spectrum until Awareness reaches the level of the soul."

"What happens then?" Larry asked.

"The process starts all over again, from a higher harmonic of red, until Awareness finally merges with the All That Is. The point is that each drop of Awareness affords a new, more elevated point from which to view—provided the being is willing to go there."

"Thank you, Zeus," the Voice said. "A lovely explanation. It also illustrates how the Higher Self assists in overcoming addiction.

"Larry, is it fully clear to you that the personality that can neutralize an unwanted energy pattern cannot be at the same level of Consciousness as the personality that created and expresses that pattern?"

"Yes."

"Can you explain why?" the Voice asked.

"I think so," Larry answered. "All of my personalities, whether they're active or dormant, were created in my local universe, as I reacted to the happenings around me. In fact, they define my subjective world. They define the way I see what's around me and how I encourage others to see me. A higher point of view, on the other hand, exists outside that world, so we could say it's nonlocal, relatively speaking. The old viewpoint is, by nature, blind to the new. From the vantage point of the new, however, it seems I can still see the old. Like going up a mountain.

"So the lower I—the persona with the problem—is stuck. It can't create a direct connection to the part of myself holding the solution because it doesn't realize that the higher part of me exists. If I don't know where it is, or what it is, how can I build a bridge to it? Yet it does exist; it's alive and well in a parallel universe, holding open the possibility for me to enter into a reality where the old patterning has never taken hold.

"I have to open myself up to my inner knowing and surrender my lower will in order to ask for the assistance of my Higher Self."

"In short," the Voice said, "You must be willing to die."

You are a child of the Universe,
No less than the moon and the stars;
You have a right to be here.
And whether or not it is clear to you,
No doubt the Universe is unfolding as it should.

— MAX EHRMANN

CHAPTER 26

Redefining Reality

The three waited in silence, no one wishing to interrupt the reverberations of the Voice's last words. "Such is the process," the Voice finally said. "When one walks, each step must die so the next can replace it. And so it is with all life. Death is no enemy. On this path through the densities, death becomes your greatest ally—to be welcomed, when it comes, as a dear and treasured friend. Perpetual birth in the absence of death is overwhelming; it leads only to pain and suffering. Consider, for instance, the current state of imbalance on your planet, a product of humanity's reverence for power and possessions while disdaining surrender.

"The Higher Self can be reached only by surrendering the lower will. The egoic self cannot manipulate or exploit it, for its Light/Love quotient is too bright for the lower I to handle."

"Then how do we bridge the gap?" Larry asked.

"With great humility," the Voice answered, "just as one does not pray arrogantly to one's God. Remember, the Higher Self is the priceless jewel gifted to your sixth-density self by your seventh-density self just before it turns its full attention to merging with All That Is. It is arguably the highest form of God a third-density being can commune with directly. Contact with this elevated energy is so elusive that we strongly recommend it be attempted only during states of dreaming."

"But didn't I contact my Higher Self when I was with Junie?" Larry asked. "I wasn't asleep then."

"Ah, then we have to define our terms more precisely. By 'dreaming,' we refer to any activity that establishes a bridge between your conscious and unconscious. Space/time flows into time/space along this pathway, allowing you and your Higher Self to connect. This state can be most easily achieved in sleep. However, it is also reached through deep meditation, especially with judicious use of the breath, and through other activities that call for surrender, such as channeling, deep ritual, and—though unpredictably—the use of mind-altering substances. Your ability to speak with your Higher Self in Junie's presence was largely due to her particular magic. She induced the required state in you."

"So it *is* possible to commune with the Higher Self while you're still alive and awake in the third density."

"Yes, Larry, it is," the Voice replied. "However, this state—called the magical personality—is accessible only to serious adepts who have already balanced their chakras and honed their ability to reach into the Infinite Intelligence. You will have greater success by confining your attempts to the modes of dreaming that come through sleep and meditation."

"Fair enough," Larry said, "I can read a 'no trespassing' sign as well as the next guy. What do you suggest I do?"

"The opportunities available when you link with your Higher Self are limited only by your imagination. You have only to express your clear intent and, provided it does not interfere with the lessons you are programmed to learn on this side of the Veil, it will manifest."

"Does that mean I can ask to be healed?" Larry asked.

"Yes."

"Can I ask for guidance and understanding about problems or relationships?"

"Absolutely."

"And how do the answers come?"

"In many ways," the Voice responded. "Healings, of course, are self-evident. Moreover, the reasons for a particular physical disharmony are often made clear, and the lesson that is its gift is learned, so the illness departs. With regard to guidance or understanding, the Higher Self communicates through many means, often catching your attention through synchronicities and coincidences. Words on a billboard might suddenly take on a profound meaning, or the right book might fall off a shelf at a key moment. One might overhear a key remark in a restaurant or—in your case—read a relevant fortune cookie. Perhaps a random thought suddenly appears in your mind, a line from a movie or a play sticks in your Consciousness, or a friend you haven't seen or thought about for years unexpectedly contacts you."

"If they're so diverse," Larry asked, "how will I know what to take seriously?"

"That's the easiest question you've asked yet," the Voice chuckled. "Take it *all* seriously. There is no need to travel to India in search of your guru. There is nothing in all Creation that is not your teacher, provided you are present and open to learning. Understand that virtually nothing occurs randomly. Every chance encounter, every casual remark, every serendipitous happenstance contains deeper meaning than is first apparent.

"Consider the complexity of events in a world of well over six billion people, each personally guided by his or her Higher Self—like an unimaginably elaborate, intricate multidimensional chess game with remarkably dynamic rules. Because of the Oneness of Creation, every single interaction has a direct effect—grossly palpable or exquisitely subtle—on you. Fortunately for each entity on your planet, the game is played by Grand Masters with levels of Love, Wisdom, and Power beyond your wildest conception. We promise, when you finally review your incarnation after leaving this illusion, you will be amazed at the many, many blatant messages you've ignored."

Zeus smiled, thinking of all the thirty-foot neon signs Larry had missed during their few years together. His mind echoed the famous words of Matthew Henry, "None so blind as those that will not see." But honoring the process and Larry's Free Will, he said nothing.

"How do I become more aware of them?" Larry asked.

"By not being so consumed by the magnitude of your daily drama that you fail to appreciate the wonders surrounding you at all times," the Voice replied. "By learning to listen, treating everyone you meet as if he or she was an avatar. By relinquishing the need to seek rational answers to the enigmas of life. By focusing less on being interesting and more on being interested. But by far the greatest way to open up to the riches offered you moment by moment is to reverse your third-density instincts and learn to think with your heart and love with your mind.

"In Zeus's words, the key is to show up—to be as present as possible. You cannot be completely in the now if ingrained patterning and prejudgments control you. So cultivate the art of not knowing. It is up to you to find and celebrate the uniqueness of each aspect of Creation. We suggest you play this simple game: Wherever you find yourself at any moment, try to observe three things you have never noticed before. Look for them in the people you encounter, in your physical surroundings, and most especially in your own thoughts."

The Voice allowed this advice to sink in for several moments before continuing. "Very well, then. We shall complete the Myth of Creation by briefly mentioning the seventh density, also called the gateway cycle. Here the Consciousness of those who enter from the sixth density discerns the sacramental nature of all aspects of Creation. From that point forward, the process is shrouded in mystery. From the little we know, it seems the social memory complex accumulates such a high degree of spiritual mass that it turns away from all concepts of personal identity. It surrenders fully to the gravitational force calling from within as it coalesces into the zero point of All That Is. The outward, physical manifestation of this metaphysical state is what your scientists call a black hole. Then, in the eighth density, Consciousness becomes one with its original source. All Creation cycles back in this way, merging into the All That Is—before reemerging in the first density within a new octave of Creation."

"So it's a continuous process?" Larry asked.

"There is no way to answer without misleading you," the Voice replied. "In the eighth density, time as we know it collapses completely. The transition from the eighth density into a new form of experience is neither linear nor simultaneous. The succeeding creative expression simply unfolds from an unimaginable timelessness. That is all we can say.

"And so ends our little journey through Creation. We offer it not as fact to be accepted blindly but as a proposition for you to consider. In this period of extreme uncertainty, it is urgent that your peoples embrace a larger mythology than your present teachings offer. You must discard the conclusion that you are powerless in an infinite universe and cease measuring your worth by how well you please others or meet society's expectations. It has become dangerously counterproductive to wallow in the illusion of separation and alienation—from each other and from Creation itself. Can you not hear the insistent ringing? It is time to awaken and greet a dawn you have never before encountered."

"You make it sound ominous," Larry said.

"That is not our purpose," the Voice replied. "We do not

intend to direct choice or interfere with Free Will in any manner. Rather, we wish you to appreciate that the third-density experience on this planet is rapidly approaching the end of its cycle. We want you to realize that those who wish to make the transition must make certain decisions.

"Our discourse is intended not to underscore the failings of humankind, but quite the opposite. Those entities who respond to the call and wander outside of Plato's cave will surely discover for themselves what you are learning here, that humankind and God are one.

"Consider humankind's extraordinary legacy of architects and writers, painters and performers, inventors, scientists, mathematicians, philosophers, musicians, and dreamers. Are their works—given the self-imposed limitations of the Veil—any less grand than the galaxies? We think not. The spark of the logos thrives in each of you, though it is hidden under layers of conditioned beliefs.

"Perhaps you can now appreciate the limitations of your physicists' attempts to explain the Universe. Even quantum theories only create more questions than they answer. Infinity can not be perceived by the finite. No telescope, no matter how powerful, can see to the edge of the Universe. The Universe will always appear to be expanding in direct proportion to one's ability to view it, the red shift factor notwithstanding."

"I thought the red shift proves that galaxies are hurtling away from each other," Larry said.

"Not really," the Voice replied. "It's just a convenience latched onto by modern science to lend credence to the Big Bang—an attempt to describe mysteries, vast beyond comprehension, in terms that human beings already accept. If your scientists would review their data without preconception, they might find that the intrinsic red shift of a quasar or a galaxy is not related to velocity. In other words, it has nothing whatsoever to do with receding galaxies. One of your scientists, Halton Arp, almost took a step in the right direction when he suggested the shift might be linked to a galaxy's relative age. But because he relies on current scientific concepts, he, too, fell in the trap of seeking a physical explanation for a nonphysical event. The red shift does appear to manifest in discrete steps over time, but this is not a function of chronological age. Rather, it is due to the increase of spiritual mass acquired as a local galaxy evolves. What meaning can distance or velocity possibly have in an infinite universe?

"So you see, Larry, in your quest for heightened Awareness, always seek another way of seeing things. Do not rely solely on your senses or intellect. Even lightning, which Zeus so beautifully described to you earlier, is not what it appears to be. In all matters of inquiry, never settle. No matter how far you believe you have come or how much you think you understand, you are only on the surface. Always go deeper.

"The potential for further discussion is almost as infinite as Creation itself, but the shadows are beginning to lengthen. It is now time for you and Zeus to begin your journey back to your home on this planet. It has been a privilege to share this teaching and learning experience with you both. We have gained much from this exchange. Perhaps we shall meet again. For now, we bid you farewell. *Espavo*. Go forth rejoicing in the power and peace of the One Infinite Creator. Adonai."

"Thank you," Larry said. "Thank you. This has been, without a doubt, the most extraordinary school I've ever attended. You've given me much to think about. If you don't mind, I'd like to ask you a few more questions. A few areas of confusion still remain."

"Just a few?" Zeus remarked. "Come now, laddie, this is no time to be modest."

But the energy of the Voice had vanished as unexpectedly as it first arrived. Larry and Zeus found themselves once again in their physical bodies, sitting on rough, bare ground in the concave depression of a cliff face. Shadows had indeed engulfed the entire area, and the air was considerably cooler than Larry remembered. His body felt stiff as he gingerly stood up and began to stretch.

"Do they all just suddenly appear and disappear like that?" Larry asked.

"Don't know," Zeus drawled. "Can't rightly say I've met 'em all. Least ways, not up close and personal like this. Makes a dog wonder."

Zeus and Larry walked side by side, silently picking their way around the spill of boulders. The scattering of Joshua trees dotting the barren landscape were barely catching the last caress of the late afternoon sun. At last, they reached the marked trail that looped around Hidden Valley. It was Larry who spoke first. "Zeus, what did the Voice mean—that lightning is not what it appears to be?"

"You're insatiable," Zeus replied.

"Well, the Voice did tell me to go deeper."

"Can't you give it a rest, kiddo? Why not get out of your head for a while and enjoy the walk? This has got to be one of the most beautiful places on the planet and you're not seeing a single rock or tree."

"They're gorgeous," Larry replied, running his hands over the ridges of a nearby boulder, "and since they've been here for the last umpteen million years, my guess is there's a good chance they'll still be here next month."

"Ah, but will you?"

"What do you mean by that?" Larry asked.

"I'll let you work out that morsel for yourself," Zeus replied.

"You've got to be the intellectual equivalent of a nymphomaniac. What does it take to satisfy you?"

"Physically or mentally?"

"Okay, you win," Zeus said. "Let's dive into the deep end one last time before we leave the energy of Joshua Tree. You recall the Love, Wisdom, and Power triangle? What do you suppose these three cosmic principles really are?"

"From what I remember, Love is mastered in the fourth density; Wisdom, which balances Love, is gathered in the fifth; and Power, which unifies Love and Wisdom, is attained in the sixth."

"And the beat goes on," Zeus said.

"What do you mean by that?" Larry demanded.

"You speak as if answering a test question—carefully defining the surface. What you're looking for lies deeper. Remember the Voice's advice to think with your heart and love with your mind. You might want to give the Voice's meditations on the three sides of the Great Triangle a try—especially if you expect to get the meaning behind the words I am about to use."

"Calling Love, Wisdom, and Power 'principles' is misleading, because it suggests that one can grasp the essence of this Great Cosmic Triangle with the intellect. They are not theoretical concepts. Each is an aspect of the All That Is—three interlocking pieces of a puzzle that combine to form the unity of the Infinite One. Love is Infinite Consciousness, Wisdom is Infinite Intelligence, and Power is the innate ability to Create.

"Earlier I used the illustration of waves on the surface of a pond forming interference patterns."

"Yes, I remember that," Larry said.

"Now, imagine the water as an omnidirectional plasma—like a cosmic, multidimensional game board—where these three interact. How do you suppose the logos manifests galaxies? Through intentional design. It manipulates the wave patterns of

Love, Wisdom, and Power in the potential flux of hyperspace to create precise interference patterns. When these are frozen in the illusion of space and time, presto! Cosmic arrays of apparent realities, in all their multifarious expressions, take their appointed places in the Grand Experiment!"

"I think I'm getting the idea," Larry said, "though I can't begin to imagine the level of intelligence required to hold it all together."

"There's no way you can, so don't even try," Zeus said. "It'll help, though, if you substitute 'Awareness' for 'intelligence.' This Love-Wisdom-Power model of Creation opens up a whole new understanding of the nature of the cosmos. Space is not, as your scientists once believed, a vacuum. It is living, throbbing, holographic Consciousness. That's why information is instantly and universally available. That's why there are solar winds and heliospheres. That's what makes ESP and channeling possible. That's what our host in the rocks meant by saying every single interaction throughout all Creation has a direct effect on you."

Noting Larry's silence, Zeus continued, "Why do I get the distinct impression you're not following me here? Let me take another approach. Until your scientists grasp the significance of Consciousness, they are better off accepting the electric model of cosmos suggested by the plasma physicists. It's a more elegant platform from which to explain cosmic curiosities such as recurring spiral structuring, galactic magnetic fields, and the dynamic movement of galaxies."

"I don't get it," Larry interjected, "what's all this got to do with lightning?"

"I digress not, little chickadee. You just hang in there. We're about to discuss lightning as an effect of cosmic orgasm. It'll just be gift wrapping if you haven't grasped how the Universe operates. Stay with me, now."

"Okay, sorry."

"So hold onto your image of a charged electrical plasmic Universe made up of Consciousness, Infinite Intelligence, and the Power of Intention. Instead of thinking of stars as gigantic thermonuclear engines, try them on as electrodes in a galactic glow discharge—great concentrated balls of lightning. What looks like activity—sunspots and solar flares and the like—is essentially determined by their electrical environment, which can change suddenly. Every star is actively communicating with its galaxy's central sun and with other parts of the cosmos. They're not atomic furnaces; they're great beings, the sublogoi of Creation.

"This brings us to the object of your insatiable curiosity—the nature of lightning. Lightning is really a dense stream of luminous plasma manifested as a powerful electric discharge. When you see a great jagged burst of electricity explode from the sky, where does the electric charge really come from? What I said the other day—that it comes from static electricity built up in storm clouds—was pretty simplistic. But given your understanding at the time, it was the best I could do. Besides, it made for a helluva story!"

"Thanks. And now you're going to tell me the tooth fairy doesn't exist?"

"No way, José. I no spoil 'joo foone para toda el Tequila een Tijuana. I gonna turn 'joo fairy into some pretty hot, chili-pepper mamma. 'Joo bet."

Larry chuckled as Zeus continued, abandoning his south-of-the-border accent.

"Guess what? Your government has several low-light photos of the upper atmosphere that conclusively prove—since seeing is believing to the beltway boys—that while you are enjoying the lightning lightshow below the clouds, there's a simultaneous above-the-clouds plasmic discharge that reaches up to seventy kilometers above the planet's surface. Now, what tree lives high enough to create the necessary positive ionic charge, do you suppose?"

"The Tree of Life?" Larry quipped.

"Cute. And not so far removed from what's actually happening, I might add. Toss out the belief that lightning is created in the clouds. It simply ain't so. Clouds are merely a convenient pathway for electricity originating in space to descend to Earth. Keep in mind that your planet, together with its solar system and galaxy, is speeding through the vast, dynamic electrical plasmic medium of the Great Cosmic Triangle."

"Talk about the potential for a sparking good time!" Larry said.

"There'll be a hot time in the old town tonight," Zeus quipped to the tune of the old refrain. "It means that the Sun and Mrs. O'Leary's cow may not be the only source of Earth's thermal and electrical stimulation. If your planet freely exchanges its energetic favors with every good-looking hunk of cosmic plasma it encounters, can you imagine how that might affect weather patterns? As I said, your scientists actually have photographs showing the illicit discharge between the ionosphere and the center of a hurricane. Scandalous!"

"But everyone knows weather comes from the sun," Larry said. "As the sun heats up the oceans they get warmer and stir up the air above them. This creates wind, which in turn creates weather."

"Then tell me, little hummingbird, how come there is weather on the sun? Who heats her buns? Besides, last time I checked her out, I didn't find too may oceans—or cows for that matter. While you're at it, perhaps you'll explain how come Neptune, one of the more distant planets from the sun, has the most violent winds in the entire solar system. And how do your little theories explain away the huge dust devils and planet-wide dust storms peppering Mars? Exactly why do your astronomers observe spokes in Saturn's rings or St. Elmo's fire dancing over the tops of Venusian mountain ranges?

"No, my little mosquito, these are not caused by the sun. They're merely part of the outward pyrotechnic display caused by interesting interference patterns. It's the clash of planes in a great cosmic joke."

"Pretty soon," Larry said, "you'll soon be calling me your little molecule! Why are you stressing all this weather stuff?"

"Ah, so!" Zeus replied. "Since we are about to leave the energetic hospitality of Joshua Tree, perhaps it's time for us to join together alpha and omega to make a complete sacred circle—not unlike the one we encountered soon after we got here. Let's go back a few days. Why did you leave work early last Friday and make tracks towards Phoenix?"

"My despondency over the terrorist attacks last Tuesday," Larry answered.

"And do you not see the connection between what I have been telling you and 9/11?" Zeus asked.

"No, I'm afraid I don't."

"Then allow me to fill in the gaps. If we live in an electric Universe, and if the sun and all the planets are significantly affected by plasmic interference patterns, how do you suppose they affect all other life forms, which are also electric in nature?"

"I'm not sure I get the question," Larry said.

"Fair enough," Zeus said. "Do you grasp the idea that the sun is not a burning ball floating in empty space, but the visible manifestation of an energy nexus—or a major confluence of interference patterns, as your scientists might say—in the electrical plasmic ethers?"

"Yes, I've got a picture in my mind—a Universe made up of a multidimensional, plasmic electrical field that manifests all the created objects in space, such as planets, stars, comets, and galaxies," Larry answered.

"Good," Zeus said. "Then what does that make you?"

"Oh, my God!" Larry exclaimed. "Me too?"

"Every one of us," Zeus said. "Every rock, every tree, every bird, fish, and drop of dew. Every entity that ever lived in any of the infinite subsets of the many densities. What are these, if not the products of interference patterns in the same plasma field, albeit on a smaller scale? You're not very different from your sun—a projected electrode of Consciousness linked to the Infinite Hologram by the silver thread of Love. . . . My, how poetic," he mused. "Even if it doesn't quite say it all, it sure sounds pretty. You think I'm ready to publish?"

"Oh, cut it out," Larry replied. "This stuff is tough enough without you making light of it."

"Why thank you, Larry, what a kind thing to say. To think I've created Light—which, in a sense, is exactly what I'm talking about.

"How you choose to see yourself is little more than a function of the position you choose along your continuum of existence, defined by the I's of infinity. You can look out into the heavens from here on Earth and explore the Unknowable Mysteries, or you can turn the telescope around and view Creation from the point of view of All That Is, who's exploring life behind the Veil through you. Either way, you discover that a part of yourself has been projected from the larger You into this remarkable dualistic illusion. How can any biochemical/electric entity—whether it be the sun or an ant—move through the electrical field of plasmic Consciousness without interacting with it?"

CHAPTER 27

What You *See* Is What You Get

Zeus let his last question negotiate its own way into Larry's mind. The concepts it proffered were so deeply intertwined with every aspect of his master's identity that suggestions or interference of any kind at this stage were unthinkable.

"What a weird way to look at things," Larry mused after several minutes' thought. "When I hold the picture of the plasmic field of Creation in my mind, it's like seeing myself watching me pretending to be me. It's surreal! How am I supposed to hold that vision and not go bonkers?"

"What makes you think all of us haven't gone off the deep end eons ago?" Zeus asked.

"No, seriously," Larry protested, "how do you expect me to dive into the dissociative world of quantum num-num and continue operating as a functional human being at the same time?"

"Mind rephrasing that?" Zeus jested. "I get the distinct impression that you're suggesting humans are sane. Surely, you don't mean that, do you?"

"Zeus, you're confusing the hell out of me," Larry said.

"Why not try being the *you* watching yourself pretending to be confused?"

"Why don't you try chewing your own tail for a change!" Larry blurted out, surprising only himself.

"Now there you've got me," Zeus responded. "The sheer weight of your intellect leaves me breathless. Why didn't I think of that? Of course, the Uroboros—the alpha consuming its own omega, the full circle of Creation manifesting the infinite One. How elegant! I now sit at your feet, a humble student eager to learn."

"Zeus you're driving me nuts!"

"Now you've got *me* confused. You just wrapped up the entire mystery of All That Is in a simple metaphor and still you want more. Man, don't you listen to anything you say?"

Larry burst out laughing—there was no other suitable container for his mounting anger.

"Ah, there you are," Zeus remarked. "Thought we'd lost you for a moment. Ain't teetering on the edge a hoot? Take anything too seriously and *wham*—you're ass over tea kettle in pea soup— whatever that's supposed to mean. The trick of this balancing act is to envelop yourself in the protective coat of humor while never losing sight of the lessons you learned with Junie. Be able to play at investigating the cosmos, be able to play at being a biped, and remember all the while they're both games. They involve you only to the extent you infuse them with your own intention and attention. You are safely outside of any illusion as long as you remember."

"That's where the Veil comes in?" Larry asked.

"Bull's-eye!" Zeus replied, mimicking the Voice in the rocks. "Now do you grasp the simplicity of it all? The Veil is a gossamer energy field now being buffeted by a unique sector of plasmic Consciousness specifically programmed to rend the fabric of forgetting. This is triggering the opportunity to remember, which means letting go of your old patterning. Unfortunately, for the majority of your populace it seems to be having the opposite effect."

"Is that what's making people freak out all over the planet?" Larry asked.

"What do you think?" Zeus responded, giving Larry room to explore his own question.

"I think I'm getting an idea of what you've been driving at. As the Veil progressively thins, humans must feel as if their favorite Linus blanket is being wrenched away. That's got to be scary stuff! It's no wonder people are losing it. It's almost as if humanity is desperate to act out its disowned, suppressed parts before time runs out.

"Maybe *that's* it!" Larry said, making it clear that a new penny had dropped. "Maybe it *is* about time! I've noticed that days and weeks seem to be streaming by faster and faster. It's like we're catapulting toward a zero point. Is that what's causing the planet-wide angst?"

"You're on the right track," Zeus responded. "Time is not an isolated constant. It does appear to constrict as Consciousness approaches the shift from one density to another. The days ahead will be increasingly challenging for humankind. The compression is already abrading much of the social veneer, exposing the underlying tangle of unresolved issues. People will find 'faking it' more difficult as their true colors are exposed. You'll see an unprecedented resurgence in fundamentalism and nationalistic chauvinism in a last-ditch attempt to reinforce the old paradigm."

"Ah," Larry said, "like the ancient Chinese curse, 'May you live in interesting times!'"

"You've been chewing on too many of those sugary fortune cookies, kiddo. The closest that saying ever got to China is in your mind. The only Chinese proverb that even comes close is 'Better a dog in times of peace than a man in times of war.' Your version is right out of science fiction. In fact, that's exactly where it first showed up, more than a half century ago, in Frank Russell's story 'U-Turn.' But that's a moot issue. Me dog. You man. Time chaotic. What's a poor doggie to do?

"Let me offer instead Julius Caesar—liberally paraphrased, I might add, by William Shakespeare:

> Why, man, he doth bestride the narrow world
> Like a Colossus, and we petty men
> Walk under his huge legs and peep about
> To find ourselves dishonorable graves.
> Men at some time are masters of their fates:
> The fault, dear Brutus, is not in our stars,
> But in ourselves, that we are underlings.

"Each person on your planet now finds himself, or herself, at a choice point—to arise as the Colossus or to slink back into the pettiness of the lower egoic realm. The stars have done their work and the baton has been passed. Nonparticipation is no longer an option.

"Perhaps at times over the past few days you thought I was harsh with you or made fun of some of your answers. I was only holding up a mirror so you could see yourself from another point of view. For though you consider yourself an individual, Larry, you—like every other human on this planet—are also the macrocosm. Every insight you attain accrues to the collective. When you soar, you raise the vibration for the entire planet. When you settle for mediocrity, humanity ebbs back to its old patterning. A great deal is at stake. And I love you too much to support anything but your best."

For the next several minutes, the two were simply man and dog making their way back to the parking lot after spending some time in nature. Larry watched Zeus as he crisscrossed the desert floor, sniffing at random rocks and shrubs, his tail erect as if pointing to something of great significance. He found himself puzzling how it would feel to be a sixth-density being in a dog's body, checking out the markings of others' territories.

Zeus suddenly returned to Larry's side. "Funny, I was just wondering the same thing about you. Gotta admit, it can sure be fun once we learn to get out of our own way. And there, sweet prince, lies the rub. These *are* challenging times. Transitioning through the condensing plasma is profoundly affecting the planet herself. Her Consciousness has already shifted into the fourth density, and she can barely support the polarized, dualistic vibrations of third-density beings."

"That's probably why psychic futurists are predicting volcanic eruptions and earthquakes in the time ahead," Larry proposed.

"Prediction is a tricky business," Zeus replied. "Some seers say that California is going to sink into the ocean and Phoenix is about to become a major seaport. Some predict that recent volcanic eruptions and major quakes—with a magnitude of 7.7 or higher—are just precursors of what lies ahead. But the problem isn't so much in the accuracy of their predictions as in the dissemination of their conclusions. It's no coincidence that so many humans are now connected by a worldwide information grid. But that's a double-edged sword that cuts with alarming swiftness and power.

"Consider, Larry, that Creation is not random. Intention always precedes manifestation. Or, to quote one of the key isms from the *Interdimensional Survival Manual*:

What you see is what you get.

"The planet's been enduring regular seismic jolts since the beginning of its existence at a rate of something like twelve million earthquakes in any twelve-month period. Only a hundred or so per year are disruptive to your societies, and the most destructive in terms of human lives aren't among the most recent.

"To borrow one of Wall Street's CYA disclaimers, however, past performance is no guarantee of future behavior. What happens—or doesn't happen—next will be a direct product of the collective human vision and expectation. Looking into the Akashic records, which are now available to you too, all I want to say at this time about earthquakes and volcanic eruptions is, it's gonna be interesting!"

"Well, what about the crazy weather patterns?" Larry asked. "I suppose you're going to tell me they're figments of the collective imagination as well?"

"Whoa there, good buddy," Zeus responded. "Let's not throw everything into the same pot and call it reality. As far as the abnormal weather is concerned, it's a plague that's already been visited upon the multitudes. Why? Humanity is now reaping the toxic yield of centuries of thoughtless activity. The skies and oceans that once looked like limitless dumping grounds are in danger of being supersaturated with poisons. Scientists are only now stating publicly what science has known for decades: second-hand smoke kills just as surely as smoking itself. When will people finally admit that second-hand water and soil—the legacy of your unconscious modern societies—are equally deadly?

"You know that ritzy section of town you like to walk me in?"

"You mean Bel Air?" Larry answered.

"Well, the air there ain't 'belle' at all! How can otherwise intelligent people shell out outrageous sums to raise their families in one of planet's more toxic spots?"

Larry smiled to himself at the irony.

"Over the coming years," Zeus continued, "you're going to be exposed to a lot of stories—some built on fact, others on speculation. You'll be hearing about Nibiru, or Planet X, said to be a rogue planet that circles your sun every 3,600 years or so. Its orbit is off-plane, clockwise, and elliptical, while the rest of the planets travel counterclockwise. Nibiru is said to have caused the Great Flood of your Bible and to have brought with it demigods who fought over gold mines in Africa. Such tales, like the events flowing out of 9/11 and many others you will be exposed to, may engender panic and fear in some.

"It will be up to each person to assign an appropriate plane of reality for each story. Certainly Nibiru and the many predicted events have meaning in the mythic and metaphorical realms. Don't discard them as childhood fantasies just because they challenge your rationality."

"But 9/11 did happen. And it shocked the entire world," Larry said. "Was that just a random act of terror, or does it have a deeper meaning?"

"You're still asking questions of the mind and ignoring input from your higher Consciousness," Zeus answered. "The answer isn't hanging out in the intellect. But since you've asked, I'll provide a few clues. Are you familiar with random number generators?"

"Yeah," Larry responded. "Aren't they the machines that spit out a constant series of totally random numbers?"

"There's a little-known ongoing experiment, called the Global Consciousness Project, in which thirty-seven of these RNG devices are connected to computers located all over the world. Each computer independently uses the generated numbers to 'flip' two hundred virtual coins at a time, and they upload the data every five minutes to the project's website. You'd expect the results to come out fairly even—roughly a hundred heads and a hundred tails each time. The experiment's supposed to determine if global-scale events that bring the thoughts and feelings of great numbers of people into coherence can influence otherwise independent, 'unthinking' machinery. In other words, can Consciousness be measured?

"Don't laugh. The concept isn't all that radical. Parapsychologists have shown that certain gifted people can actually influence the throw of dice. China boasts of a large number of psychic Indigo Children who can affect all manner of physical objects. Quantum physicists have long accepted that the observer influences the outcome of an experiment. So why shouldn't the focus of millions of people disrupt the random patterning of a number generator?"

"Well, what happened?" Larry asked. "Did the last Tuesday's events show up on the RNG radar screen?"

"You bet they did!" Zeus said. "Big time. And the anomalous data lasted for hours. Now, skeptics might say all the radar and cell phone activity right after the tragedies must have affected the RNGs. But they can't so conveniently explain away the fact that the data starting displaying nonrandom patterning a few hours *before* the events took place! Once again, Consciousness shows itself as neither linear nor local in nature.

"The fabric of the entire Creation is woven of threads of Consciousness. Or, as Empedocles once said, 'The nature of God is a circle of which the center is everywhere and the circumference is nowhere.' We are all connected in ways so inextricably intimate, the drunken chicken antics of your illusion would be laughable if it weren't for the pandemic pain and suffering rippling out from your planet."

Suddenly Zeus became uncharacteristically serious. "You yearn to help humanity move on to the density of Love and

Compassion, but right now that seems impossible. Do you know what you and your brothers and sisters are failing to see?"

"No. I wish I did," Larry answered.

"The majority of those who will eventually hear or read your words live in relative comfort and security. The little they know of the suffering that plagues much of the rest of the world comes from sanitized news bytes on CNN. The few who are moved by the anguish may contribute money or time, attend benefits, sign petitions, but then they continue with their normal lives. They hear the cries as if muted and they're screened from feeling the pain, for that is how events are meant to be perceived on your side of the Veil.

"Those in the higher densities perceive a different reality. The sounds of the six o'clock news travel through a particulate medium, so no matter how loud the cries are at first, eventually their wave vibrations cannot overcome the inertia of the medium, and silence returns. This is not so with the energy of pain and suffering. When these tortured pebbles are cast into the plasma of Love, Wisdom, and Power, they create interference patterns that ripple through all Creation. These do *not* dissipate. They're not weakened by time and distance. And they cause great concern for those learning to master Love in the fourth density. Perceiving the personal tragedies played out on this planet with selfless tenderness and understanding, they feel compelled to help in any way possible. Such is the nature of Compassion."

"We must look pretty pathetic from on high," Larry said. "But given our unwillingness to let go of our deeply ingrained ways of seeing things, wouldn't you agree the odds are pretty much stacked against us?"

"Yes and no," Zeus replied. "When you try to predict what the flock will do, it's a complete crapshoot. However, it isn't about the collective anymore. That's the gift of 9/11."

"You *are* nuts," Larry said. "Why would you call 9/11 a gift?"

"I expected you'd see it yourself by now," Zeus replied. "Our friend in the rock gave you a pretty good clue, describing the events of 9/11 as either a great tragedy that needs to be mourned or an unparalleled opportunity that needs to be seized—depending on one's point of view. On the surface, the world was presented with four commercial airliners commandeered by Islamic terrorists bent on teaching the United States and the rest of the 'infidels' a lesson. Their sheer audacity called the bluff of America's invincibility and exposed a basic flaw in the matrix that all the posturing and saber rattling can't hide. The net result is that, for a moment, everyone felt as vulnerable as the twin towers. When those two buildings collapsed into a heap of twisted rubble, so did the certainty of humanity.

"Now let's revisit these events on a deeper level. If all of you are one, then, despite what your elected leaders say, there is no 'us and them.' There's just a collective family of humanity, inexorably linked, hurtling through space together on this fragile sphere. When you went back and observed the world as it was on September 10, you found most people living lives of quiet desperation, driven by fear and uncertainty. Collectively, humankind was no better off than the ostrich, lying flat on the ground feigning death when it's frightened. I'm here to tell you that no matter how tight you shut your eyes, the monster won't disappear. The time has come to face the bogeyman and make sense of a life that, for the vast majority of humans, has no real relevance beyond their structures of belief.

"Once the planes hit the buildings, the world ceased to make sense to a great many people. Many, no doubt, will return to the fold, marching in lockstep to the beat of chauvinistic war drums and outrage. Some will not. It is to those who are no longer willing to buy a pig in a poke from the well-heeled merchants pedaling yesterday's wares that you must speak. To these folk, 9/11 was not an isolated event that pitted terrorism against democracy; it was an unmistakable symbol—stunningly visible to billions all over the world—proclaiming that humanity is in big trouble.

"With the untimely death of some three thousand individuals, 9/11 accomplished what the deliberate slaughter of six million men, women, and children in Auschwitz, Bergen-Belsen, and other Nazi extermination camps could not. September 11 has commanded the attention of humanity even as a million sub-Saharan Africans starve to death each month in total anonymity and the two-mile-high cloud of toxic pollutants shrouding Asia from Afghanistan to Sri Lanka goes unreported, though it threatens the immediate well-being of over 20 percent of the globe's population.

"Are those who die in Africa or Europe or Asia of less value than those who perished in New York or Virginia or Pennsylvania? I think not. Yet only 9/11 has managed to stop the implacable machinery of events dead in its tracks. *That* is its greatest gift. For the briefest instant in the history of your world, 9/11 disrupted the deeply ingrained flow you just spoke of. Routines were not just interrupted; they were completely overturned. People were brutally shaken from their semisleep to face, for the first time, the horror of their own creation. And most, thank God, did not like what they saw. As Walt Kelly aptly observed through the voice of Pogo, his ingenuous swamp possum, 'We have met the enemy and he is us.'

"For a moment, Larry, put yourself in the position of this planet's collective oversoul."

"What exactly is that?" Larry asked.

"It's not all that mysterious," Zeus replied. "The Higher Selves of every third-density being on this planet are connected and communicate with each other through the Infinite Universal Hologram. Each one knows what's happening not only with its own lower self but with the billions of other lower selves sharing the third-density experience. Is it inconceivable that they might act collectively?"

"Now I see what you're driving at," Larry replied. "Given the current state of affairs on the planet and the limited amount of time remaining, what else could they have done to get our attention? From that perspective, I can see why you call 9/11 a gift. But isn't such a deliberate act of terror a blatant violation of Free Will?"

"Interesting question," Zeus replied. "You just touched on one of the major dilemmas facing a sixth-density guide: how to create options without compelling a particular action. That's why all the signposts your Higher Self places along your every-day path are oblique. And that's why true channeling from the higher realms is always equivocal, allowing wiggle room for interpretation. If channeling comes as a directive, you can bet something's amiss!

"As I said yesterday morning, the Prime Mandate of Creation—senior even to Love itself—is Free Will. No Higher Self can violate this law, no matter how urgently it wishes to warn or help its third-density self. That's why the events of 9/11 are open to interpretation. Those who want to hold tight to the old paradigm will probably use the attacks to justify further acts of hostility. Others may react with despair, confusion, anger, pride, outrage, and a whole host of other reflexive emotions. We honor each and every choice. Collectively, we ask only that each choice is made as consciously as possible.

"September 11, in spite of its sudden and dramatic impact, is completely equivocal. Whether it evokes compassion or fear, love or revenge, sorrow or joy, is simply a function of selecting a point along the I-continuum from which to view. There's no correct answer. Any decision allows the All That Is to know itself more completely. The question at hand is simply: what will your choice be?"

Larry stopped dead in his tracks, mulling Zeus's last question over and over in his mind. He turned to face his most remarkable dog, who gazed back at him with his head cocked expectantly.

"Amazing," Larry thought. "Whoever I thought I used to be I certainly ain't any longer. Whatever I decide to be I get to choose right here, right now. Absolutely amazing!"

He dropped into thought. If one thing was true of his adventures over the past three days it was that nothing had been random. Every act, every word, every nuance was deliberate and had been carefully weighed before it was added to the stew.

Now the trick was for him to be sufficiently present to grasp the message's meaning. Larry focused on Zeus's last words as he visualized a seesaw in perfect balance. On the left side he placed the words "sorrow," "fear," and "revenge." On the opposite side "love," "compassion," and "joy." He did the same with "constriction" and its opposite, "expansion," then "separation" and "unity." There was ample room on each side for him to sit and cause that side to descend into the operative reality defining his existence. Viewing the two sets of options arrayed before him, his choice was crystal clear.

But something else niggled at Larry's mind. He searched inwardly for several moments before recalling Zeus's exact words: "It isn't about the collective anymore. That's the gift of

9/11." If nothing was random, what did these words really mean?

Fragmented thoughts from previous conversations barraged his mind until Zeus interrupted: "Stop trying to work this out, kiddo. Just let the ideas wash over you like a cool shower. Acknowledge whatever seems to stand out and let it go as soon as another concept grabs center stage. Your mind can't help you with this one. Let your heart do the thinking."

The trickle of thought soon became a torrent: "I think, therefore I am. I believe, therefore I am. I am righteous, therefore I am. I am a good lawyer, therefore I am. I am noticed, therefore I am. I stand for something, therefore I am. . . . If I define myself by what others perceive me to be, how can I alter that definition without risking annihilation at some level? Death makes way for birth. I need to become reborn. I need to die!"

Larry emerged from his inner journey with a start. "That's it!" he said. "It *isn't* about the collective anymore. All the labels that define me as part of a group—however wonderful or noble—have to fall away. It *is* all about the individual, the one buried inside every human being on the planet. It's all about me and what I choose to do!"

Larry looked straight at Zeus as he spoke the words that would shape the rest of his time in the third density. "The time for collective action has passed. I now know that I don't need anyone's permission to act. I don't need consensus or anyone's agreement. All I ask from others, if they're willing to give it, is their support. The fate of the world literally depends upon what I decide to do. And that's equally true for anyone else who feels the same way."

"Bravo!" Zeus responded. "Now you're getting what I meant when I said that although you and others are beginning to perceive yourselves as individuals, you're also the macrocosm;

every insight each of you gains belongs to the whole. With the Veil now so incredibly thinned, all humanity has access to resources that boggle the imagination. Anyone with the courage to leave the flock can attain levels of information and powers of manifestation that make your old comic book superheroes pale into insignificance."

"What do you mean by that?" Larry asked.

"Uncle. Stop. I give up," Zeus teased. "Enough with all these questions already."

"Don't pass this off on me," Larry chided, "you're the one who dangled the bait. Did you really expect me not to ask?"

"I'm just concerned you're approaching sensory overload."

"Don't worry," Larry quipped, "I died from sensory overload yesterday. Remember?"

Zeus chuckled. "So you did. I forget that I dialogue now with the eternal Phoenix. Okay then, Big Bird, since you're such a smarty pants, tell me something: what makes one person intelligent and another dumb?"

"Genes?" Larry answered.

"Sorry, Levi Strauss has nothing to do with it." Larry groaned as Zeus continued. "Don't knock the humor, my little peacock. Without it you would never be able to handle the intricacies of intelligence."

"*What? What? . . . What? What?*" Right on cue.

"Ah, I see your fellow fine-feathered friend has found you floundering afresh," Zeus commented, acknowledging what was to be What-What's last appearance of the weekend. "Permit me to explain to both of you the mysterious nature of intelligence.

"As you know, everything that occurs throughout Creation is recorded in the limitless hologram of Consciousness. What you actually experience day to day is mirrored in countless parallel universes, where alternate realities—the choices you almost made—play themselves out. These nonlocal O-worlds are usually held at bay by the barriers programmed into the Veil of Forgetting. Your Higher Self—itself a source of wisdom and information—decides on the nature and strength of these barriers before assisting a portion of its Awareness into the third density.

"You getting any of this?" Zeus suddenly inquired.

"Yeah, I'm still in working mode. You're suggesting that there are thousands of other little Larrys living out my fantasies in parallel universes—probably having more fun than I am right now."

"And reaping all the consequences of that fun," Zeus replied. "The piper always gets his due. It's your ability to access the other realities that's the key here. Basically, the more permeable the barriers, the greater the third-density being's intelligence quotient. Accessing alternate realities not only increases the information input, it also provides a greater range of simultaneous viewpoints. That's why intelligent people tend to be great lateral thinkers. However, this advantage can be a very slippery slope, as leaky margins can't easily be secured, so uninvited cascades of data constantly bombard one.

"Another danger—of particular interest to you, I might add—is the ease with which intelligent people fall into the pit of arrogance. Intelligence in and of itself is merely an attribute, like height or complexion or eye color. Don't believe you belong to some sort of mythic aristocracy merely because you have access to alternate realities.

"The ability to dip into parallel universes can be managed two ways: You either block it by retreating into a fundamental set of beliefs so your chakras have a reinforced set of filters to defuse the unwanted flow of data, or you adopt a playful mechanism to safely handle the clash of disparate planes of information."

"Ah," Larry said. "You must be referring to humor. The parallel universe model would explain how a single word or situation can evoke so many different mind pictures at once."

"And why puns are so delightful to those who make them and so agonizing to those who don't," Zeus responded.

"And what happens when a person chooses neither option?" Larry asked.

"Typically," Zeus answered, "they go off the deep end. And as one of your recent movies suggested, 'a beautiful mind' is a terrible thing to waste. Those who dare play with the worlds around the corner walk along a very narrow ledge. The line separating you from the psychopathic serial killer, wife beater, predatory priest, or drug dealer is more easily traversed than you imagine.

"Don't start thinking: there but for the grace of God go I. For in fact, by the grace of God, each of those sociopaths *is* you. Whatever you now choose to do you're choosing also for the part of you that is them."

"My God!" Larry exclaimed. "Now I finally got the last lines of Rocky's rap."

"I thought you got them earlier," Zeus teased.

"No. No. I mean this time I *really* got it! This time I went deeper and totally grasped the difference between gratitude and omnitude."

"And?"

"Gratitude is thanks for what I have. Omnitude is thanks for what I am."

"And what are you, Larry?"

"Incredibly blessed to bear Conscious witness to Creation."

Zeus simply smiled.

The two walked in silence to the parking lot to begin their journey back to Los Angeles. There was nothing more to say. Zeus jumped into the rear of the SUV, settling into the warm comfort of his blankie as his master took the wheel. Larry turned left onto Park Boulevard, driving slowly north toward the ranger station at the entrance of the National Monument. Part of him was clearly reluctant to leave the magic of Joshua Tree.

As he negotiated a left turn in the road, he was almost blinded by the light of the setting sun. Maybe Zeus was right—he had succumbed to sensory overload. His imagination began running wild as he rubbed his eyes in disbelief. His heart raced to such an extent that he was barely able to pull the car onto the shoulder and stop the engine. "My God," he thought, "is this what's it's like to have a heart attack?"

The palpitations subsided almost as suddenly as they came. But the images didn't. The clouds radiated unimaginable colors and swirled in impossible directions, displaying one shape upon another in an unending kaleidoscopic array. There were mountain vistas that gave way to cityscapes that dissolved into trees, then animals, then human faces. Suddenly Larry's mind exploded with the syncopated sounds of familiar piano chords. Looking down at him from the glowing sky was the unmistakable smiling face of John Lennon, round glasses and all. Then came the words:

> Imagine there's no countries,
> It isn't hard to do,
> Nothing to kill or die for,
> No religion too.
> Imagine all the people
> Living life in peace. . . .
> You may say I'm a dreamer,
> But I'm not the only one,
> I hope someday you'll join us,
> And the world will be as one.

Larry sat in stunned silence, only the slow, rhythmic rise and fall of his chest providing tangible proof of life. By the time he realized that his beloved dog was at his side, gently licking his right cheek, night had fallen completely.

"Zeus . . . ," Larry stammered, the words barely taking form in his mouth, "did you hear that? Did you see what I saw?" Zeus only wagged his tail and nuzzled more insistently into his master's face. "Zeus, talk to me!" Larry's stomach dropped as he faced a new possibility. "It can't have been just a dream, it was too real. I remember it so clearly, I can almost reach out and touch it. Zeus, say something!"

The absolute silence of the high desert mocked his throbbing thoughts.

Somehow he made his way down the rest of Park Boulevard to the intersection at route 62. It was while staring at the red light, waiting for it to change, that he heard the words confirming that the last few days weren't just a figment of his imagination.

"Lighten up already, you're giving me a headache."

The day will come when,
After harnessing space, the winds, the tides and gravitation,
We shall harness for God the energies of love.
And on that day,
For the second time in the history of the world,
We shall have discovered fire.

— Pierre Teilhard de Chardin

⊚ ACKNOWLEDGMENTS

Whenever I'm asked, "Where are you from?" I never truly know what the person means and usually respond playfully, "What's your context?" just in case the question is meant more deeply than simply inquiring where I was born or where I now live. It rarely is. However, the few exceptions have helped form my life, and for these I am eternally grateful.

It's impossible to thank all those who contributed to the writing of *Going Deeper*. There are those without whom this book might never have been written. My profoundest thanks to Jack Barnard, who first challenged me to have the courage to commit, then called me every week for months to make certain I hadn't wavered; to Jean Houston, who taught me that no matter what treasure I sought, it wasn't nearly enough and who incessantly insisted that we all stop theorizing, roll up our sleeves, and get to work; to Carolyn Bond, a caring, devoted, and totally professional editor who lovingly demanded that I be at least partially responsible for bringing the reader along on my fantastic voyage.

This book flowed through me rather than out of me. I have obviously been assisted by many who came before, on whose shoulders I humbly and gratefully stand. It's no great feat to see farther when you are buoyed up by the efforts of those who paved the way. The many extraordinary beings who, through their writings, seminars, and discourses, added straws to my wondrously tangled pile: Ram Das, Brugh Joy, Verna Yater, Indira, Ra, Buddha, Christ, Lao-tse, J. J. Hurtak, Clif Sanderson, Mae Wan Ho, L. Ron Hubbard, Lefty Willner, and so many others whose concepts and teachings continue to shape my being.

From a very young age, I was blessed by meeting Winkers. These glorious people somehow recognized me and shared their inner delights, letting my little mind know there were vastly more things in heaven and earth than were dreamt of in the collective philosophies of my immediate world. The term "Winker" comes from a science fiction short story I read in my teens entitled, "When Two Soothsayers Pass, They Invariably Wink." That's how I learned there were basically two kinds of people in the world, the Winkers and the Wankers. Although I prefer to play among the former and let the latter sort out their own affairs as best they can, I don't succeed nearly as often as I'd like. Too many times each day, I find myself firmly entrenched in the Wanker camp, arms akimbo, with both feet planted firmly in the mire of judgment. The best I can do is giggle myself out of there as fast as my little Awareness units will take me. Why, after all these years, I still take myself seriously, only God knows.

Toby and Bernie Feinstein, my surrogate parents who lived next door, opened the doors to worlds otherwise unknown to recently arrived immigrants steeped in the traditions of Europe. Toby led me through the bizarre worlds of Isaac Asimov, Ray Bradbury, and my favorite of all, Theodore Sturgeon. I grew up to the fading bars of Rossini's *William Tell Overture* heralding the thundering hoofbeats of the great horse Silver! I fell asleep each night listening to Long John Nebel interviewing self-proclaimed geniuses (I fully agreed), like Lester del Rey and other superminds of the time, as they discussed the world around the corner. Jean Shepherd was my first acknowledged guru. His late-night radio monologues, delivered flawlessly in beguiling, smoothly flowing streams of consciousness, mesmerized my innocence.

If I had a predisposition to be curious before I came to planet Earth, by the time I was thirteen I had so completely swallowed the bait (hook, line, and sinker) that it became part of my living matrix. I no longer sought the Great Mystery, I craved it. I bought an endless succession of books—mostly because their authors or subject matter impressed me. I confess now to having collected far more than I read. It was sometimes difficult for me to get past the first few chapters. Then came Alice! To Charles Lutwidge Dodgson, a.k.a. Lewis Carroll, I owe the comforting knowledge that somewhere, out in the vastness of inner space, a voice answers. Following shortly behind the tales of Wonderlands and Looking Glasses were the writings of Lao-Tze and the wondrously unstructured world of the Tao. It has been written (or spoken, or I made it up) that "If one mans asks of the Tao and another responds, neither understands." I immediately adored the concept, and to this day, if someone were to inquire about my religious persuasions, I would proclaim myself "a born-again Taoist," relishing the oxymoronic paradox of it all. It don't mean a thing if it ain't got that swing.

L. Ron Hubbard and Scientology beckoned irresistibly, and I, curious as the proverbial cat, responded. Priscilla, the wonderful lady with whom I was sharing my life at the time, became a full-time staff member and I became a part-time dilettante, receiving and dispensing auditing sessions. I studied the world according to Ron, listening to endless hours of unedited, rambling tapes dating back to Hubbard's early days in Philadelphia and East Grinstead, England, reading mimeographed memos printed in various colors of the rainbow denoting their office of origin, and practicing TRs (Training Routines) designed to turn me into me a more proficient auditor. Even to this day, I remain impressed by the vast body of work Hubbard produced and the training I received. But in the end, it was simply another stepping stone along my journey, and I found early on that I traveled lighter by not collecting the stones in my backpack.

In time, I tried various mind-altering substances with varying degrees of success. I remember my first experience with magic mushrooms. I was with my wife, Arianne, in an almost deserted state park not far from San Diego. We found a totally secluded spot in the woods visible only from passing satellites and the occasional INS helicopter scouring the border for illegal aliens. As the first slivers of altering consciousness radiated through my brain, I panicked, took off all my clothes, and made a serious attempt to burrow back into Arianne. Eventually, unable to maintain control, I submitted totally and relaxed into the experience. What transpired blew my mind! I was connected to some vast pool of Cosmic Consciousness that invited me to explore any aspect of Creation that interested me. We discoursed for hours as I was shown how realities (apparent universes) are created and how we select the role each of us chooses to play in the drama. When I asked how it was permissible for me to be given such intimate knowledge, the voice actually laughed, reminding me that I took part in the original process. It was my first tangible introduction to the Oneness of Creation.

There came a point when my mentor asked whether I would like to see the "next octave of creation." Might as well ask a starving man if he would like a meal! I was taken outwards (if there was such a thing as direction) into an ever-brighter light. Suddenly the intensity overwhelmed my insatiable curiosity and I recoiled in pain. For the second time the voice laughed, letting me know I had much yet to do before I could enter these refined realms.

I tried 'shrooms a few times afterwards, expecting to recreate the magnitude of the first experience, but with disappointing results. I will most probably not try them again. There's actually no need because the connection made with Higher Intelligence that day in the state park has never left me, and we dialogue about this and that often. The Cosmic Intelligence, whom I lovingly call "The Guys," has been with me every step of the way as this book unfolded. No one is owed a greater debt of trust, love, and admiration. I am truly blessed by having this remarkable source always by my side. As I wrote these last words, I was asked to remind my gentle readers that this powerful ally patiently awaits them all.

Please do not take my personal story as an advocacy of psychedelics. It is not. I tried marijuana only once, with rather unfortunate results. Smoking weed totally blocked my channel of communication with The Guys for thirty days. It was definitely not worth the price of a few bars of mirth, which I can hum any time I choose. My favorite train to ride out of this realm of ordinary consciousness is the breath. I was one of early rebirthers following the techniques of Leonard Orr. My first experience with this remarkable technique of breathing was with Jeremy Burnham, a British expatriate, during one of my visits to Johannesburg. In my very first session I had a clear image of Jesus, Sai Baba, and Baba-ji (the patron saint of rebirthing) standing arm and arm, radiating waves of love to me and the rest of the world. Suddenly, the structured arena of "ologies" and "isms" became wondrously irrelevant, and if not enlightened, I certainly became, at the least, somewhat lightened by the experience.

The weekend of my first rebirthing transported me irrevocably across the Rubicon, and there was no looking back. I have since spent time with Stanislaus Grof, whose holotropic breath work uses carefully selected music and the collective, focused energy of the group to take rebirthing into the very adult realm of psychotropic adventure land. Interesting stuff! The extended breath sessions with Grof were interspersed with deep Buddhist meditations led by Jack Kornfeld—like jumping successively from a steaming sauna into the snow. Definitely a mind bender. Try it sometime.

My road to discovery began in earnest in late 1984, when I left my conventional life in the United States and moved to Australia. I was fortunate to meet two extraordinary South Africans, Brian and Esther Crowley, who welcomed me into their home as a family member (I stayed with them for quite some time as a house guest), and it was they who introduced me to the sacred chants in the five power languages (Ancient Egyptian, Hebrew, Sanskrit, Tibetan, and Chinese) revealed by J. J. Hurtak in his seminal book *The Keys of Enoch*. A group of us, led by Brian and Esther, meditated every week, intoning the Words of Power while visualizing world peace. I can't say, given the current state of affairs, that the results are anything to brag about— but at least I now know why.

Brian coauthored several books with J. J. Hurtak. One title, published in 1986, *The Face on Mars: Evidence of a Lost Martian Civilization,* has photos I took of murals when I visited Vusamazulu Credo Mutwa (one of the spiritual leaders of the Zulu) while he still lived in the black township of Soweto, just outside of Johannesburg. It was Brian who first introduced me to J. J. and Desiree Hurtak. I was privileged to spend several days with them touring ancient wats (temples) in Thailand, energetically linking these abandoned places of worship with power spots across the planet by intoning the sacred chants—an activity I have never stopped doing. After attending the First (and only) Paranormal Healing Conference held in Baggio City, the Philippines, I returned with J. J. and Des to Sydney, where Dr. Hurtak took a small group of us through the entire text of *The Keys*. This experience shaped the course of my life since.

A year later, Arianne joined me in the Land of Oz (Australia), and we explored the outback in a 1972 Toyota Corona with no air conditioning. We made the pilgrimage to Uluru (known to tourists as Ayer's Rock), southwest of Alice

Springs in the center of nowhere. This vast monolith that totally dominates an otherwise featureless plain is still under the protection of the Anangu, the traditional landholders of the region. It is one of the most powerful parts of Aboriginal *tjukurrpa* (mythology of creation as well as the rules of interaction within society), with many sacred dreamings centering there. It was fitting that our ascent up this hallowed shrine was the starting point of our adventures. For an hour and a half, Arianne and I had the rock to ourselves. The top was deserted, and we were able to meditate without interruption or distraction of any kind. It was there that we both first caught a glimpse of the path we would be following for the rest of our lives.

Our meanderings through the back and beyond of the Australian bush took us through Katherine, Kakadu, and Darwin before bringing us to the small town of Freshwater in Far North Queensland, just outside of Cairns. With our visas about to expire, we needed to leave the country so we could return. Although unintelligible to me at the time, this process makes perfect sense to bureaucrats, and I am eternally in their debt, as it facilitated what came next. We could not go to Indonesia (Bali was our first choice) as they would not recognize Arianne's South African passport. Our options were to fly to Port Moresby in Papua New Guinea (not, according to the locals, the garden spot of the world) or—for almost the same airfare—get a round-the-world ticket. We chose the latter, taking as much time and visiting as many places as the rules of the fare permitted. In short, Arianne and I spent a full year circling the planet.

We began our odyssey in Cairns and went to (among other places) Hong Kong, Thailand, Singapore, Italy, Greece, France, England, the U.S.A., then back to Australia. We returned to Cairns 365 days after we set out. The journey led us from one adventure to another. The teachers along the way are at once too numerous to mention and too important to ever forget.

In our five weeks in Hong Kong (we were provided with a beautiful, rent-free apartment on Wyndham Street, just a short walk up from the Star Ferry), we were privileged to work with Dr. Clif Sanderson, recipient of the Albert Schweitzer Prize for Humanitarian Service to Medicine for his tireless work with children suffering from the aftereffects of Chernobyl. It was through Clif—a brother and treasured friend—that Arianne and I were first introduced to intentional healing, entity work, and Feng Shui. While in Hong Kong, I was initiated into the Ling Su by Dr. Wilson Wang, a local physician who had discovered several powerful techniques that allowed mere humans to break the manifestation barrier. It was through his tutelage that the world of intentional creation was opened, and for the first time, I was permitted to tap into the processes used by various mystery school adepts in the conduct of their sacred ceremony. It was getting increasingly obvious that there were many beings, in every part of the planet, that could easily pierce the apparent limitations of this world behind the Veil whenever they chose.

Of all our adventures on our round-the-world jaunt, our five months in Israel may have had the greatest impact on me and, ultimately, on this book. Our extended stay there provided the opportunity to appreciate the inner core of the Sabra, as Israelis are often called. The term takes its name from the fruit of the sabra cactus—thorny on the outside but sweet and tasty inside. Nothing describes the typical Israeli more perfectly: on the outside, bombarding each other with the four A's: arrogance, anger, aggressiveness, and assertiveness; on the inside, displaying a reverence for life unmatched anywhere else in the world. How do these people live, knowing that any day they or their children might be attacked by the Russian-roulette mentality of wanton terrorism? To the fullest! Why they greet each other with the traditional *shalom*—peace—is beyond me. To my mind, the traditional *l'chiam*—to life!—would be better suited. But what do I know?

It was in Israel that another medical doctor changed my life. Dr. Eli Lasch was a pediatrician working in Gaza alongside Palestinian physicians, helping to heal the artificial rift inherited through the whims of birth. One day, Eli arrived at our door with a four-volume set of books. They were almost 8 ½" x 11" in size, saddled-stitched (with two staples through the spine), and typewritten rather than set in a conventional publisher's type-face. The title of each volume was the same: *The Law of One*. Only the volume numbers changed, denoting the sequence in which they were meant to be read.

The books were transcripts of a series of communications received by a small group in Louisville, Kentucky, commencing in mid-January 1981. The channel was Carla L. Rueckert; the questioner was an Eastern Airlines pilot, Don Elkins; the scribe was James McCarty. Together these three highly intelligent, extraordinary people made up a group called L/L Research. The information source called itself "RA, an humble messenger of the Law of One."

I began reading RA's words the day Eli gave me the books. In short order, they became so perfectly melded into my con-sciousness that I could no longer speak, act, or think without their influence. To a very large extent, the Universal Myth of Creation and related insights contained in this book flow from the teachings of RA. I am indebted to this earthly/extraterres-trial team beyond measure. Each rereading of their work seems to be the first, presenting me with layer upon layer of fresh, undiscovered information begging consideration. It is through their collective example that I came to appreciate the infinite depth of the journey and the joy it holds for each of us willing to take the risk.

When I first read *The Law of One*, I felt like Sleeping Beauty being wakened from her one-hundred-year sleep by the kiss of a prince. I was in psychic shock for nearly two weeks, and it was only through the combined efforts of two remarkably gifted healers visiting Israel from the United Kingdom, Zorika and Pat, that I was once more able to form coherent sentences—although some would still argue otherwise.

On my trip around the world, I stopped in Louisville and spent too brief a time with Carla and Jim. I would have liked to have met Don as well, but he died several years before I got there. I think of them often—especially Don—and the sacrifice each still makes to continue their work.

During our stay in Israel, Arianne and I studied healing with Israel Carmel and visited several times at the home he shared with Phyllis Schlemmer, author of *The Only Planet of Choice—Essential Briefings from Deep Space*. It was she who indirectly introduced me to Dr. Andrija Puharich (author of several best-selling books including *Uri, The Sacred Mushroom,* and *Beyond Telepathy*) and the Council of Nine, whom she channeled. Their story—involving Phyllis Schlemmer, Andrija Puharich, J.J. Hurtak, Israel Carmel, Sir John Whitmore, and the Council of Nine—is depicted in a then nearly impossible-to-find book entitled *Briefing for the Landing on Planet Earth*, written by Stuart Holroyd and published in soft cover by Corgi Books. It was also published in a hardcover edition by W. H. Allen & Co. under the title *Prelude to the Landing on Planet Earth*. Both editions are currently unavailable, and amazon.com does not even list them, though it acknowledges eighteen other out-of-print titles by the same author.

By the time I arrived in England, where both books had originally been published a few years earlier, they were nowhere to be found. Bookstore personnel recalled that both editions were excellent sellers and seemed genuinely surprised that they were no longer on their shelves. Used bookshops (including most along the Strand in London) had nary a copy. The plot thickened when I called the publishers. Corgi said they had removed all the remaining copies from general distribution and shredded them. No one seemed to know exactly why. W. H. Allen denied ever having published the book in the first place.

Dr. J.J. Hurtak had given me my first copy of the book—a xeroxed facsimile of the W. H. Allen edition. The only edition I now have in my possession—the Corgi paperback version—came from a small collection of spiritual books in a library in the little town of Atherton, Australia. I traded my entire six-volume set of *The Life and Teachings of the Masters of the Far East* by Baird T. Spaulding for it. Each of us thought we had gotten the better of the bargain—which, in my book, is as good as it gets.

I've recently discovered that Phyllis Schlemmer has reprinted the book with the title: *The Nine: Briefing From Deep Space*. You can find it on her web site: www.theonlyplanetofchoice.com /newbook.htm. Once you've read it, you will have a better understanding of why the publishers might have been encouraged to remove it from circulation. By nature, I am not particularly fond of conspiracy theories, not because I think they are untrue but because they distract. I have met too many people along the way who have gotten so caught up in the drama of chemtrails, ELF transmissions, the HARP project, the reptilian puppet masters and their Illuminati, Bilderburg minions, and the like that they have completely lost sight of the larger picture.

I was reminded of the need to maintain perspective some years later when Dr. Eli Lasch gave me a hand-typed piece of paper on which he had written a poem entitled "The Fetters," which ends:

> We are all like puppets on a string
> Torn here and there
> As if by winds
> Where is the puppeteer?
> I ask
> I want to pull the strings
> At last

Even those pulling strings are but puppets dancing the steps dictated by more distant puppeteers.

Our trip around the world also took us to Findhorn, the new-age community established in 1962 in the northern reaches of Scotland. Unlike so many of both its predecessors and its imitators, Findhorn thrives to this day, constantly reinventing itself, finding new relevant forms of expression. I'll save the extraordinary stories of our misadventures there for another campfire. It was there that I was taught a technique that facilitated intentional encounter with one's Higher Self. For this alone, Findhorn has more than earned a special place in my memory. And that was but one of its many gifts.

Another gift was the Findhorn bus that transported Arianne and me past Loch Ness, across the Isle of Mull, to the Inner Hebridean island of Iona. This singular fragment of land is a mere 3.4 miles long and 1.7 miles wide. Yet walking it was one of the most intimate moments I can recall spending anywhere on earth. There's a sense of timelessness on Iona that suffuses those who come seeking her blessing. She is one of the great wise ones, having, for 2.9 billion years, staunchly held her presence against the incessant pounding of the restless sea seeking to reclaim her. The wisdom she holds is almost unparalleled on earth.

A special debt is owed to two remarkable people, Hal Stone and Sidra Winkelman-Stone, who developed voice dialogue, an exceptionally effective, elegant form of therapy that successfully bridges the gap between mundane psychological issues and the cosmological concerns of universal archetypes. Junie's interactions with Larry is based in large measure on the Stones' work. So is my relationship with Arianne. It has allowed two otherwise headstrong, singular individuals the wisdom to share without compromise, love without reservation, and laugh at our many selves every step of the way.

My debt list is, of course, endless. Perhaps like Kefa, the synagogue's janitor, I should simply recite the alphabet and request all that read these acknowledgments to rearrange the letters to spell out their own names. Even the plants growing outside my office window speak to me of wisdom. I have come to acknowledge all Creation as my teacher. Every person I meet, every animal I see, every tree, every blade of grass informs me. It is said, "When the student is ready, the guru appears." I ask only to be made ready every moment of my waking and sleeping life—a true chela (student) of the universe. How can any of us look at the stars and not wonder? How can any of us look at each other and fail to see God?

All things said, nothing has impacted me more profoundly than the process of midwifing *Going Deeper*. May the result—this book—in some small (or large) way do the same for you.

In love and light, and in service to the One Infinite Creator.
I wish you Love,
Jean-Claude

P. S. There's always another tale to tell when exploring the infinite ways the universe weaves its magic. For example, take the cover of this book. When it became apparent that *Going Deeper* would be staged in Joshua Tree National Park, I began researching in earnest. Although I had visited the park several times over the years, I knew little about its history and geology. While surfing the Internet for notes to download, I came across the stunning photograph—a juniper tree and a white tank monzogranite boulder catching the last rays of a setting sun—that now graces the book's cover.

Two hours later, I visited the first annual art show held in my hometown, Rancho Mirage, California. I was stunned to see the very same photo hanging on display. And I met Ellie Tyler, the gifted, sensitive photographer who had captured the magic of the moment. She had spent days trying to get the positioning and the light exactly right, to no avail. Then, on a whim, she crossed a few yards to view the rock and tree from the opposite direction. The perfect photo instantly revealed itself. It had been there all the time, waiting for her to shift the point from which she was viewing.

My egoic I didn't know at the time that the two objects in the photograph would become central characters in the book or that Ellie's process of discovery would be its major metaphor. There was much else that I didn't know until I began to let the book write me. But that's another story altogether.

◉ SUGGESTED EXPLORATIONS

SOURCES

Your journey through *Going Deeper* offers you the opportunity to shift the point from which you view. Each vantage point along the way provides new information. Every epiphany simply defines a new place from which to let go and delve even deeper. Your greatest allies are intense curiosity and the willingness to transcend judgment.

Going Deeper peeks behind the curtain of conventional wisdom. As you become comfortable exploring the concepts that lie well outside the prepackaged sound bites of our cultural institutions, you will be increasingly free to link hands with like-minded Wanderers who, like you, are in varied stages of remembering.

People tell me that each time they read this book they are surprised by the concepts and information that appear to them for the first time, as if they had not read them before. I invite you to experience this phenomenon for yourself.

The concepts explored in *Going Deeper* are drawn from the excellent work of others, alongside my own experiences and the constant source of downloading from higher consciousness that is available to us all. The following are some avenues you may wish to investigate:

The Law of One

L/L Research offers information for spiritual seekers, the RA material and Law of One books, and a home for Wanderers. *The Law of One* is a series of channelings that began in the 1970s and continue, in modified form, to this day. The information provided by the three extraordinary and dedicated souls at the heart of L/L Research (Don Elkins, Carla L. Rueckert, and Jim McCarty) forms the basis of much of the material in *Going Deeper*.

L/L Research is devoted to discovering and sharing information for the spiritual advancement of all humankind. The L/L Research website offers transcripts and publications from weekly channeling and meditation sessions. A visit to the website will open the doors to endless exploration.

L/L Research
P.O. Box 5195
Louisville, KY 40255–0195
Phone and fax: (502) 245–6495
http://www.llresearch.org/
contact.us@llresearch.org

Voice Dialogue

The process that Junie facilitates for Larry is based entirely on an exceptionally elegant form of therapy called Voice Dialogue. This outgrowth of Jungian analysis was conceived and developed by Drs. Hal and Sidra Stone. Their seminal books (including *Embracing Our Selves: The Voice Dialogue Training Manual,* and *Partnering: A New Kind of Relationship*) have redefined our understanding our inner world. Voice Dialogue and its offshoots, Relationship and the Psychology of Selves, can be used by individuals for their own personal growth or by professionals in the fields of psychotherapy, counseling, personal coaching, and business and organizational consulting. The Stones' psychospiritual approach to consciousness and transformation includes an in-depth study of the many subpersonalities that make up the psyche, plus work with dreams, archetypal bonding patterns, and body energy fields.

Voice Dialogue International
P.O. Box 604
Albion, CA 95410
Phone: (707) 937–2424
Fax: (707) 937–4119
http://www.delosinc.com/
delos@delosinc.com

The Foundation for Mind Research

Few people have contributed more to shifting the consciousness of this planet than Jean Houston, Ph.D., who, along with her husband, Dr. Robert Masters, was instrumental in establishing the Foundation for Mind Research in the 1960s. The foundation's purpose is to identify, describe, understand, and gain productive access to the myriad potentials of the human mind-body system. In short, it is endeavoring to map the genome of consciousness.

Dr. Houston is a brilliant thinker, a captivating speaker, and the author of numerous books (including *Mystical Dogs: Animals as Guides to Our Inner Life,* and *Jump Time: Shaping Your Future in a World of Radical Change*). One of the great transformational figures of our age, she has had a profound influence on my life as well as the lives of thousands of other seekers. Her Mystery School—now available on both the west and east coasts of the United States—has nurtured and midwifed many social artists (Jean's endearing term for those who emerge from the herd to make their contribution to the planet). The writing of this book is in no small measure the result of her inspiration and encouragement. Among the gifts she gave me was the realization that extraordinary beings—like Jean—are readily accessible to those willing to make the effort.

Jean Houston
PMB 501
2305-C Ashland Street
Ashland, OR 97520
Phone: (541) 488–1200
Fax: (541) 488–3200
http://www.jeanhouston.org/
info@jeanhouston.org

The Plight of Wanderers

Wanderers are highly evolved souls who have lovingly come from the higher densities (mainly the sixth) to be of service on this planet in human form. If you are one of these beings, the material in this book will trigger your memories and begin the process of awakening to who you truly are.

The Wanderers' more concentrated level of consciousness is an energetic mismatch with the vibrations of the third density. These higher-density beings do not penetrate the Veil of Forgetting with the same ease as third-density beings. As a result, they often feel like fish out of water—somewhat alienated socially, psychologically, and physically, faintly aware that Earth is not their real home. They frequently suffer any one of a host of physical ailments, loosely termed allergenic or autoimmune conditions, in which the immune system mistakenly attacks the cells, tissues, and organs of the person's own body.

The following is a partial list of autoimmune diseases:

Nervous system – multiple sclerosis; myasthenia gravis; autoimmune neuropathies such as Guillain-Barré syndrome; autoimmune uveitis

Blood – autoimmune hemolytic anemia; pernicious anemia; autoimmune thrombocytopenia

Blood vessels – temporal arteritis; anti-phospholipid syndrome; vasculitides such as Wegener's granulomatosis; Behcet's disease

Skin – psoriasis; dermatitis herpetiformis; pemphigus vulgaris; vitiligo

Gastrointestinal system – Crohn's disease; ulcerative colitis; primary biliary cirrhosis; autoimmune hepatitis

Endocrine Glands – type 1 or immune-mediated diabetes mellitus; Grave's disease; Hashimoto's thyroiditis; autoimmune oophoritis and orchitis; autoimmune disease of the adrenal gland

Multiple organs, including the musculoskeletal system – rheumatoid arthritis; systemic lupus erythematosus; scleroderma; polymyositis, dermatomyositis; spondyloarthropathies such as ankylosing spondylitis; Sjögren's syndrome

From one standpoint, almost all chronic (and a great many acute) conditions can arguably be considered autoimmune or allergic disorders. Here's why: Modern medicine tends to view the body in terms of a biochemical model. Thus to address a disease, it attempts to create chemical compounds (drugs) that either intervene by blocking biological pathways or combat what are perceived to be invading pathogens.

Seen from a higher perspective, the body is a bioelectrical entity, existing simultaneously as the projector (nonlocal) and the projection (local). This view holds that we coexist in many dimensions at the same time. What we perceive as "reality" is but an energetic projection emanating from a higher aspect of our selves. Obviously, a medical condition that involves only the projection (such as a broken bone or an acute pathogenic condition) can be successfully treated in the local universe. But what about a projector-based condition? These "diseases" arise from energetic mismatches—akin to moiré patterns—triggered when local stimuli create interference patterns with the misaligned data imprinted in the person's chakras. This is precisely what causes an inappropriate allergenic-autoimmune response. Notably, this occurs most often in higher-density beings who that have been subjected to the Veil of Forgetting.

Attempting to rectify in local space/time what amounts to a programming error in the chakras usually brings limited results. While it is beyond the scope of this book to diagnose or suggest treatment of any kind, it would be remiss not to offer alternatives that have helped countless Wanderers repattern their energetic matrixes. For instance, this is precisely what energetic healing and prayer accomplish. Great intentional healers (psychic surgeons, shamans, faith healers, Reiki and Quantum Touch practitioners, and others) all over the planet employ these techniques with excellent results.

There are several ongoing remote services (which operate successfully even if you are thousands of miles distant) that can keep your energetic body in tune. Two of these are: the Quantum Resonance System, offered by Mony Vital, Ph.D. (Energetic Balancing, P.O. Box 1070, Del Mar, CA 92014, phone: 888-225-7501; energeticliberation@att.net, http://www.energeticliberation.com); and the AIM Program offered by the Energetic Matrix Church of Consciousness (phone: 877-500-3622; info@energeticmatrix.com, http://www.energeticmatrix.com.).

Several other recent advances in energetic healing are achieving impressive results:

NAET – Nambudripad's Allergy Elimination Techniques

According to the research conducted by Dr. Devi S. Nambudripad, M.D., most illnesses (including headaches, back aches, joint pains, addiction, PMS, indigestion, cough, and body aches) are caused by undiagnosed allergies. When left untreated, allergies can become serious life-threatening illnesses. NAET offers a distinct alternative for relief from lifelong conditions.

In her excellent book, *Say Goodbye to Illness,* Dr. Nambudripad explains that whenever blockages occur within the energy pathways, the brain sends warnings to the body in the form of pain, inflammation, fever, heart attacks, strokes, abnormal growths, tumors, and various other physical, physiological, or psychological discomforts. If the symptoms are minor, blockages are minor. If the symptoms are major, blockages are major. Minor blockages can be unblocked easily, whereas major blockages take a long time to unblock.

NAET is an innovative and completely natural method for regaining better health, often with permanent freedom from allergies and the diseases arising from those allergens. For more information, visit: http://www.naet.com.

QXCI-SCIO

The Quantum Xrroid Consciousness Interface (QXCI) / Scientific Consciousness Interface Operations (SCIO) is a nonlocal biofeedback device that allows the local body to dialogue with its nonlocal counterpart to identify areas of energetic interference. I have personally experienced quite a few sessions on this computer-based system with astonishing results. I have also witnessed many other people shift lifelong conditions in a matter of a few weeks with the help of the QXCI/SCIO. The device operates in a language that the energetic/electrical body understands but the mind cannot follow.

To learn more about the QXCI/SCIO, visit: http://www. quantumlife.com or http://www.qxciscio.com.

Low-Level Laser Therapy

Since all Creation flows from Love and Light, why should it be surprising that coherent light (such as a laser) is used with excellent results in a wide variety of medical procedures? New advances are regularly being made in the field of Lasik (laser-assisted *in situ* keratomileusis) surgery, helping people to see clearly without glasses. See: http://www.fda.gov/cdrh/lasik.

What isn't nearly as well publicized is the benefit of sending coherent light into the body at varying depths. I have been receiving this type of low-level laser therapy for some time and am very impressed with the results. I have also witnessed others experiencing what appears to be unexpectedly quick relief for a host of painful conditions.

The following are some of the reported benefits:

Blood pressure – 80% positive results in a test of 30
     patients with hypertension
Tennis elbow – complete pain relief and restored
     functionality in 82% of acute cases
Fibromyalgia – 66% reported pain relief and better
     mobility
Headache/migraine – most patients report complete
     relief within minutes
Lower back pain – 71% effective.
Rheumatoid arthritis of the hand – improves grip
     strength; reduces morning stiffness

I have also personally experienced excellent results on a wide range of skin conditions (including the potentially serious ones) and witnessed several cases in which the low-level laser was used following major dental surgery to completely eliminate pain and greatly speed healing. To learn more about this therapeutic

option, go to: http://www.laser.nu/ and http://users.med.auth.
gr/~karanik/english/vet/laser1.htm, or search *low-level laser
therapy* on the Internet.

When it comes to using any of these nontraditional techniques, do your homework, ask questions, and be advised by your
inner knowing. You already know what doesn't work for you.

Please note that the medical information contained in this
book is not intended as a substitute for consulting your physician. Any attempt to diagnose and treat an illness using the information in this book should be done under the direction of a
physician or qualified health practitioner who is familiar with
the techniques involved. These notes are presented for educational purposes only and to stimulate further inquiry and
research. All matters regarding your health should be supervised
by your health practitioner.

EXPLORING THE INFINITE

There has never been another time like this. Never before has
there been immediate and intimate access to the wealth of
knowledge that is now stored and shared on the worldwide web.
Never before have virtually all the arcane secrets of hidden secret
societies been made so public and available. However, this
wealth of information is a two-edged sword. The freedom of
information on the Internet allows equal access to misinforma-
tion. There is no way that you, acting from your lower egoic self,
can reliably sort the wheat from the chaff.

Fortunately, you are never alone on your journey. Each of us
has access to exquisite inner guidance that unfailingly leads us
and illuminates our path. You have to contribute only three
things to the process: faith in the oneness of all Creation; trust in
the still, small voice that beckons; and the courage to be intensely
curious.

As Zeus so wisely counsels Larry, if what you find can be written or spoken, it isn't what you ultimately seek. However, the written and spoken word can act as arrows pointing to paths of exploration. As you journey, believe nothing. After all, belief is the lowest form of information processing—akin to a hypothesis in scientific study. Accept nothing, for in acceptance you barter your Free Will. Simply be guided by your curiosity and desire to explore.

Each new concept is a stepping stone. Some advance you, others lead to dead ends. There is no need to judge any of them. As you come upon a new thought, just store it on a shelf in your mind. If it is meant for you, it will find its own way to connect with other thoughts and enter into your consciousness. If not, let it be.

The Internet is a doorway to the infinite. How can you not yearn to peek through it?

⊚ GLOSSARY

Akasha. See **Akashic records.**

Akashic records. An amorphous universal filing system where every thought, word, and action of every human is recorded. These energetic patterns are imprinted on a subtle substance called Akasha (or soniferous ether). The Akashic records—also called the Cosmic Mind, the Universal Mind, the collective unconscious, and the collective subconscious—are a place where all thoughts from each subconscious mind are available to be read by other subconscious minds. Many people claim it is easy to access the events recorded on the Akasha, making clairvoyance and psychic perception possible. However, reading the Akashic records generally requires altered states of consciousness induced by certain stages of sleep, extreme physical weakness or illness, drugs, and meditation.

All That Is. The One Supreme Infinite Creator. The Oneness. That which is beyond any concept of God. The infinite cosmic hologram of which every aspect of Creation is an inextricable part.

Arp, Halton. American astronomer, born March 21, 1927, noted for challenging the theory that the red shifts of quasars indicate their great distance from the earth.

Atlantis (adj. Atlantean). An island nation located in the middle of the Atlantic Ocean some 11,000 years ago, said to be populated by a noble and powerful race whose rulers controlled much of Europe and Africa. According to the writings of Plato (in his dialogues *Timaeus* and *Critias*), Atlantis was the domain of Poseidon, god of the sea. The legend says that at first the Atlanteans lived simple, virtuous lives, but greed and power slowly overcame them. This angered Zeus greatly, and in one violent surge, the island of Atlantis, its people, and its memory were engulfed by the sea. New-age versions of the story refer to the misuse of advanced technology, crystals, and other sources of immense power as the reason for the island's demise.

Awareness continuum. See **I's of infinity.**

ayahuasca. *Quechua Indian:* "Vine of the dead." A hallucinogenic substance derived from a mixture of two plants and varying in potency according to the skill of its maker. While each shaman has his own secret formula for the mixture, true ayahuasca always contains both beta-carboline and tryptamine alkaloids, the former (harmine and harmaline) usually obtained from the *Banisteriopsis caapi* vine, and the latter (N, N-dimethyl-tryptamine, or DMT) from the leaves of the *Psychotria viridis* bush. Neither is normally psychoactive in oral doses, but the combination of the harmala alkaloids in the *Banisteriopsis caapi* vine, embodying powerful short term MAO inhibitors, and the DMT-containing *Psychotria viridis* leaves produce what has been described as one of the most profound of all psychedelic experiences.

barista. Someone professionally trained in the art of espresso preparation, or someone who excels at espresso making regardless of their training.

boytchik, zay gezunt. *Yiddish: boytchik*—affectionate term for boy; *zay gezunt*—stay well, goodbye, bless you (often said when someone sneezes).

brain/mind. A method of processing information that theoretically combines input from the intellect (the left-brained, rational, thinking mind) and the intuition (the right-brained, creative mind). In humans operating at the lower, egoic level, usually one portion dominates, limiting or totally blocking the countervailing input of the other portion. Unlike the heart/mind (which see), the brain/mind operates at the local (see space/time) level without the benefit of input from nonlocal (see time/space) sources.

catalyst. In chemistry, an agent that provokes or precipitates a reaction and enables it to take place under milder conditions, such as a lower temperature. In metaphysics, an outside stimulus that enables a being to observe, react, and learn. Typically, catalysts (incarnational experiences) are organized to repeat until the being has processed the information sufficiently to gain the requisite awareness.

chakra. A physical or spiritual energy center in the human body according to yoga (Hindu/Buddhist) philosophy. These are the storehouses of various imprints and distortions (which see) reflecting the individual's experience within the illusion (which see). They are also the contact points through which the Universe and the individual interact. The seven major chakras run vertically up the middle of the body, starting at the perineum and extending just above the crown of the head.

chi più sa, meno crede. Italian: The more one knows, the less one believes.

chonic. Referring to CHON, the acronym for carbon-hydrogen-oxygen-nitrogen, the requisite components of biological life.

CMS. An acronym for chonic (which see) myopic syndrome—the inability of scientists to consider intelligent life outside of the conventional view of biological form.

Council of Nine. The members of the Council of Nine (often called simply "the Nine") represent the nine expressed aspects or principles of creation, part of the universe's sacred geometry.

They are not, and never have been, in physical form. They form a nonlocal (see time/space) presence that permeates the universe so as to maintain the balance of Creation. They have significant interest in Earth at this time because of the impending shift into the fourth density (see densities) and the particular aspect of the Grand Experiment (which see) that affords humans on planet Earth the opportunity of accessing and directing Free Will for the first time.

crevolution. A coined word combining (and mocking) the seemingly opposed theories of evolution and creation.

density. Any one of the eight levels of Awareness defining the eight levels of Creation. Each density is subdivided into seven dimensions, each of which is again divided into seven, ad infinitum. The octave of densities contain successively higher quantities of light energy or spiritual mass, thus offering infinite Consciousness (All That Is), in the form of the individuated Awareness, a plethora of conditions under which to experience itself.

The first density is the realm of the elements—water, minerals, air. The second density is the domain of plants and animals. The third density is the human condition. The fourth—the density the Earth is shifting into—is the classroom of Compassion. The fifth density balances the lessons of the fourth with Wisdom. The sixth is the unifying density in which the path of service to self and the path of service to others (which see) merge. In the seventh, or gateway, density the individuated Awareness as part of a social memory consciousness (which see) gains access to the Great Mystery. The eighth density represents the Creator. Each density offers a unique range of catalyst (which see) designed to satisfy a particular curriculum. As the lesson of each successive density each is mastered, the individuated Awareness progresses to the next density until it is finally reunited with the Creator in the eighth density, only to emerge anew into yet another octave of Creation while simultaneously reentering into the first density of the cycle just completed.

distortion. A state of variance from the pure state of the One Supreme Infinite Creator. All Creation—beginning with Free Will and Love/Light through the manifestation of galaxies and intelligent life forms—is distortion. Distortions are evident at every level of conciousness and in all the densities, providing limitless opportunities to experience and learn.

ego/soul/God continuum. See **I's of infinity.**

espavo. Lemurian: Literally, thank you for taking your power. Used as a greeting for both "hello" and "goodbye." The word's vibrational matrix helps people reconnect to ancient memories of their true origin.

eureka. From the Greek *heureka:* I have found (it). The exclamation attributed to Greek mathematician and inventor Archimedes on discovering a method for determining the purity of gold.

foigel. Yiddish: Smart guy.

Free Will. The first distortion (which see) of the One Supreme Infinite Creator. Free Will allows Awareness to self-determine its range of experience and is available to all consciousness in the third density (which see) and above. Free Will differs from free choice. The latter is a function of preference or bias based on belief or reaction to previous physical, mental and/or emotional experience. Free Will deals with the larger picture and advances the individuated Awareness through the densities. If the eight densities were a chess board, Free Will would determine the way the piece moves from one square to another; free choice would determine where in the square the piece would like to rest.

Gerris remigis. Species name of the common water strider of the insect order: *Hemiptera* (true bugs); Family: *Gerridae* (water striders). A water bug that looks a lot like a big mosquito walking on the surface of ponds, slow streams, marshes, and other quiet waters.

goomba. Slang: A companion or associate, especially an older friend who acts as a patron, protector, or adviser. Probably alteration of Italian *compare,* meaning godfather.

Grand Experiment. The experience of individuated human Awareness within the third density (see density) on planet Earth. The perception of space/time (which see) reality that forms when one passes through the Veil of Forgetting (which see). Also called the illusion, reflecting the experience of those who have passed through the Veil. The distortions of the Veil create the impression of separation from source and the apparent realities of duality and polarization, affording a rich environment for a wide range of mental, physical, emotional and spiritual experiences unavailable to individuated Awareness in the other densities.

Great Cosmic Triangle. Conceptual equilateral triangle representing the completion of the lessons gleaned from the fourth (Love/Compassion), fifth (Wisdom), and sixth (Power) densities (which see). Love/Compassion, Wisdom, and Power interact as the building blocks of Creation. Mastery at balancing the three sides of the triangle opens the doorway to the realization that All is One.

harvest. The end of each density cycle, when those participants who have mastered the lessons of the cycle move to the next density. Akin to graduating after having taken the full curriculum and passing the final exams.

heart/mind. A method of processing information that synthesizes the data streams from both the rational, intellectual brain and the emotional, feeling brain (see brain/mind). Because the heart/mind operates at the nonlocal (see time/space) level, it transcends the perceptions of the egoic I (see I's of infinity), which tend to be based on emotion, personality, and preferences. Instead, it processes incoming information in terms of archetypes or universal "truths to arrive at a higher, more balanced state of understanding. The heart/mind is in constant two-way communication with the collective Consciousness, the All That Is (which see).

I-continuum. See **I's of infinity.**

I's of infinity. The infinite continuum of points from which an Aware being views (see point from which one views). These range from the lower, egoic human I (see Grand Experiment), where the individuated Awareness perceives itself as separate from All That Is (which see), to the point of view of God, in which all Creation is recognized as one. The lesson of each density (which see) requires that beings advance progressively higher, releasing old viewpoints as they gain greater perspective on the meaning and purpose of Creation.

illusion, the. See **Grand Experiment.**

infinite continuum of I's. See **I's of infinity.**

Jainism. A religion of India—historically traceable to the *jina* (*Sanskrit:* saint) Vardhamana Mahavira of the 6th century B.C. —having scriptures, temples, an organized religious practice or system of worship, and a monastic class. Jainism maintains that while gods control the realm of time and matter, no being higher than an absolutely perfect human soul is necessary for the creation or moral regulation of the universe. Jainism also teaches the personal ideal of the *kevalin* (*Sanskrit:* one who is set free from matter—a liberated soul), achievable through usually numerous lives in the pursuit of right knowledge, right faith, and right conduct, which includes *ahimsa* (*Sanskrit:* refraining from harming or taking the lives of others) and veneration of the *jina*s (often involving images).

kinesiology, applied. A system using muscle testing to evaluate neuromuscular function as it relates to the structural, chemical, and mental and physiologic regulatory mechanisms. Originating within the chiropractic profession, applied kinesiology has multidisciplinary applications.

Kofutu. See **Mantura.**

Kojiki. Japan's creation myth, compiled in 712 C.E. by O No Yasumaro. The quest for Izanami in the underworld is reminiscent of the Greek demigod Orpheus's quest in Hades for his wife, Euridice, and, even more, of the Sumerian myth of Inanna's descent to the underworld.

kundalini. *Sanskrit:* Derived from *kundala,* ring. The yogic life force that lies coiled at the base of the spine until it is aroused and sent to the head to trigger enlightenment.

Law of One. Everything in the universe is One. Infinity is One. All aspects of Creation are facets on the infinite diamond of All That Is. All Consciousness is drawn from the One (see Myth of Creation) and continually returns to the One in a never-ending dance of self-exploration.

Light/Love. The energetic flow informing every aspect of Creation while connecting it and drawing it back to All That Is. In the

Myth of Creation (which see) Free Will (which see) is the primary distortion (which see) of Oneness. Free Will, requiring a force with which to express itself, manifests Love as its primary distortion. Love, in turn expresses Light, which then expresses form. Conversely, when the vibration of matter is sufficiently raised. it becomes first Light, then Love, and ultimately returns through Free Will back to the Oneness. Consequently each aspect of Creation is expressed in terms of its Light/Love quotient, which becomes progressively brighter as one advances back to Source. See also Love/Light.

local time. See **space/time.**

Love/Light. The transposition of "Light/Love" (which see) so as to emphasize the Love element over the Light. Love/Light is the enabler, the power, the energy-giver. Love/Light depicts the creative thrust of manifestation that occurs when Light has been impressed with Love. By contrast, Light/Love completes the circuit by expressing the flow of Creation back to source.

maiven. Yiddish: Expert, connoisseur, authority. Often used sarcastically.

Mantura. A system of intellectual and spiritual development, developed in ancient Atlantis, embracing twelve general areas of study, including Kofutu. The system was mastered by Atlantean Tanra Samati Tamarasha. When his physical life ended in the cataclysm that destroyed Atlantis, he was anointed Master of the Kofutu System and made Keeper of the Kofutu Symbols. The teachings have recently been transmitted to Earth through the channelings of Frank Homan.

mind/body/emotion/spirit complex. A term referring to individuated third-density (which see) Awareness, or human beings, reflecting the fact that each human is a four-tiered energetic form. While these four factors are functionally inseparable, each operates in its own field, allowing the human being the full range of experience in which to process the catalyst (which see) of each incarnation. Each experience is first offered to the spirit portion of the complex; if the lesson is too subtle and is missed, it is passed on to the emotional/mental (mind) portion. If the lesson is also missed there, it is passed on to physical level—frequently as an accident or illness.

mishegas. *Yiddish:* Craziness. Example: What kind of *mishegas* is that?

Myth of Creation. The unfolding saga of the Creator's desire to know itself more completely. From the Oneness sprang Free Will, which emanated Love. From Love came Light, and from the out-pouring of the Love/Light energy, drawing from the infinite intelligence of All That Is, all Creation came into being. Our physical universe, defined by the eight densities, is but one of an infinite series of universes through which the Creator explores new and varied aspects of its being.

namaste. *Sanskrit:* Literally, salutations to you. Used as a greeting for both "hello" and "goodbye."

Nine, the. See **Council of Nine.**

nonlocal time. See **time/space.**

Omnitude. A coined word meaning "beyond gratitude," referring to appreciation of what one is rather than what one has.

Oneness. See **All That Is.**

oy. Yiddish: Abbreviation of the interjection *oy vey* or *oy vey is mier.* Generally expressing a negative emotion ranging from tiredness or sadness to martyrdom, anger, annoyance, etc. Also used as a disapproving sigh. It's meaning tends to be contextual: the stronger the emotion, the more appropriate one of the longer forms is. Examples: *Oy, it's so hot outside.* Or: *Oy vey, three tests this week! What will I do?* But: *Your mother? Cancer? Oy vey is mier. I'm so sorry.*

path of service to others. The path of positivity, embracing selfless, openhearted giving. The seeker has the intention of serving others rather than self. At least 51 percent of one's thoughts, words, and deeds must be for the benefit of others in order to graduate from the third to the fourth density (which see) along this path. Also called the path of that which is, or unity.

path of service to self. The path of negativity, through which the seeker attempts to control others. This highly disciplined path requires at least 95 percent of one's thoughts, words, and deeds to be for personal gain in order to graduate from the third to the fourth density (which see). Also called the path of that which is not, or separation.

point from which one views. The position along the infinite continuum of I's, or the I's of Infinity (which see), from where one regards the catalyst (which see). Like the ever-changing perspectives one achieves while climbing a mountain, the successive points from which one views as one gains in Awareness offer ever-greater understanding of the panorama of Creation. The point from which one views is distinct from one's point of view, which refers to the conclusions one draws based on perception and experience.

Prime Mandate of Creation. The purpose of Creation is to allow the Creator to know itself more completely by knowing itself in all its possible aspects (see Myth of Creation). Thus the driving force behind every individuated aspect of Creation is to seek new experiences in order to learn. Since each individuated aspect of Creation is defined and limited by its Light/Love (which see) quotient, or the point from which it views (which see), it can view Creation only in terms of its own survival. Hence the Prime Mandate of Creation becomes: "What's in it for me?"

As the individual's Awareness grows and its understanding of the Law of One (which see) increases, its view of self expands until it finally realizes its identity with the One Supreme Creator.

seychel. *Yiddish:* Reason, common sense. Example: *If you had a little more seychel you wouldn't give him a single dime.*

Rachmaninoff, Sergei. Russian composer (1873–1943). His piano concerto number 3 in D minor, Op. 30, featured in the movie *Shine,* is considered by many pianists the most technically demanding work in the concerto repertoire.

Ramayana. (Pronounced rum-eye-ana). For the past two thousand years the *Ramayana* has been among the most important literary and oral texts of South Asia. This epic poem provides insights into many aspects of Indian culture and continues to influence the politics, religion and art of modern India. The story of Prince Rama (1200–1000 B.C.), considered the seventh incarnation of the god Vishnu, was recorded by Valmiki c. 400–200 B.C.

social memory complex. A group of higher-density (which see) entities—entities of the fourth, fifth, or sixth density—in which the mind/thoughts/memories of one are freely available to all. Individuals connected to such a group retain both individual and group consciousness with full awareness.

space/time, space/time continuum. Reality as it is seen within the illusion, offering the guise of linear time in which the universe seems to have a past, present, and future. Space appears to be fixed and time (as well as objects and events) move through it. Also called "local time." Compare time/space.

sweetgrass. *(Hierochloe odorata)* Used by Native Americans for scenting the floors of their tents and in ceremonies and costumes. Live plants can be grown around the house, as living incense. In Northern Europe (particularly Russia) it is known as Mary's grass, and was strewn on church steps on saints' days. Also known as zebrovka, seneca grass, holy grass, and buffalo grass.

time/space, time/space continuum. Essentially the complement of space/time (which see). This inverted view sees Creation as an Infinite Instant in which all events occur simultaneously and past, present, and future are not fixed linearly. From the perspective of a third-density (which see) being, time/space is an invisible, metaphysical reality accessed through altered states such as deep meditation, hallucinogens, or sleep. Also called nonlocal time. Compare space/time.

toomel. Yiddish: A noisy chaos. Example: *Such a toomel, I couldn't hear a single word.*

Upanishads. *Sanskrit:* Vedic treatises dealing with broad philosophic problems such as the nature of ultimate reality, humankind, and the universe.

Uroboros. *Greek:* The symbol of eternity represented as a snake swallowing its own tail.

Veil, the. See **Veil of Forgetting**.

Veil of Forgetting. The energetic barrier through which each being passes at birth. It serves to separate the being from knowing who/what it truly is, so it can experience the fullness of a mind/body/spirit complex (which see) in a highly polarized (dualistic) illusion. One of the seven veils (which see). Specifically, the energetic barrier one passes through when one takes birth in the third density. The Veil filters out Awareness of who or what one truly is, so the person fully experiences life in a mind / body / emotion / spirit complex. See also Grand Experiment.

veils, the seven. Energetic fields that define the borders separating the densities (which see). Each veil—for example, the Veil of Forgetting (which see)—is encoded with specific programs to set up the catalyst, or learning experiences, appropriate to each density.

walk-in. An entity from one of the higher densities (fourth, fifth or sixth) who makes an agreement with a third-density human to take over (enter) the human's physical body and assume the responsibilities of that person's incarnation. The human then reposes at an appropriate Light/Love quotient level in the astral realm while the walk-in advances its particular agenda of service.

Wanderer. Entity from the fourth, fifth, or sixth density (which see) who responds to calls for assistance from third-density beings. At the present time there are over 70 million Wanderers incarnate on Earth, the majority from the sixth density. Wanderers are required to come through the Veil of Forgetting, so they must rediscover their call to service during their incarnation. In arriving through the Veil, they emerge as human beings, subject to all of the challenges of the illusion. This allows them to undergo the entire process required for harvest so that they do not infringe on the Free Will (which see) of this planet's population by appearing to be evolved extraterrestrials.

JEAN-CLAUDE GERARD KOVEN is one of those rare, independent, and adventurous free spirits who successfully combines practical enterprise and cosmic mystery. He is a highly successful entrepreneur who has started and run more than a dozen businesses. During these same years, he also studied with spiritual masters and led awareness-expanding workshops on six continents.

Jean-Claude's abiding love of the mystery of Creation sent him around the world on a relentless quest to learn from a host of extraordinary masters both on and beyond this plane of existence.

What he saw and realized along the way informs his unique perspective and imbues his writing with uncommon love, power, and wisdom. Jean-Claude speaks for the millions of Light Workers who have come to this planet to help evolve the consciousness of its people. His pithy style prods and awakens the dormant memories hidden deep within each of us.

Jean-Claude lives in Rancho Mirage, California with his wife, Arianne, and Zeus—a fifteen-inch-high dog of undetermined pedigree who sits in constant meditation on his desk, offering support and unconditional love . . . as only a stuffed animal can.

QUICK ORDER FORM

Use this form to order additional copies of *Going Deeper* in the event your local bookseller is out of stock.

I would like to order:

QTY.		AMOUNT
_____	Hardbound copies of *Going Deeper* / $16.95 ea.	$_____
	California orders add 7.75% sales tax	$_____
	Shipping, Handling & Insurance ($ 4.95)	$_____
	(All books shipped via USPS Media Rate Mail in Continental USA—Hawaii & Alaska, add an additional $2.00)	$_____
	For UPS 2nd Day: $12.50, For Overnight: $17.50	$_____
	For International Air Post Orders: $20.00 for 1st book; $2.00 for each additional book	$_____
	TOTAL	$_____

_____
NAME (PLEASE PRINT)

_____
ADDRESS

_____
CITY   STATE/PROV

_____
COUNTRY   POSTAL CODE

_____
EMAIL ADDRESS

PAYMENT

❑ CHECK   CREDIT CARD: ❑ Visa   ❑ MasterCard

Card Number _____ Exp Date _____/_____

Name on Card (Print) _____

Fax orders: +1.760.321.5314
Telephone: +1.760.324.3072 (Have your Visa or MasterCard card ready.)
Email orders: orders@goingdeeper.org
Online orders: www.goingdeeper.org
Postal orders: Prism House Press, 36101 Bob Hope Drive, Suite E5/PMB305
                   Rancho Mirage, CA 92270 / USA

Please contact the publisher:

- for reseller and bulk purchase wholesale pricing
- to schedule author interviews and booksigning events
- to sponsor author lectures, workshops, and retreats.

www.goingdeeper.org